Back to the Well

Women's Encounters with Jesus in the Gospels

Frances Taylor Gench

WESTMINSTER
JOHN KNOX PRESS
LOUISVILLE · KENTUCKY

Book design by Sharon Adams
Cover design by Night & Day Design
Cover art: Christ and the Samaritan Woman, *by Prof. Dr. He Qi, Nanjing Theological Seminary, www.heqiarts.com*

First edition
Published by Westminster John Knox Press
Louisville, Kentucky

This book is printed on acid-free paper that meets the American National Standards Institute Z39.48 standard. ♾

PRINTED IN THE UNITED STATES OF AMERICA

07 08 09 10 11 12 13 — 10 9 8 7 6 5 4

Library of Congress Cataloging-in-Publication Data

Gench, Frances Taylor, 1956–
    Back to the well : women's encounters with Jesus in the Gospels / Frances Taylor Gench.—1st ed.
        p. cm.
    Includes bibliographical references and indexes.
    ISBN-13: 978-0-664-22715-9 (alk. paper)
    ISBN-10: 0-664-22715-5 (alk. paper)
    1. Women in the Bible. 2. Jesus Christ—Views on women. 3. Bible N.T. Gospels—Feminist criticism. I. Title.

    BT590.W6G46 2004
    226'.06—dc22

                                                                        2004043019

FOR MY MOTHER AND HER SISTERS

Lillian McCulloch Taylor

Nancy McCulloch Bridger

Jane McCulloch Blair

Julia Clark Calhoun
(in memoriam)

Catharine Clark Strand
(in memoriam)

Contents

Acknowledgments

This book has evolved out of engagement with these stories with many people in a variety of places, and I wish to thank all who have been part of the conversation, though everyone cannot be mentioned here. Union Theological Seminary in Richmond, Virginia, provided the impulse for the book by inviting me to lecture at their Interpreting the Faith event in 1996. The manuscript that began to take shape for that occasion grew further in preparation for other speaking engagements: Preaching Days at The Lutheran Theological Seminary in Philadelphia (1998); the 2002 HerStory Conference sponsored by Shenandoah Presbytery, Massanetta Springs, and Mary Baldwin College; weekend retreats and lectures for a number of churches. Two congregations in particular have been wonderful church homes during the writing of this book and lively forums for discussion of all the New Testament women featured here: Brown Memorial Park Avenue Presbyterian Church in Baltimore, Maryland, and The New York Avenue Presbyterian Church in Washington, D.C. Students at Gettysburg Lutheran Seminary and Union-PSCE have studied these stories with me throughout the writing of this book, ever instructing their teacher. A number of friends, some of whom read portions of the manuscript, have provided special encouragement along the way: Mary-Paula Walsh, Janyce Covner Jorgensen, Holly Hearon, Cindy Rasmussen, Robin Hogle, Barbara Osborne, Richard Nelson, Richard P. Carlson, and Kurt Noll. Stephanie Egnotovich of Westminster John Knox Press has provided wise counsel and superb editorial assistance. For all of these persons and communities, I am deeply grateful!

I owe my greatest debt of gratitude to members of my family: to my father, David W. A. Taylor, who has patiently reviewed every thought I have had about these texts and provided masterful editorial commentary every step of the way; and to my husband, Roger J. Gench, with whom I am in constant conversation about biblical texts and who inspires me weekly with his powerful preaching of them. This book on New Testament women is dedicated to five of the most important women in my life, my mother and her sisters, with gratitude for their abiding love.

Frances Taylor Gench
Richmond, Virginia

Introduction

How would you describe your relationship with the Bible? My own journey with it, in recent years, has been marked by two things in particular: (1) a fascination with women in the biblical world—how their lives and experiences are represented and refracted, and how their stories might illumine contemporary Christian life and faith; and (2) a deep appreciation of the ways in which feminist biblical scholarship has deepened and broadened engagement with the stories by articulating new questions and insights for the community of faith.

Both have prompted the writing of this book, and I would like to explain why they have become important to me. They emerge from my journey with the Bible, so let me share a few reflections on my own relationship with it—how that relationship has evolved and continues to evolve through the years—with the hope that it may stimulate reflection on the role the Bible has played in your own life and daily ministry. I will stick to the highlights and significant milestones along my way and spare you my entire personal history.

My relationship with the Bible was established well before I could read, and my earliest impressions of it were formed by a song, one of the first taught to me by my parents and grandparents and legions of faithful Sunday school teachers: "Jesus Loves Me This I Know, For the Bible Tells Me So." My grandfather, a former missionary, sang it with particular gusto, and I was greatly entertained to hear him sing it not only in English, but also in Chinese. The words of that song in both languages impressed themselves upon my mind and heart throughout my Wonderbread years and led me to embrace the Bible as the story of a love affair: the story of the love that God in Christ had for me, for all people around the world, and for the whole creation. That conviction became foundational for all my subsequent encounters with the Bible and is one I have never relinquished.

However, there have been rough moments as the relationship evolved, particularly during my teenage years when I began to read the Bible with some seriousness and found myself tremendously insulted by what I thought at the time to be Paul's view of women. For example, I didn't care for the fact that in 1 Corinthians we read that it is shameful for women to speak in church gatherings (14:35), or for the fact that the Corinthian men appeared to be advised that "[i]t is well for a man not to touch a woman" (7:1). Nor was I fond of 1 Timothy, a letter to which Paul's name is attached, which commands that no woman is "to teach or to have authority over a man" (2:12). Women, rather, are told to be silent and submissive, and to earn their salvation by bearing children (2:15). So much for justification by grace through faith alone!

My solution to this problem was simply to take my magic marker and clearly "X" these portions out of my Bible and then to record obscene remarks about the apostle Paul in the margins for future reference. But even that did not suffice when I came upon Ephesians 5: "Wives, be subject to your husbands as you are to the Lord. For the husband is the head of the wife just as Christ is the head of the church, the body of which he is the Savior. Just as the church is subject to Christ, so also wives ought to be, in everything, to their husbands" (5:22–24). When I came to Ephesians 5, I took out the scissors. These words had to be forcibly removed—excised—banished from my personal canon of Scripture. It was, I suppose, my first experience of "textual harassment,"[1] though not my last—the first stirrings of feminist consciousness. Tension crept into my relationship with Scripture. But though I began to form my own canon within the canon, reversing Marcion's inclination,[2] I by no means rejected the whole Bible.

Eventually, I made my way to a theological seminary to continue wrestling with the Bible, where my teachers did manage to rehabilitate Paul for me. Under their tutelage, I found myself largely (if not entirely) reconciled to the apostle, who much to my surprise turned out to be more of an advocate for the freedom and equality of all people in Christ than I could have imagined. Theological education, as it turned out, mellowed me considerably, and I no longer perform radical surgery on the canon.

But seminary transformed my relationship with the Bible in even more profound and positive ways that continue to impact my engagement with Scripture to this day. I began to learn a deep respect for the language and grammar of a biblical text and for the importance of the interpretive task.

The seminary I attended required that students engage the Bible in its original languages (Hebrew and Greek), and that we sit in exegetical seminars week in and week out, our noses pressed against a biblical text: parsing verbs and sweating bullets; analyzing variants and genres; establishing boundaries; attending to literary context and historical context; distinguishing between tradition and redaction; striving above all to discern affirmations of the text and hear their claim on our lives. I realized that what we were doing in those classrooms mattered profoundly—that it made a real difference in how we were to think about God and God's way with the world and our own human reality. The experience began to cultivate in me and my fellow seminarians the habits of "exegesis," which is to say that the experience began to help us learn to read a biblical text in a disciplined, informed, and faithful manner for the rest of our lives in preparation for ministry.

But life continues and learning continues, and how has my relationship with the Bible continued to evolve through my adult years, as I have entered the working world and engaged in teaching ministry? The relationship has been impacted in especially significant ways by my post-seminary evolution as a feminist. Now that I have uttered what is for many people the "f" word, which sometimes provokes allergic reactions, it might do well to provide a working definition, particularly because popular use of the word is more often informed by the likes of Rush Limbaugh than by a careful reading of any feminist writers.

Four definitions have been particularly helpful to me. Rebecca West writes, "I myself have never been able to find out precisely what feminism is. I only know that people call me a feminist whenever I express sentiments that differentiate me from a doormat or a prostitute."[3] Alan Alda perceptively noted, "A feminist is someone who believes women are people." Katharine Sakenfeld provides an encompassing perspective: "A feminist, broadly speaking, is one who seeks justice and equality for all people and who is especially concerned for the fate of women—all women—in the midst of all people. Such a definition means that issues pertinent to racism, classism, and ecology, as well as peace-making, are part of the purview of feminism."[4] Finally, Letty Russell helpfully observes: "Feminism is advocacy of women. It is not, therefore, *against* men, but only *for* the needs of women, needs that cannot be met without changes in the lives of both men *and* women. . . . It represents a search for liberation from all forms of dehumanization on the part of those who advocate full human personhood for all. . . . This means that men can also be feminists if they are willing to advocate for women."[5]

These perspectives have become increasingly important to my life and work, and I have puzzled over why they failed to engage me during my theological education. Perhaps I did not read a lot of books by women during my years in seminary; moreover, almost all of my instructors were men! I suspect, however, a simpler explanation is that I had not yet entered the working world, and thus had not yet fully pondered institutional realities. Most importantly, I had not yet experienced a faculty meeting.

So what has the emergence of feminist consciousness meant for my engagement with the Bible? Two things. First, my eyes finally opened wide to the decidedly male-centered perspective in the Scriptures, which are after all authored by men, written in androcentric (i.e., male-centered) language, and reflective of male religious experience. I do not know why this concept took so long to register fully, because I had long puzzled over Matthew 5: "Everyone who looks at a woman with lust has already committed adultery with her in his heart" (5:28). Now I had *tried* to wrap my head around this thought: "If I look at a woman lustfully I have already committed adultery with her in my heart"—but as a heterosexual female I was encountering considerable cognitive dissonance. Finally I understood: *I* am not the implied reader!

Out of this awareness has emerged a new fascination with the image and reality of women in the biblical world—with how their lives and experiences are represented and refracted. Women who appear in the biblical narrative are portrayed from the perspective of male authors. When issues that impinge upon the lives of women are described, we are hearing men describe them. Moreover, women are often nameless when they appear in the biblical narrative (such as the Canaanite woman or the Samaritan woman), or identified solely by their relationship to a man (Simon's mother-in-law, for example, or Jairus's daughter). Frequently, the women are voiceless as well. Their presence in the text is sometimes completely silent. Still, we do see and hear enough to know that they were present and active in ancient Jewish and early Christian communities. As Elisabeth Schüssler Fiorenza has observed, we see the tip of an iceberg,[6] but what is submerged? They are part of our history—part of our story. Indeed, they are our foremothers in the faith. I have come to appreciate Ann Lane's observation that "If we try to understand the past and leave women out, we have learned only a partial history"[7]—a partial story.

Second, my engagement with the Bible and my preaching and teaching of it have been greatly enriched by Christian feminist scholarship, which has brought so many new questions, insights, and perspectives to the reading of old, familiar stories. This scholarship has also helped me return to issues present in my gut from the beginning, when I stood before the Bible with scissors in hand, and wrestle more constructively with the question of how to appropriate a book that has proved to be profoundly liberating but also profoundly oppressive at times in the lives of Christian women.

The emergence of feminist consciousness has by no means soured my relationship with the Bible or lessened its importance in my life and ministry. It has in fact reinvigorated the relationship, for I have found myself in full agreement with theologian Letty Russell, who says this:

> In spite of the patriarchal nature of the biblical texts, I myself have no intention of giving up the biblical basis of my theology. The Bible has authority in my life because it makes sense of my experience and speaks to me about the meaning and purpose of my humanity in Jesus Christ. In spite of its ancient and patriarchal worldviews, in spite of its inconsistencies and mixed messages, the story of God's love affair with the world leads me to a vision of new Creation that impels my life.[8]

I am deeply grateful to Russell for that observation and return to it periodically for encouragement and inspiration to continue on my journey as Reformed, biblical, and feminist.

One final important and closely related milestone in my journey with the Bible has been a growing recognition of the importance of social location in the act of biblical interpretation. All of us bring our own political, gender, racial, and religious biases to a biblical text, which affect not only what we see, but even the questions we think to ask. Whenever I read the Bible, for example, I read it as a white, female, heterosexual, Calvinist baby boomer, a southerner, a feminist, and a died-in-the-wool Democrat. Listening carefully to those who stand in different places, see different things, and bring different questions to their reading of the Scriptures thus becomes very important.

The importance of social location was impressed upon me as I began to work several years ago on the epistle of James—an epistle many Western Christians have long regarded as the junk mail of the New Testament—or as Martin Luther put it, an "epistle of straw." I was astonished to learn however, that this most neglected of books in Western culture (the "first world") turns out to be a very popular book among many "third world" Christians, who have perceived within that straw much nourishing grain. Listening closely to their readings of James opened my eyes to social, political, and economic dimensions of the book that I had not seen and could not see before. Reading the Bible in the company of others, near and far, thus becomes a richer and deeper experience than reading it alone!

This book emerges out of this ever-evolving journey with the Bible, and is written for those who, like me, are eager to learn more about women in the biblical world, to engage stories of our foremothers in the faith, and to reflect on the import of these stories for our own Christian life and faith. This book is also written for readers who wish to engage many of the new questions, insights, and perspectives that feminist biblical scholarship has brought to a reading of these stories—and who are open to engagement with perspectives from other quarters as well that may deepen and broaden understanding.

Who might such readers be? I have a variety of readers in mind: female and male, and religious professionals (pastors and educators) as well as lay readers—any who engage in serious, in-depth study of biblical narratives. I hope, for example, that this book will be a resource for preachers and teachers who engage the texts on a regular basis in the practice of ministry, but who may have had limited exposure to new research emerging in connection with biblical women and to feminist biblical scholarship in particular. The book may serve as a textbook for college or seminary courses dealing with women in the biblical world or the four Gospels. It is also designed for use by laypersons and groups interested in substantive Bible study. I try to present technical matters in an accessible fashion, and include study questions with each chapter to facilitate group discussion or individual reflection. I hope all readers will find this book a useful resource by which to familiarize themselves with feminist biblical scholarship and its relevance for contemporary Christian life and faith.

One of the many contributions of feminist biblical scholarship to the reading of biblical narratives has been the rereading and reevaluation of stories featuring women. In the chapters that follow, we confine ourselves to the Gospel narratives and examine six stories that feature women in encounter with Jesus:

The Canaanite Woman (Matt. 15:21–28)
A Hemorrhaging Woman and Jairus's Daughter (Mark 5:21–43)
Martha and Mary (Luke 10:38–42)
A Bent Woman, Daughter of Abraham (Luke 13:10–17)
The Samaritan Woman (John 4:1–42)
A Woman Accused of Adultery (John 7:53–8:11)

Other stories could have been included, for these women are not the only ones who appear in the Gospels; but in the interest of in-depth engagement with each story, I have chosen these six texts. Each chapter includes an initial encounter with the text that dives deep; I provide attention to matters of language and grammar, structure, form, and literary and historical context. In some cases, the history of interpretation demands special attention, for portraits of women in the New Testament are often clouded by considerable interpretive litter and need to be rescued from androcentric interpretations that have deeply affected Christian imagination. In several instances, the danger of anti-Judaic interpretive options needs addressing as well. In each chapter I aim to engage readers with new angles of vision provided by recent biblical scholarship—feminist scholarship in particular. A variety of interpretive perspectives, problems, and possibilities emerge in connection with each of the texts, and we consider ways in which these stories can inform Christian life and faith and the practice of daily ministry.

Finally, let me share a few of the presumptions that informed my writing of this study. I presume that biblical stories are texts of transforming power with much to teach us about God's way in the world and our own human experience, which does not necessarily mean they are praiseworthy in every respect. Biblical stories may present problems as well as possibilities with which we must wrestle. But in wrestling with, and sometimes against, their claims, we are engaged by the living God, and in this sense the texts are experienced as "holy" Scripture. I do not necessarily assume that the women presented in the texts are role models (though some of them may turn out to be), for this approach would limit what they have to teach us.[9] I also assume that biblical texts are multivalent, bearing a range of meanings and possibilities. Indeed, we explore a variety of interpretive perspectives on each text. So let us go back to the well in Samaria and other ancient biblical sites to reconsider the women who appear there. As we engage the stories and new angles of vision upon them, may they bring us, too, face-to-face with Jesus.

Questions for Discussion or Reflection

How would you describe your own relationship with the Bible? What are your earliest memories of it? How has the relationship evolved through the years? What have been the significant milestones in that relationship along the way?

Is the word "feminist" a positive word in your vocabulary? Why or why not?

What do you think of the definitions of a "feminist" offered by Rebecca West, Alan Alda, Katharine Sakenfeld, and Letty Russell? Do they describe you? Does any one of them better reflect your feelings?

How would you describe your own social location? What are some of the characteristics of your reality and experience that you bring to a biblical text—that affect what you see and the questions you think to ask?

When you think of all the women who appear in the Bible, which ones intrigue you the most and why? Which biblical woman would you most like to have a conversation with when you get to heaven—and what would you like to talk with her about?

Chapter One

The Canaanite Woman

Matthew 15:21–28

Jesus left that place and went away to the district of Tyre and Sidon. Just then a Canaanite woman from that region came out and started shouting, "Have mercy on me, Lord, Son of David; my daughter is tormented by a demon." But he did not answer her at all. And his disciples came and urged him, saying, "Send her away, for she keeps shouting after us." He answered, "I was sent only to the lost sheep of the house of Israel." But she came and knelt before him, saying, "Lord, help me." He answered, "It is not fair to take the children's food and throw it to the dogs." She said, "Yes, Lord, yet even the dogs eat the crumbs that fall from their masters' table." Then Jesus answered her, "Woman, great is your faith! Let it be done for you as you wish." And her daughter was healed instantly.

Jesus' unexpected encounter with the Canaanite woman proved to be a defining moment in his ministry. The evangelist Matthew later told her story to the early Christians of his community in order to help them define their own ministries carried out in Jesus' name. The woman was an outsider with a demon-possessed daughter, and the story of her encounter with Jesus in Matthew 15:21–28 is one of the most remarkable in that Gospel. Indeed, it is extraordinary among all the Gospel stories in that it is one of the few in which a woman character is granted a significant voice. In Matthew's narrative, this account offers only the second time that the voice of a woman is heard speaking out loud (cf. 14:8).

Mark was the first to record the story (Mark 7:24–30). As the evangelist Matthew retold it to his own community some years later, he reshaped, altered, and edited the story in significant ways. Compare their accounts:

1

Mark 7:24–30

24 From there he set out and went away to the region of Tyre. He entered a house and did not want anyone to know he was there. Yet he could not escape notice,

25 but a woman whose little daughter had an unclean spirit immediately heard about him, and she came and bowed down at his feet.

26 Now the woman was a Gentile, of Syrophoenician origin. She begged him to cast the demon out of her daughter.

27 He said to her, "Let the children be fed first, for it is not fair to take the children's food and throw it to the dogs."

28 But she answered him, "Sir, even the dogs under the table eat the children's crumbs."

29 Then he said to her, "For saying that, you may go—and the demon has left your daughter."

30 So she went home, found the child lying on the bed, and the demon gone.

Matthew 15:21–28

21 Jesus left that place and went away to the district of Tyre and Sidon.

22 Just then a Canaanite woman from that region came out and started shouting, "Have mercy on me, Lord, Son of David; my daughter is tormented by a demon."

23 But he did not answer her at all. And his disciples came and urged him, saying, "Send her away, for she keeps shouting after us."

24 He answered, "I was sent only to the lost sheep of the house of Israel."

25 But she came and knelt before him, saying, "Lord, help me."

26 He answered, "It is not fair to take the children's food and throw it to the dogs."

27 She said, "Yes, Lord, yet even the dogs eat the crumbs that fall from their masters' table."

28 Then Jesus answered her, "Woman, great is your faith! Let it be done for you as you wish." And her daughter was healed instantly.

Notable differences emerge from a comparison. Chief among them is that Matthew has expanded the conversational component of the story. The encounter becomes much more of a dialogue in Matthew than it is in Mark, as the woman is given more direct speech. In Mark 7:25–26, for example, the narrator tells us that a woman came and fell down at Jesus' feet and begged him to cast the demon out of her daughter. In Matthew 15:22, however, we hear her own voice: "Just then a Canaanite woman from that region came out and started shouting, 'Have mercy on me, Lord, Son of David; my daughter is tormented by a demon.'" In fact, the woman addresses Jesus three times. Jesus answers twice, and disciples also appear and address Jesus in the Matthean text. Matthew's story is thus much more of a dialogue than is Mark's.

Other significant differences are also apparent in Matthew's retelling. For one thing, the woman is identified not as "Greek" (*Hellēnis*; "Gentile" in the NRSV) or "Syrophoenician" as in Mark, but as a "Canaanite." For another, Jesus articulates his job description in verse 24, pointedly stating that the foreign woman and her daughter fall outside its purview. Moreover, the one rejoinder to the woman's plea found in both Mark and Matthew is harsher in its Matthean version, for whereas Mark's Jesus suggests that the children are to be "fed first," Matthew's bluntly states that "It is not fair to take the children's food and throw it to the dogs." Finally, Matthew's account is distinguished by an emphasis on the woman's great faith (v. 28). These and other editorial fingerprints upon the text deserve special attention as interpretation proceeds, for they embody messages the evangelist wishes to convey.

The story's genre is difficult to pigeonhole. It has all the earmarks of a miracle story (and in particular, an exorcism), in that it describes a miraculous event—following the sequence of problem, resolution, and proof—but the dialogue, rather than the healing, stands at the heart of the story. A story about a healing appears to have been expanded by a pronouncement story or controversy dialogue—a genre that depicts Jesus engaged in a confrontation with an adversarial person or group and climaxes in a punch line from Jesus. This particular controversy dialogue, however, has an unusual twist. Sharon Ringe has pointed out the following:

> [T]he exchange between Jesus and the woman reverses the pattern usually found in such stories. Usually a situation or event provokes a hostile question from some onlooker to Jesus, to which Jesus responds with a correcting or reproving question and then drives home his point by a concluding statement which the opponent would

be hard put to deny. In this story, however, it is Jesus who provides the hostile saying and the woman whose retort trips him up and corrects him.[1]

In other words, *she* delivers the punch line and trumps him!

Attention to the structure of the dialogue reveals another remarkable aspect of their exchange. As John Meier has noted, the story is structured around four verbal encounters[2] as follows:

> *Setting* (v. 21)
> *1st verbal encounter*—initiated by Canaanite woman (vv. 22–23a)
>   *Rebuff*: silence
> *2nd verbal encounter*—initiated by disciples (vv. 23b–24)
>   *Rebuff*: theology
> *3rd verbal encounter*—initiated by Canaanite woman (vv. 25–26)
>   *Rebuff*: insult
> *4th verbal encounter*—initiated by Canaanite woman (vv. 27–28b)
>   *Response*: "Woman, great is your faith! . . ."
> *Healing* (v. 28c)

The Canaanite woman is clearly the protagonist who initiates each movement in this story. Jesus' role is that of respondent,[3] his "answering" posture underlined four times (cf. the verb "to answer" in vv. 23, 24, 26, and 28). Moreover, his response to the first three requests is decidedly negative (highlighted in the Greek by the negative word *ouk*, or "not") and consists first of silence, followed by theological rationale, and then insult.

This heaping up of oppositions to the woman's request is striking, and as Meier suggests, we need to keep the "law of threes" in mind to appreciate this structure. Biblical narratives are often structured around patterns of three. In the story of the Good Samaritan, for example, three people come upon the wounded man by the side of the road (Luke 10), and an audience instinctively anticipates that the third encounter will constitute the climax of the story. Thus, an audience hearing the Canaanite woman's story expects that she will get three chances—and normally, after three strikes you're out! But after the third verbal engagement, the encounter is not terminated. The woman steps up for a fourth time at bat! Meier suggests that divine grace supplies the fourth opportunity.[4] But does the story not also and perhaps more clearly highlight the remarkable persistence of this woman?

Encountering the Text

Let us examine each section of the text more closely. The setting is provided in verse 21: "Jesus left that place and went away to the district of Tyre and Sidon." The verb *anachōreō*, used frequently by Matthew, suggests that his "leaving" entails "withdrawing." Jesus "withdraws," he "retires," he "takes refuge" in the face of perceived danger (cf. 2:12, 13, 14, 22; 4:12; 12:15; 14:13, where *anachōreō* is used in a similar fashion). Jesus has just been engaged in controversy with the Pharisees and scribes from Jerusalem over the tradition of the elders, his disciples' failure to wash their hands ceremonially before eating, and the things that defile (Matt. 15:1–20). On the heels of that controversy he now withdraws to the far northern regions of Galilee. He goes "into" or "toward" the district of Tyre and Sidon (pagan territory).[5] Whether he actually crosses the northern border "into" Tyre and Sidon, or rather moves "toward" the district, is not clear, for the preposition *eis* can be translated either way. The translation issue is interesting, because Matthew otherwise takes pains to emphasize that Jesus' ministry takes place exclusively within Israel,[6] and this passage offers the only occasion in Matthew on which Jesus might be depicted as stepping outside its borders. At most, Jesus merely crosses the border, because we are told that a Canaanite woman from "that region" or from "those boundaries *came out*" to meet him (italics added). Maybe *she* is the one who crosses the border. Whatever the case, although the scene changes as Jesus now withdraws and encounters the woman in the far northern border regions of Galilee, the topic remains the same.[7] Jesus has just been addressing the issue of clean and unclean, the things that defile—the central issue in Jewish and Gentile relations. Will he now practice what he preaches in one of his rare encounters with a Gentile woman?

After the setting, the first verbal encounter is narrated in verses 22–23a: "Just then a Canaanite woman from that region came out and started shouting, 'Have mercy on me, Lord, Son of David; my daughter is tormented by a demon.'" As the woman appears on the scene, apparently alone, she is not identified by name—either her own or that of a husband or father—but as (1) a Canaanite, (2) a woman, and (3) the mother of a demon-possessed daughter. In Mark, as we noted, the woman is described as "Greek" (*Hellēnis*) and "Syrophoenician" (NRSV: "a Gentile, of Syrophoenician origin"). In Matthew, however, she is described as a "Canaanite," a word that appears only here in the New Testament. The term is antiquated and the description peculiar, as there were no Canaanites around in Jesus' day! They were ancient history. Indeed, as former Swedish bishop Krister Stendahl once observed, calling this woman a "Canaanite" is like calling the Danes "Vikings"![8] But who were the Canaanites? They were the ancient enemies of Israel, the indigenous people with whom Israel battled to take possession of the promised land. By identifying the woman as a Canaanite, therefore, Matthew spotlights her for his readers as enemy, as pagan, as ethnic and religious outsider.

But what extraordinary words appear on the "Canaanite's" lips! Although clearly identified as an outsider, she appropriates the confessional and theological language of the insider:[9] "Have mercy on me, Lord, Son of David; my daughter is tormented by a demon." "Have mercy on me" is the language of the Psalms, particularly the psalms of lament, and thus the language of prayer (cf. Pss. 27:7; 30:10; 86:3; 123:3).[10] Moreover, in addressing Jesus as "Lord, Son of David," she acknowledges her trust in his divine authority and his fulfillment of all the messianic expectations associated with David's line.[11] Who would have anticipated that an "outsider," a despised enemy no less, would address Jesus with the confessional titles of early Christian communities and the language of prayer!

Matthew also highlights the public nature of her speech. In Mark, the encounter between Jesus and the woman takes place in a house, a private setting. Matthew, however, shifts the encounter to the public arena. Moreover, the woman comes out "shouting" or "screaming." In the text, the verb *krazein* ("to cry out," "to scream," or "to shriek") is in the imperfect tense, which suggests that she cries out not just once but continuously. The language thus conveys the notion of speaking too loudly,[12] of shouting, of high decibel levels. Her concern for the well-being of her daughter leads her to break all the rules of conduct for decorous women, as she enters the public domain of men and intrudes upon their company speaking loudly.[13]

What is Jesus' response? In verse 23 Matthew tells us that "he did not answer her at all." This silent rebuff is puzzling, for Jesus has not failed to respond to similar requests. Earlier, in Matthew 9, Jesus was engaged by a leader of the synagogue who sought healing for his daughter. Upon restoring the girl to life, in the very next scene Jesus healed two blind men who followed him, crying loudly, "Have mercy on us, Son of David!"—echoing the Canaanite woman's cry. So why the silent rebuff in this instance? Because she is Gentile? This did not prevent the healing of the Roman centurion's servant nor the Gadarene demoniacs in Matthew 8. What is the difference in this case? Is it because this particular Gentile is also a woman who dares to approach and importune him loudly in the public arena?

In Matthew's version of this story, the woman is rebuffed not only by Jesus, but also by his disciples, who react to her presence by initiating the second verbal encounter in verse 23b. They do not address Jesus as "Lord," as does the Canaanite, but petition him nonetheless: "Send her away, for she keeps shouting after us." The language of their entreaty is ambiguous, for it can be translated as "Dismiss her," "Send her away" (NRSV), or "Release her," "Send her away satisfied," "Give her what she wants" (NJB). So which is it? Do the disciples entreat Jesus to get rid of her, to get her off their backs? Or do they intercede for her, touched by her plight? On the one hand, "Send her away" is more consistent with the portrait of the disciples, who also implore Jesus to "send the crowds away" in 14:15 and seek to prohibit even the approach of children in 19:13–15. On the other hand, Jesus' negative rejoinder to their request ("I was not sent except to the lost sheep of the house of Israel") implies that they had in fact urged him to "give her what she wants." Of course a measure of truth may be present in both. As parents of young children attest, sometimes one "gives them what they want" precisely to "get them off one's back"! Thus, perhaps a plea for riddance (i.e., "do something for her quick") seeks to expedite her departure.[14] Whichever the case may be, the imperfect verb tense suggests that the disciples' request of Jesus is a repeated, insistent one (i.e., "they kept urging him, saying . . ."). One senses that the disciples are, at the very least, annoyed by the woman's noisy behavior and wish her to go away quietly, as the TEV translation suggests: "Send her away! She is following us and making all this noise!" They wish for peace and public decorum. Also, ponder the visual image that the verse conveys: "Send her away, for she keeps shouting out after us!" What picture do you see? They are moving—not stopping—and she is following along, trailing them, crying out behind them.

Again the woman is rebuffed, this time by means of a theological rationale, for Jesus' second response in verse 24 is this: "I was sent only to the lost sheep of the house of Israel." Only Matthew records this response, which, to be sure, is consistent with the Matthean Jesus' restrictive mission directives to his own disciples in his missionary discourse in 10:5–6: "Go nowhere among the Gentiles, and enter no town of the Samaritans, but go rather to the lost sheep of the house of Israel." With similar words Jesus now conveys his own sense of divine commission and necessity[15] and his sense that ethnic boundaries define the mission he has embraced.[16] These words express a troubling ethnic exclusivism on Jesus' part, but perhaps we ought not to hear them solely in these terms. Do they not also give expression to the urgency that impels him? Matthew has earlier described how deeply Jesus has been moved by the perilous situation of his people: "When he saw the crowds, he had compassion for them, because they were harassed and helpless, like sheep without a shepherd" (9:36). Indeed, they are "lost sheep" (10:6; 15:24) desperately in need of rescue. Thus, those human beings he perceives as the neediest are identified as the primary focus on his mission.[17] Moreover, faced with the pressing needs of a substantial group, may Jesus not also wrestle with prioritizing needs as he faces competing demands on his energies and attention?[18] For all of these reasons, a lone Gentile woman and her daughter would seem to fall outside the purview of his urgent and divinely ordained job description.

But if Jesus and the disciples are still moving, and she is trailing along, crying out behind them, their procession encounters a roadblock in verse 25: "But she came and knelt before him saying, 'Lord, help me.'" Again, the visual imagery is significant, for it appears that the Canaanite halts further movement by physically prostrating herself before Jesus. Moreover, the significance of Matthew's language in this third verbal encounter should not escape us, for the verb which describes her action is one of the evangelist's favorites: *proskyneō*, which means "to kneel," but also "to worship." The Canaanite does more than just kneel before him. She also worships him, and the imperfect verb tense suggests that she does so repeatedly. Over and over the evangelist Matthew uses the verb *proskyneō* to convey that Jesus is the worthy object of our worship (cf. 2:2, 8, 11; 8:2; 9:18; 14:33; 15:25; 28:9, 17); indeed, it is one of the distinctive emphases of this Gospel. That fact is here acknowledged by an outsider—a Canaanite woman—who cries out to Jesus again in the language of faith and prayer: "Lord, help me." This cry, like her worship, is a repeated one (signaled by a present-tense participle). Like the psalmist who also prays in this manner, she is at the end of her rope (cf. Pss. 69:1–18; 79:9; 109:26; 119:86). Matthew heightens the element of prayer and the woman's role as a petitioner. Both her language and her posture are those of Christian liturgy, and once again the Canaanite demonstrates her dependence upon and confidence in Jesus. She is absolutely certain that Jesus can heal her daughter if he is so inclined.

The third rebuff of the woman, however, pointedly indicates that he is not inclined, for Jesus answers in verse 26: "It is not fair to take the children's food and throw it to the dogs." Make no mistake about it: Calling someone a dog, then as now, was no compliment (cf. 1 Sam. 17:43; 24:14; Matt. 7:6; Phil. 3:2; Rev. 22:15)! Jesus' third rebuff of the Canaanite is undeniably a sharp insult. Indeed, as John Meier notes, "nowhere else in the Gospel tradition does Jesus address a sincere petitioner with such harsh, insulting language."[19] "Dogs" was apparently a term that Jews used to refer to groups overtly hostile to God's people or law (see 1 Sam. 17:43; Ps. 22:16; Prov. 26:11; Isa. 56:10–11).[20] (It was not a term of scorn for Gentiles or pagans in general, a racial slur, as many commentators aver.) Some commentators try to take the edge off of its use by arguing that because the word "dogs" appears here in the diminutive form, the reference is therefore to "little dogs," "house dogs," or "puppies," which places everybody under the same roof. Nevertheless, this language is offensive! Indeed, as T. A. Burkill notes, "As in English, so in other languages, to call a woman 'a little bitch' is no less abusive than to call her 'a bitch' without qualification."[21]

Moreover, as we have noted, Matthew's version of this saying is even more offensive than Mark's. In Mark, Jesus says, "Let the children be fed first, for it is not fair to take the children's food and throw it to the dogs." In Matthew, that dogs are to have their turn later is not implied. The insult is clearer and sharper. This picture of Jesus is frankly offensive and troublesome, raising an interpretive issue to which we shall return, one that has consumed much of the scholarly attention focused on this text.

Turning now to the fourth verbal encounter and the story's climax, given the "law of threes," one expects the story to conclude with the third exchange. (Three strikes and you're out!) But despite the fact that she has been rebuffed three times, the amazingly persistent woman comes back again in verse 27 for a fourth time: "She said, 'Yes, Lord, yet even the dogs eat the crumbs that fall from their masters' table.'" "Yes, Lord," she says, thereby acknowledging the urgency and priority of his mission to Israel's lost sheep.[22] Still, by addressing him as "Lord" for a third time (cf. 15:22, 25, 27), she continues to assert that he is Lord not only of Jew, but also of Gentile. Moreover, she takes up Jesus' insulting word and uses it to argue against him, subtly reshaping the metaphor to include her own need and her daughter's within the purview of his mission. Perhaps, as Gerd Theissen suggests, she hears a promise in the brush-off: "Behind the sharp refusal, she can hear a positive attitude to children expressed in the image. And when she acts on behalf of a child, she is only putting into practice what is praised in the image within the saying."[23]

Whatever the case may be, her reply ingeniously shifts the image from frugality (of bread sufficient for the children alone) to abundance.[24] She speaks of the masters' table[25] so lavishly supplied that food falls to the floor and feeds the dogs beneath; note, too, that the word for "master" and "Lord" are one and the same in Greek (*kyrios*). The "children's bread" is thus the Lord Jesus' to give.[26] The fact that the word "lords'" or "masters'" appears in the plural form may imply recognition not only of Jesus but also of God as her Lord, as Stephenson Humphries-Brooks suggests: "she understands the table as the table of the final banquet presided over by God and the Son of Man that includes all, despite accidents of ethnicity, gender, or status" (see 22:1–14; 25:1–13).[27] In sum, with this striking rejoinder, the Canaanite bears witness to a God of abundance, rich in mercy, who supplies bread aplenty for all.[28] And she continues to invoke the Lord's abundant mercy for the healing of her daughter.

This brings us to Jesus' final response in verse 28: "Then Jesus answered her, 'Woman, great is your faith! Let it be done for you as you wish.'" The emphatic "then" suggests that we have reached a turning point as Jesus (who is finally named) now addresses the Canaanite woman directly for the first time. Indeed, only with this fourth and final response is Jesus' speaking to her explicitly stated, and the fact that his remarks are prefaced with "Woman" suggests that he speaks with strong emotion.

Matthew's edits are evident upon this conclusion to the story. In Mark, Jesus says: "For this saying (Greek *logon*) you may go your way," stressing the woman's argument and teaching.[29] Matthew's emphasis, however, is on her persistent faith, an emphasis even more apparent in Greek, where in terms of word order both the word "great" and "your" are highlighted. Jesus' final saying also features a triple "you":[30] "Great is your faith. Let it be done for you as you wish." Jesus thus honors the woman and her faith, her unshakable confidence in him, and her insight into the inclusive power, presence, and mercy of God.[31] Her great faith stands in pointed contrast to the "little faith" exhibited by Peter in the preceding chapter (14:31) and by the disciples in the following one (16:8). The woman's faith foreshadows the response of the Gentiles to the gospel, a faith that overcomes barriers which the risen Jesus himself explicitly removes after his death and resurrection, when he commissions his disciples to "Go therefore and make disciples of all nations" in Matthew's closing scene (28:16–20).

New Testament scholar Joanna Dewey makes a striking observation that is well worth pondering as we consider the conclusion of this story:

> The narrative portrays *Jesus being bested by a woman*, and *changing his behavior* on that account. This is the only instance in the extant tradition of Jesus being taught by someone, and that someone is a woman who should not properly be speaking to him at all. As a result of her speech, [or in Matthew, as a result of her persistent faith,] Jesus ignores the fundamental boundary between Jew and Gentile.[32]

Similarly, Judith Gundry-Volf notes that Jesus, inspired by the woman, "rises up to her faith in him as Lord of Gentile as well as Jew."[33] As Krister Stendahl puts it, Jesus says, "What hutzpah!" "He hails the Gentile hutzpah and makes an anticipatory exception."[34]

Finally in verse 28 Matthew reports that "her daughter was healed instantly."[35] In Mark, the woman's daughter is healed at a distance: when the woman goes home, she finds the child lying on the bed, and the demon gone (Mark 7:30). Matthew, however, reports an instantaneous healing. Is the daughter at home, or has she been there all along, by her mother's side?

Angles of Vision

Having examined the text closely, let us now stand back from it and consider three interpretive lenses, or angles of vision, that may help us focus our reflection on its message and significance for our lives: Jewish/Gentile boundaries, gender boundaries, and socioeconomic boundaries. The discussion also addresses the humanity of Jesus and the troubling picture of him that the text presents, a matter that has long confounded interpreters.

Jewish/Gentile Boundaries

The first interpretive lens is Jewish/Gentile relations. This issue was a sensitive one for the Matthean church, a mixed congregation with a sizeable Jewish-Christian constituency. Many factors point to a Jewish-Christian presence, such as the evangelist's penchant for "Jewish-like" phraseology ("righteousness," "kingdom of heaven," etc.), a portrait of Jesus that highlights Jewish lineage and expectation ("Son of Abraham," "Messiah," "Son of David," "King of Israel," "Emmanuel," etc.), Jesus' concentration on Israel, and the earnest attitude he takes toward the law and the tradition of the elders.[36] Christians of Gentile origin were apparently also increasingly found in the congregation,[37] and in fact the community stood at a turning point in its life, poised for a new venture in Gentile mission.[38]

This text no doubt provided guidance for the Matthean church in its relations with Gentiles, which is perhaps why the disciples play a role in Matthew's version of the story. The querulous disciples may represent Jewish-Christians who were opposed to, or did not understand, the entry of Gentiles into the church.[39] One can also imagine that the Canaanite woman would have been cheered and claimed by the Gentiles seated in Matthew's pews as one of their own! Viewed from this angle of vision, the story celebrates both God's faithfulness to Israel and the power of boundary-crossing faith.[40] The account celebrates the miracle of the faith of Gentiles as that which gives them access to healing and salvation. That faith, seen as the miraculous gift of God, justifies the inclusion of Gentiles in the church and its mission. This dimension of the good news is still important in this text, for those of us who continue to encounter the story are, after all, mostly Gentile Christians. As Paul reminds us, we are "wild" olive branches that have been grafted onto Israel's cultivated olive tree. As Karl Barth affirmed, we Christians are "guests in the house of Israel"— "new wood grafted onto their old tree."[41] This text continues to affirm that mystery, celebrating both God's faithfulness to Israel and the power of boundary-crossing faith.

This issue of inclusion is further highlighted by the context in which the story appears, for two feeding stories stand in close proximity to it: a feeding of a Jewish crowd of five thousand in the immediately preceding chapter (14:13–21) and a feeding of a Gentile crowd of four thousand among the episodes that follow (15:32–39). That the second feeding is a feeding of a Gentile crowd is indicated in 15:31 by the reference to the fact that "they praised the God of Israel." The contrasts between the Canaanite woman's story and the second feeding story are particularly striking. Though Jesus initially ignores the Canaanite woman, in 15:32 we hear him say of four thousand Gentiles: "I have compassion for the crowd." Though his disciples sought to "send her away," in 15:32, Jesus states explicitly: "I do not want to send them away hungry." In response to the faith of a Gentile woman, Jesus appears to have expanded the original scope of his ministry. Moreover, in both feeding accounts framing the Canaanite's story, there are abundant leftovers—twelve baskets after the first feeding (14:20), and seven baskets after the second (15:37)—bringing to mind her plea for crumbs. Thus, clearly, "divine provision for Israel can be extended to gentiles, and . . . Israel will still have no lack."[42] So lavish are God's blessings and the abundance of God's table that even after the children are fed, enough bread remains for all.

Interestingly, the evangelist Matthew adds a postscript to both feeding stories, explicitly noting that about five thousand and then four thousand are fed, "besides women and children" (14:21; 15:38). Thus, there is ample room for women and children at the table. Furthermore, the bread theme is central throughout Matthew 15:1–16:12. It begins with a controversy with the Pharisees over eating bread with unwashed hands (15:1–9) and discourse on the things that defile (15:10–20), continues with Jesus' encounter with a Canaanite woman which raises the question of the possibility of bread crumbs for Gentiles (15:21–28), and is followed by the feeding of four thousand (15:32–39) and a warning about the yeast of the Pharisees and Sadducees (16:5–12). This connecting thread of food and bread that runs through this section of Matthew's Gospel may account, in part, for the odd nature of Jesus' reply to the Canaanite woman's entreaty. Jesus speaks to her of "bread," though she has asked for healing. As Theissen notes, "the food metaphor could be conditioned by the fact that common meals often occasioned a debate on the relation between Jews and Gentiles."[43] The bread metaphor also has patent sociopolitical implications in the context of a Roman imperial system that ensured the elite's food supply at the expense of the poor. As Warren Carter notes, in the feeding stories "Jesus enacts God's will that hungry people be fed" and "an alternative system marked by compassion, sufficiency, and shared resources."[44] In so doing, he anticipates "the abundance of God's future new creation and empire."[45]

The issue of Gentile/Jewish relations has been the traditional lens by which to examine the Canaanite woman's story. For centuries, the story has been read as a model of salvation history—that is, the story of God's saving acts, which proceeds from the Jews to the Gentiles. Moreover, the faith by which Gentiles gain access to healing and salvation has often been spotlighted as the story's central theological affirmation. The Protestant Reformers, for example, turned repeatedly to the Canaanite woman for a dramatic illustration of the nature of faith.[46]

What does one learn from her example? That faith "is not a quality which takes its support from what can be perceived. . . . Its essential character must consist, therefore, in a trusting despite the evidence of eye and ear."[47] Indeed, the Canaanite appears to embody the definition of faith proffered by Hebrews: "faith is the assurance of things hoped for, the conviction of things not seen" (Heb. 11:1). Interestingly, only two persons in Matthew are lauded for their "great faith," and both are Gentiles: a Roman centurion (8:10) and a Canaanite woman (15:28).

Gender Boundaries

The Canaanite's story is multivalent—rich in nuance and complexity. In recent years, feminist scholars have surfaced a second interpretive lens that can expand our reflection on the story: gender. The one who approaches Jesus is not only a foreigner, she is also female, although commentators have devoted far more attention to the former feature of her portrait than the latter.[48]

As we have noted, Jesus has not failed to respond immediately when approached by other Gentiles in Matthew's story (see Matt. 8:5–13, 28–34). But in this one instance he hesitates, and one cannot but wonder: is it because this particular Gentile is also a woman?[49] Feminist scholar Elaine Wainwright has highlighted this angle of vision, arguing that "the subversive power of this story goes far beyond the traditional boundary breaking with which it is associated—namely, Gentile mission. It invites the hearer to break the bonds of gender-stereotyping and bias and demand miracle in human life, particularly in female human life."[50] Wainwright identifies two struggles within the Matthean community inscribed in this text: (1) conflict over mission to the Gentiles, but also (2) conflict surrounding women's roles, that is, women's participation in the liturgical and theological life of the community.

Several indicators of this second conflict can be found in Matthew's version of the story. One is the location of the encounter in Matthew: the public arena. As Wainwright reminds us, in first-century Mediterranean culture, the public arena was the domain of men; women's activity was limited to the private, domestic sphere. Thus, the Canaanite's success as a woman in the public arena is an indicator of a significant gender question in the story.[51]

The second indicator is the language placed on the woman's lips. As we have noted, in Matthew's version of the story she is accorded direct speech. Moreover, she addresses Jesus using christological titles such as "Lord" and "Son of David" and in the language of prayer. As Wainwright observes, this language represents the developing liturgical and theological formulations within the Matthean community, and thus offers another clue that the text is concerned not only with ethnic questions, but also with gender questions.[52]

To the clues highlighted by Wainwright, others can be added: the woman's liturgical posture of "kneeling" (15:25); the woman's explicit reference to the "masters' table" or "lords' table" and her right to be fed there, which calls to mind the central table in the worship of the church; and the explicit inclusion of "women and children" in the eucharistically cast feeding stories that precede and follow (14:21; 15:38). All of these clues are the evangelist Matthew's editorial fingerprints on the text. They suggest that Matthew's community may have struggled with the role of women within the liturgical and theological life of the community. The fact that the Canaanite is endowed with liturgical and theological speech and activity would appear to affirm women's significant participation within it.[53]

The heaping up of objections to the woman's request is significant in this connection, as is Matthew's introduction of disciples into the scene. Perhaps the peevish disciples represent those in the community opposed not only to mission to the Gentiles, but also to women's active leadership in community life. In sum, Wainwright suggests that the Canaanite woman "is the catalyst and hence the 'foremother' not only of Gentile Christians but also of women freed from all restrictive and oppressive socioreligious bondage."[54] She is symbolic of the struggle of Gentiles and women for participation within the life of new Christian communities. Moreover, her story may reflect the catalytic influence of women in enlarging the ethnic boundaries of the early Christian community. Elisabeth Schüssler Fiorenza calls attention to this possibility, noting how striking it is that a theological argument against limiting the Jesus movement to Israel alone is attributed to a woman: "That such a theological argument is placed in the mouth of a woman gives us a clue to the historical leadership of women in opening up the Jesus movement to 'Gentile sinners' (Gal. 2:15). The story of the Syro-Phoenician [Canaanite] makes women's contribution to one of the most crucial transitions in early Christian beginnings historically visible."[55] Is this not intriguing speculation?

Schüssler Fiorenza, like Wainwright, holds up the Canaanite woman as symbolic of the struggle of women for participation within the life of the Christian community, and in so doing further assists us in appreciating the contemporary significance of her story. Schüssler Fiorenza says this, for example, about the entrance of feminist biblical criticism into the world of theological education and scholarship:

> Like the woman in this gospel story, feminist biblical interpretation meets resistance when it seeks to enter scholarly discourses on equal terms. In recent years, feminist biblical interpretation has continually sought to enter the "house" of biblical criticism as an "insider" to interrupt biblical criticism's androcentric isolation and to challenge its prevailing discourses. Yet, like the woman in Matthew's Gospel, such attempts to enter the discourses of the discipline on equal terms often receive no response at all—"but he did not respond to her word"—or they are met with the reaction of Jesus' male disciples, who wish to send the woman away because her voice is too loud and noisy.[56]

Christian feminists who have tried to make their voices heard in the church or the academy can appreciate this connection between their own experience and that of Matthew's Canaanite! Schüssler Fiorenza also urges Christian feminists to heed her example in that she "does not enter the house and interrupt Jesus [as in Mark]; rather she 'comes out' and 'shouts after' Jesus and his disciples." Following her lead, "feminist biblical interpretation must position itself in the public-political center of church and academy, rather than on the boundaries."[57] Schüssler Fiorenza highlights intriguing connections for Christian women to ponder, for in connection with the struggles of contemporary women within the church and the academy to have their voices heard, the Canaanite continues to be a powerful symbol.

Although Elaine Wainwright and Elisabeth Schüssler Fiorenza share some perspectives on this text, feminists do not speak with one voice. In other words, no such thing as "the feminist interpretation" exists for this text or any other. Feminists represent a variety of perspectives, methodologies, and opinions, which is certainly the case in connection with Matthew 15. Indeed, Schüssler Fiorenza notes that in her classroom, "when trying to assess whether the story advocates patriarchal values and visions, feminist students usually disagree":

> Those who argue that the narrative is not patriarchal point to the fact that the woman is the major protagonist in this story, that her argument convinces Jesus, and that her daughter was healed. But at what cost, other students ask. The woman does not challenge the ethnic-religious prejudice of Jesus but confirms it with "Yes Lord." She doesn't argue for equal access; she begs for crumbs. Thus she accepts second-class citizenship which she herself has internalized. She acts like a dog who is grateful, even when kicked. Hence it is not surprising that commentators praise her for her humble submission. This is indeed a sacred text that advocates and reinscribes patriarchal power-relations, anti-Jewish prejudices, and women's feminine identity and submissive behavior.[58]

Problematic aspects of the text have also been highlighted by postcolonial feminist interpreters, who are attuned to ways in which texts may reflect imperialistic values and visions as well as patriarchal ones. Postcolonial studies take "the reality of empire—of imperialism and colonialism—as an omnipresent, inescapable, and overwhelming reality in the world,"[59] inscribed in both ancient texts and modern interpretations of them. Musa Dube illustrates this point in her sobering reading of the Canaanite woman's story, which, in her view, has frightening implications when read as a narrative that foreshadows the church's mission to the nations. For one thing, it "sanctions the traveling to and entering foreign nations by divinely authorized travelers"[60] and upholds the superiority of some races to others. For another, the foreign "other" is marked as one of the Canaanites, who in the memories of Israel were to be invaded, conquered, and dispossessed. Moreover, she is seen to be in desperate need of the divinely empowered traveler and takes all the initiative in their encounter, seeking and beseeching him for salvation. She is also portrayed as accepting the social category of a dog assigned to her and agreeing to stay under the table and pick up crumbs, where she presents no threat to the children's bread. Jesus grants her request on these conditions.[61] Is there not a disconcerting ring of truth to these observations? Dube's reading alerts us to ways in which Matthew's vision of mission may embody imperialistic values and strategies, lest we reinscribe them in our theology and practice of mission.

The Canaanites' history of dispossession by the Israelites is also central to a study of the text by Leticia A. Guardiola-Sáenz, who provides an alternative reading of the story by reading it in solidarity with the displaced and recasting it from the Canaanite's point of view: "I hold that the Canaanite woman is not a humble dog begging for crumbs. She is a dispossessed woman who has awoken from her position as oppressed, and now is coming to confront the empire and demand her right to be treated as a human being."[62] In this confrontation, she challenges the excluding ideology of chosenness, asks for restitution, and humanizes the oppressor by her presence. Postcolonial readings such as these help us acknowledge our blind spots and expand our reflection upon this complex narrative.

Contemporary readers should ponder their own impressions of the story. Do you celebrate the woman's initiative, her persistence in the face of overwhelming rejection, her public voice? Do you also want to attend to problematic aspects of the story that may not be life-giving? Continue this discussion with people in your own Christian community, and you will no doubt encounter further interpretations. Women with children, for example, are often untroubled by the seeming willingness of the Canaanite to accept crumbs and second-class status. As they note, when your child is seriously ill and you are desperate, nothing else matters. You would do anything, say anything within your reach to gain healing for your child. Indeed, some will appreciate the Canaanite's politically astute appropriation and subversion of the dominant discourse and its structures to achieve just ends. Still other contemporary women would clearly pursue a different strategy when faced with a similar affront. As one unidentified Hispanic woman comments: "The woman in the Bible needed help. She realized Jesus could help her and nothing was going to stop her. It was not very nice, as a matter of fact, it was terrible of Jesus to tell her that she could not eat from the bread that was on the table. She could only have crumbs. If it had been me, I would have answered him that I have every right to eat from the bread on the table. We do not want just the crumbs, no."[63]

In considering these varied perspectives and our own impressions, we are reminded of the multivalence of biblical texts and of the ways in which our understanding is enriched by hearing the perspectives of others within a wider interpretive community. In reflecting on the text, we would also do well to reevaluate traditional interpretations of the Canaanite. It is striking, for example, that within the history of (largely male) interpretation of this text she has frequently been held up as a model of humility and submissiveness. But does not close attention to her dogged persistence in the face of repeated rejection suggest that she is anything but humble and submissive? And is not the boldness of her approach an arresting feature of her portrait? F. Gerald Downing has highlighted this point: "A woman in late antiquity approaches a strange male and speaks first, without being invited to. Then, in the ensuing exchange, apparently she comes out best. There are not many parallels in ancient texts to the bold approach, very few instances indeed where a woman wins an argument with a man."[64]

At the close of this chapter, we also consider the Canaanite's epitomization of a great tradition of Israelite prayer: that of arguing with God and demanding a response. As Gail O'Day has observed, "the faith she embodies is not a faith of submission, but of robust boldness and vigor." Indeed, her story "shows the power and possibility inherent in boldly insisting that God be faithful to God's promises."[65]

Socioeconomic Boundaries

If ethnic and gender differences are integral to the Canaanite's story, so also are socioeconomic ones. Gerd Theissen has drawn attention to the likelihood that the woman Jesus encountered was upper class, urban, and well-educated. The evangelist Mark describes the woman as "Greek" (*Hellēnis*; Mark 7:26), thereby indicating, as Theissen notes, the social class to which she belonged: "Knowledge of Greek language and culture point to a member of the upper class, since Hellenization had first affected the people of higher status everywhere."[66] A further inkling of her affluence is found at the conclusion of the story, when she returns to her home and "found the child lying on the bed, and the demon gone" (Mark 7:30). The word for "bed" is not the usual one, *krabattos* (transportable "mattress," "straw tick," the poor person's pallet), but rather *klinē* ("couch," a piece of furniture).[67] These clues, which provide a glimpse into her household, are intriguing and compelling.

Thus, Theissen believes, when the woman comes out from the city of Tyre and encounters a rural itinerant preacher from the Galilean backwaters, two very different socioeconomic worlds collide. Indeed, Theissen finds in Jesus' harsh response to her a reflection of the bitter relationships between Jews and Gentiles in the border regions between Tyre and Galilee and urban-rural tensions. Tyre, as Theissen reminds us, was a wealthy coastal city that profited from extensive trade with the whole Mediterranean region. However, Tyre was located on an island with limited arable land. Thus, throughout its history the city depended on agricultural imports from the rural Galilean hinterlands, which served as its "breadbasket" (cf. Acts 12:20). Indeed, "The economically stronger Tyrians probably often took bread out of the mouths of the Jewish rural population, when they used their superior financial means to buy up the grain supply in the countryside."[68] Jesus' words to the woman may therefore reflect "a bitterness grounded in real relationships"[69] and would have been heard as follows: "First let the poor people in the Jewish rural areas be satisfied. For it is not good to take poor people's food and throw it to the rich Gentiles in the cities."[70] Indeed, Jesus may be drawing on a common saying that condemned this exploitative situation. Theissen's study of the cultural context leads him to conclude:

> If the considerations developed here are correct, the miracle would not consist in healing someone far away, but in the overcoming of an equally divisive distance: the prejudice-based distance between nations and cultures, in which the divisive prejudices are not simply malicious gossip, but have a real basis in the social, economic, and political relationships between two neighboring peoples. The Syrophoenician woman accomplishes something that for us today seems at least as marvelous as the miracle itself: she takes a cynical image and "restructures" it in such a way that it permits a new view of the situation and breaks through walls that divide people, walls that are strengthened by prejudice.[71]

In light of Theissen's analysis, we must ask: Does envisioning the woman as well-educated, urban, and upper class alter our perception of the story in any way? If so, how? Is she "part of the group in that region whose policies and lifestyle would have been a source of suffering for her mostly poorer, rural, Jewish neighbors,"[72] as Sharon Ringe suggests—an oppressor rather than one of the oppressed? If so, perhaps "her reply relinquishes the place of privilege" and "moves her into the place of receiving only what is left over—the place where the poor of the region have always been."[73] Perhaps her role as a member of an economically dominant, exploitative group explains why Jesus responds to her harshly, as Nicaraguan peasants from Solentiname instinctively recognize: "She must have been a rich old woman." "She must have been an oppressor."[74] Whatever the case may be, Theissen reminds us that the boundary-crossing dimensions of the text may be far more complex than we might have initially imagined.

These three interpretive perspectives, taken together, may expand our reflection on the text and help us explore its manifold connections with our lives. The Canaanite woman's story invites us to ponder the ways in which ethnic, gender, and socioeconomic differences and prejudices continue to be reflected in our own human experience. Moreover, the story invites us to ponder the role of human initiative and persistence in challenging and overcoming differences and prejudices. As Judith Gundry-Volf perceptively observes, in some biblical stories (such as John 4), "the divine gift of the Spirit breaks down barriers between people and leads to reconciliation and fellowship." In others, however, such as the one before us in Matthew 15, "human insistence on divine mercy, which is blind mercy, dramatically reverses a pattern of exclusion."[75] Similarly, Elizabeth Moltmann notes that this story "shows how human beings meet and how they can help each other to grow, to mature, and to become whole."[76] Viewed from this perspective, Jesus is not the only one who engages in ministry in this story. As we shall have occasion to note below, the Canaanite woman also engages in ministry—on behalf of Jesus and her daughter.

The Humanity of Jesus

One last issue begs for attention. The unflattering portrait of Jesus presented in Matthew 15:21–28 troubles many Christians. A desperate mother approaches Jesus, seeking healing for her sick daughter, and how does Jesus respond? Not in the compassionate manner we might have expected. First, he completely ignores her: "he did not answer her at all" (15:23). She persists, and he then provides a theological reason for his refusal to engage her: "I was sent only to the lost sheep of the house of Israel" (15:24). When she continues her entreaty, Jesus rebuffs her yet again with sheer insult: "It is not fair to take the children's food and to throw it to the dogs" (15:26). Nowhere else in the Gospel tradition does Jesus respond to a sincere petitioner in such a harsh, insulting manner.

So troubling is Jesus' response to the Canaanite woman that interpreters have gone to great lengths to rationalize it and rehabilitate the frankly offensive image of Jesus that the story presents. Considerable attention has also focused on the question of whether the story has any historical core—that is, whether it represents an actual encounter in the life of the historical Jesus. Varied solutions have been offered.

Some people have argued that Jesus was simply tired and having a bad day. After all, his encounter with the Canaanite follows on the heels of intense conflict and argument with the Pharisees; as he "withdraws" to the northern border regions of Galilee, he finds a clamorous woman intruding upon his solitude.

Others argue that Jesus' response to the woman is not really as offensive as it first sounds, for he does not compare the woman and her daughter to "dogs" but to "puppies"—adorable house dogs—which places everybody under the same roof! Still, as noted earlier, this language is offensive and no compliment. As Theissen observes, "all exegetical attempts at improvement are a waste of time and show that even the moral sensitivity of some Christian exegesis has 'gone to the dogs.'"[77]

More frequently, the argument is made that Jesus was "testing" the woman's faith—probably with a twinkle in his eye! But would such a test not then render Jesus a "hypocrite," one whose speech and action are inconsistent?[78] The Matthean Jesus denounces hypocrisy so vigorously (cf. 6:2, 5, 16; 22:18; 23:13–36) that one is hard-pressed to find the "testing" theory persuasive.

Could it be that we come face-to-face in the story before us with the very real humanity of Jesus? Could it be, as Sharon Ringe suggests, that the story reflects "an incident in Jesus' life when even he was caught with his compassion down"?[79] And is the story not also remarkable in presenting us with a Jesus who learns something from his encounter with another and changes his mind? As we have noted, this story is the only one in the Gospel tradition in which someone appears to change Jesus' mind about anything! Though Jesus has refused to engage her, stating emphatically that his ministry is restricted to Israel (15:24) and further distancing her with an insult (15:26), in the end the woman wins both his admiration and the healing of her daughter.

Many scholars insist that we read the story as being not about the historical Jesus, but rather as reflecting early Christian debates about the legitimacy of the Gentile mission. In other words, they argue, the story did not originate in an actual incident in Jesus' life and ministry, but instead was created by first-generation Christians to address a problem they faced, and to ground a solution to it in Jesus' own ministry. Jesus' sharp words of rejection are therefore not his own, but those of an early Christian group that wanted to bar Gentiles from access to the community. When all is said and done, the fact that Jesus extends himself in ministry to a Gentile instructs the Christian community to do likewise.

Gerd Theissen, however, questions this interpretation and asks, "Why should an early Christian group attribute to Jesus an opinion that it has rejected, if it wants to combat that opinion in the minds of other Christians?"[80] Sharon Ringe also rejects the argument that the story originated in early Christian missionary conflicts: "It is hard to imagine why the church at any stage of its development would want to present the Christ it confesses in such a light!"[81] Thus, Ringe is led to a conclusion with which I concur:

> The shocking quality of the portrait of Jesus . . . suggests to me that instead of composing this story to address contemporary church problems, the early church . . . made the best of a bizarre tradition about Jesus which it received. The very strangeness and the offensiveness of the story's portrayal of Jesus may suggest that the core of the story was indeed remembered as an incident in Jesus' life when even he was caught with his compassion down.[82]

Mark and Matthew no doubt found the remembered story instructive as their communities debated Gentile mission. Indeed, Matthew further shaped the story so that it might address this very problem (among others) more explicitly. But I cannot imagine that the evangelist or the church would have created the incident out of whole cloth. "The criterion of embarrassment" that "historical Jesus" scholars refer to lends further support to this conclusion. As John Meier explains, "The point of the criterion is that the early Church would hardly have gone out of its way to create material that only embarrassed its creator or weakened its position in arguments with opponents."[83] In the case of Matthew 15, the church appears to have faithfully transmitted an embarrassing incident in Jesus' life rather than yield to "convenient amnesia."[84]

Some Christians will not be able to accept this interpretation, this por-

trait of a Jesus who is less than perfect, who participates in human prejudice, who is consequently instructed by another, and who changes his
mind. Other Christians, however, will embrace it as a reminder of Jesus'
full engagement with our own human reality and struggle and find in it
good news. Theissen grasps both the difficulty and the possibility in a nut-
shell: "Perhaps you will say, 'Can we still believe in such a Jesus, a Jesus
who is not perfect, a Jesus who is put to shame by a foreign woman toward
whom he has behaved inhumanly?' I think that this is the only Jesus whom
one can trust. We can only trust a Jesus who allows a woman to draw him
out of his prejudices. Only in such a Jesus do we recognize a human
face."[85]

Similarly, some Christians will insist that the focus of interpretation
must remain on the ministry of Jesus and the text's witness to him as the
saving presence of God. Other Christians, however, will also want to celebrate the ministry of the woman to Jesus and her daughter by her faith—
her "act of trust, of engagement, risking everything." Sharon Ringe makes
this point:

> That act has the effect, as the story is told, of enabling Jesus to see
> the situation in a different way. That new perspective appears to free
> Jesus to respond, to heal, to become again the channel of God's
> redeeming presence in that situation. Whatever provoked the initial
> response attributed to Jesus . . . it is the Gentile woman who is said
> to have called his bluff. In so doing, she enabled him to act in a way
> apparently blocked to him before. Her wit, her sharp retort, was
> indeed her gift to Jesus—a gift that enabled his gift of healing in turn,
> her ministry that opened up the possibility of his.[86]

Perhaps both dimensions of the story and both ministries can, in the
end, be honored when the dialogical nature of Matthew's story is fully
respected and taken into account. The evangelist Matthew, as we have
noted, has reshaped the story in significant ways, most notably by expand-
ing its conversational component so that it becomes much more of a dialogue than in Mark. In so doing, Matthew has evoked a strong biblical
tradition: that of arguing with God and demanding a response. This tradition is embodied in the experience of Abraham, of Job, and of the
prophets, but finds its chief expression in Israel's psalms of lament.
Indeed, the majority of prayers in Israel's psalter are psalms of lament,
psalms of startling boldness and candor, in which believers take God by
the lapels, so to speak, speak honestly of the pain of human experience,

and demand God's faithfulness to God's promises. The biblical presentation of this tradition of prayer suggests that God welcomes this dialogue, and that to argue with God in this manner is in fact an act of faith—an acknowledgment of the presence of a second party in our lives in whom we hope. This presentation also suggests that both parties are shaped by the dialogical encounter and communion. Yahweh's mind was often changed by such remonstrance (see, for example, Exod. 32:14; Gen. 8:21; Jonah 3:10; Job 42:7–17).

Gail O'Day has argued persuasively that the Canaanite woman stands in this tradition of prayer, that in fact her story is "a narrative embodiment of a lament psalm": "Matthew has shaped her words to reflect the traditional, candid speech of Jews before their God."[87] As O'Day observes: "Israel's placing of needs and hurts before God was an act of faith in God's presence and ability to respond. The Canaanite woman's act of placing her need before Jesus was also an act of faith."[88] O'Day also writes that

> Jesus was changed by this woman's boldness. Just as God is impinged upon by Israel's pleas, so is Jesus impinged upon here. The Canaanite woman knows who Jesus is and holds him to it; she will not settle for a diminishment of the promise. She insists that Jesus be Jesus, and through her insistence she frees him to be fully who he is. . . . Using the idiom of Israel's lament, Matthew narrates a story that shows the power and possibility inherent in boldly insisting that God be faithful to God's promises. . . . The Canaanite woman's faith insisted on the fulfillment of the gospel promise, and Matthew asks that we, like Jesus himself, listen to her and be transformed through a faith like hers: persistent, vigorous, and confident in God's faithfulness to God's promises.[89]

The dialogical framework in which the story is cast and the biblical tradition of argumentative prayer in which it stands suggest that both parties in the conversation merit our reflection as we explore the story's connections with our own lives. May the Canaanite woman continue to inspire in us the same boldness in prayer and persistence in faith that clings to God's promises. May the God who has drawn close to us with a human face bless us also with a saving presence. And may their mutual story help us imagine and define our own daily lives as ministry that crosses boundaries dividing the human family, so that we, too, may bear witness to the inclusive power, presence, and mercy of God.

Group Study Suggestions

Begin with a dramatic reading of Matthew 15:21–28. Assign roles to
a narrator, a Canaanite woman, and Jesus, and ask the rest of the
group to read collectively the disciples' line.

Following the reading, ask participants: What impressions emerged
as you heard the story, and what questions does it raise for you?

Explain that Mark was the first to record this story, and that the evangelist Matthew retells it for his own community. In his retelling,
he makes editorial alterations in order to address issues of concern
in his community and to give expression to his own theological
convictions. Ask group members to compare Matthew's version of
this story with Mark 7:24–30. What differences emerge from the
comparison?

Proceed with any of the questions for discussion/reflection below.

Questions for Discussion or Reflection

With whom do you identify as you hear this story, and why? Where
would you place yourself in the scene?

In what ways do you identify with the Canaanite woman? With the
disciples? With Jesus?

Where do realities reflected in the text intersect with your own experience? What word does the text address to the reality or experience you have identified?

What do you make of Jesus' harsh saying: "It is not fair to take the
children's food and throw it to the dogs"? Of the variety of interpretations proffered, which do you find most persuasive? Why?

The story spotlights a variety of boundary issues that continue to
divide the human family: ethnic and religious boundaries, gender
boundaries, socioeconomic boundaries, urban-rural boundaries.
How are these boundaries reflected in your own life experience
and community? What do you learn from this story that can
inform your encounter with them?

In your view, is the story life-giving to women? Or does it reinscribe
patriarchal values and norms? How so?

In your view, does the story convey imperialistic values and troubling
implications for the church's mission? Why or why not?

Does your perception of the story change to think of the woman as
upper class, urban, and educated? To think of the story as an

encounter between the first world and the third world? How so? What insights are gained?

Do you think of the Canaanite woman as oppressed or as an oppressor?

As you hear Jesus' harsh saying in verse 26, where do you locate yourself within it? Do you envision yourself among the children at the table, receiving choice portions—or among the dogs who eat the crumbs that fall from the table? Why? Consider the following suggestion by Megan McKenna:

> As residents of the First World, using the bulk of the world's resources, we are the ones at the table and everyone else is under the table, as dogs, feeding on the leftovers that we throw their way. The conversation between Jesus and this woman reveals on a deeper level the realities of politics, economics, religion, racism, and nationalism that existed then and exist now. The brief encounter of these two human beings reveals to us today what is happening, what shouldn't be happening, and what could be happening.[90]

What do you think of McKenna's observation and what does it contribute to your reading of the story?

Frederick Dale Bruner suggests that the presence of the disciples in this scene can remind us that "The church can turn people away as well as attract them."[91] In a similar vein, Gerd Theissen observes that some of the worst barriers between people are those barricades people build up by referring to God: "I am sent, but not to them!"[92] What do you think of these observations?

Is it difficult for you to accept the interpretation that Jesus learns something from his encounter with the Canaanite woman and changes his mind as a result? Why or why not? Does the text, in your view, present a very human portrait of Jesus? Why or why not? What does the humanity of Jesus mean to you? What do you learn about Jesus from this story?

Have you known mothers with chronically ill children? Think of those women. What does this lens contribute to your reading of the story? Does it strike you as odd that she cries to the Lord: "Have mercy on *me*. . . . [M]y daughter is tormented by a demon. . . . Lord, help *me*"? Why or why not?

What does the strong biblical tradition of lament and of arguing with God contribute to your reading of the story? How can this story inform your own practice of prayer?

What new insights have emerged for you from your engagement with the Canaanite woman's story? What questions would you like to ask her or Jesus?

Resources for Further Study

Dube, Musa W. *Postcolonial Feminist Interpretation of the Bible.* St. Louis: Chalice, 2000.

Guardiola-Saenz, Leticia A. "Borderless Women and Borderless Texts: A Cultural Reading of Matthew 15:21–28." *Semeia* 78 (1997): 69–81.

Gundry-Volf, Judith. "Spirit, Mercy, and the Other." *Theology Today* 51 (1994): 508–23.

Humphries-Brooks, Stephenson. "The Canaanite Women in Matthew." In *A Feminist Companion to Matthew*, edited by Amy-Jill Levine with Marianne Blickenstaff, 138–56. Sheffield: Sheffield Academic Press, 2001.

Meier, John. "Matthew 15:21–28." *Interpretation* 40 (October 1986): 397–402.

O'Day, Gail R. "Surprised by Faith: Jesus and the Canaanite Woman." *Listening* 24 (Fall 1989): 290–301. Reprinted in *A Feminist Companion to Matthew*, edited by Amy-Jill Levine with Marianne Blickenstaff, 114–25. Sheffield: Sheffield Academic Press, 2001.

Patte, Daniel. "The Canaanite Woman and Jesus: Surprising Models of Discipleship (Matt. 15:21–28)." In *Transformative Encounters: Jesus and Women Re-viewed*, edited by Ingrid Rosa Kitzberger, 33–53. Leiden: Brill, 2000.

Perkinson, Jim. "A Canaanitic Word in the Logos of Christ; or The Difference the Syro-Phoenician Woman Makes to Jesus." *Semeia* 75 (1996): 61–85.

Ringe, Sharon. "A Gentile Woman's Story." In *Feminist Interpretation of the Bible*, edited by Letty Russell, 65–72. Philadelphia: Westminster, 1985.

———. "A Gentile Woman's Story, Revisited: Rereading Mark 7.24–31a." In *A Feminist Companion to Mark*, edited by Amy-Jill Levine with Marianne Blickenstaff, 79–100. Sheffield: Sheffield Academic Press, 2001.

Schüssler Fiorenza, Elisabeth. *But She Said: Feminist Practices of Biblical Interpretation.* Boston: Beacon, 1992.

Theissen, Gerd. "Dealing with Religious Prejudices: The Example of the Canaanite Woman (Matthew 15:21–28)." In *The Open Door: Variations on Biblical Themes.* Trans. John Bowden. (Minneapolis: Fortress, 1991), 40–46.

———. *The Gospels in Context: Social and Political History in the Synoptic Tradition*, 60–80. Trans. Linda M. Maloney. Minneapolis: Fortress, 1991.

Wainwright, Elaine. "A Voice from the Margin: Reading Matthew 15:21–28 in an Australian Feminist Key." In *Reading from This Place.* Vol. 1, *Social Location and Biblical Interpretation in Global Perspective*, edited by Fernando Segovia and Mary Ann Tolbert. Minneapolis: Fortress, 1995.

———. "The Gospel of Matthew." In *Searching the Scriptures.* Vol. 2, *A Feminist Commentary*, edited by Elisabeth Schüssler Fiorenza. New York: Crossroad, 1994.

Chapter Two

A Hemorrhaging Woman and Jairus's Daughter

Mark 5:21–43

When Jesus had crossed again in the boat to the other side, a great crowd gathered around him; and he was by the sea. Then one of the leaders of the synagogue named Jairus came and, when he saw him, fell at his feet and begged him repeatedly, "My little daughter is at the point of death. Come and lay your hands on her, so that she may be made well, and live." So he went with him.

And a large crowd followed him and pressed in on him. Now there was a woman who had been suffering from hemorrhages for twelve years. She had endured much under many physicians, and had spent all that she had; and she was no better, but rather grew worse. She had heard about Jesus, and came up behind him in the crowd and touched his cloak, for she said, "If I but touch his clothes, I will be made well." Immediately her hemorrhage stopped; and she felt in her body that she was healed of her disease. Immediately aware that power had gone forth from him, Jesus turned about in the crowd and said, "Who touched my clothes?" And his disciples said to him, "You see the crowd pressing in on you; how can you say, 'Who touched me?'" He looked all around to see who had done it. But the woman, knowing what had happened to her, came in fear and trembling, fell down before him, and told him the whole truth. He said to her, "Daughter, your faith has made you well; go in peace, and be healed of your disease."

While he was still speaking, some people came from the leader's house to say, "Your daughter is dead. Why trouble the teacher any further?" But overhearing what they said, Jesus said to the leader of the synagogue, "Do not fear, only believe." He allowed no one to follow him except Peter, James, and John, the brother of James. When they came to the house of the leader of the synagogue, he saw a commotion, people weeping and wailing loudly. When he had entered, he said to them, "Why do you make a commotion and weep? The child is not dead but sleeping." And they laughed at him. Then he put them all outside, and took the child's father and mother and those who were with him, and went in where the child was. He took her by the hand and said to her, "Talitha cum," which means, "Little girl, get up!" And immediately the girl got up and began to walk about (she was twelve years of age). At this they were overcome with amazement. He strictly ordered them that no one should know this, and told them to give her something to eat.

The stories of Jesus' encounters with a hemorrhaging woman and with Jairus's daughter demand joint consideration, for the one is told entirely within the other.[1] The intertwining of the stories invites us to compare the two and to interpret them together. The parallels and contrasts between the two stories illumine and enrich the reading of each.

Some of the connections between the two stories are easily found. The number "twelve," for instance: "There was a woman who had been suffering from hemorrhages for twelve years" (v. 25), and a little girl raised from the dead who was "twelve years of age" (v. 42). Is this simply a catchword used to link the stories in the oral tradition, or does it convey something significant about the association of the two women? The precise significance of the numerical link eludes us, but speculation abounds. Perhaps the bleeding disorder has meant for the woman an inability to conceive and give birth for twelve years, just as Jairus's daughter faces death at the point when she physically comes of age and can become a source of new life. The restoration of both women to their life-giving capacity may in that case image "the generative and nurturing power of God."[2] The number twelve may also establish a subtle contrast with the disciples and provide a "clue to the identity of Jesus' true family."[3] The only use of the number twelve prior to this scene is in relation to the disciples (3:13–19; 4:10), who, in contrast to the hemorrhaging woman, prove to be deficient in faith (cf. 4:35–41). Perhaps the woman and the girl represent the people of Israel, symbolized by twelve tribes, who experienced both "individual and social hemorrhaging and near death" as effects of subjection to Roman imperial forces. The story might then convey that "God's restorative powers are working through Jesus" to mediate new life to Israel, to lead the people "to their recovery from the death-dealing domination by Roman imperial rule."[4]

Other connections between the two stories are apparent as well. Both, for example, depict desperate situations and use the same key terms. The verb *sōzein*, for example ("to save" or "to make well") figures prominently in each. Jairus implores Jesus to come and lay his hands on a dying daughter "so that she may be made well, and live" (v. 23). Likewise, the hemorrhaging woman says, "If I but touch his clothes, I will be made well" (v. 28), and Jesus confirms that this has in fact taken place when he says, "Daughter, your faith has made you well" (v. 34).

"Faith" is also a central reality in both stories, as each links the effectiveness of Jesus' power to the faith of the persons involved. Indeed, Mark elaborates in the story of the hemorrhaging woman the meaning of the faith called for in the story of Jairus's daughter. Jesus exhorts Jairus to follow the woman's example: "Do not fear, only believe" (v. 36). And both women are healed by touch. In fact, the verb "to touch" is highlighted by repetition, appearing four times (vv. 27, 28, 30, 31).

Shifting now from similarities to contrasts, we note that the stories juxtapose two extremes on the socioeconomic scale. As Ched Myers has observed, "the little girl had enjoyed twelve years of privilege as the daughter of a synagogue ruler"; the woman "had suffered twelve years of destitution."[5] Moreover, the little girl has a male kinsman, a concerned father, who approaches Jesus directly and pleads in her behalf. The woman, however, approaches Jesus in a covert fashion, speaks only to herself, and is apparently alone. However, at the end of her story, she too receives a male kinsman and is claimed by Jesus as a "daughter": "Daughter, your faith has made you well" (v. 34). Bear these contrasts and connections in mind and ponder their significance in reading the story.

Finally, structure, form, and context further set the stage. In terms of structure, the two stories are roughly parallel. As Gerald West observes, "In each case the woman is defined by her social location; in each case the woman is in need; in each case Jesus responds to her need; . . . in each case there is contact, touching, between Jesus and the woman; in each case Jesus speaks to the woman; in each case there is healing and restoration of the woman to the community."[6] Moreover, both stories are miracle stories in that they describe miraculous events. Both contain the three structural elements of the miracle story form (problem, solution, and proof), and in each case the standard pattern has been expanded in significant ways. The additions are easy to spot and are noted as we examine the text more closely, for they give expression to convictions that the storyteller wishes to convey.

In terms of their shared literary context, the stories appear within a subsection of Mark's Gospel that stretches from 4:35 to 6:6. Within this subsection, Mark narrates four spectacular miracle stories back to back, each of which demonstrates that Jesus has extraordinary power. First, Jesus shows his control over chaotic nature by stilling a storm (4:35–41). Then he restores to health and wholeness persons afflicted with the most severe illnesses, exorcising a legion of unclean spirits from a tortured demoniac (5:1–20) and healing a woman who has bled incessantly for twelve years (5:25–34). Even death is conquered by his power, as Jairus's daughter is raised to new life (5:21–24a, 35–43). Thus it is clear that "No power—whether nature, demons, human illness, or death itself—can withstand the kingdom" or rule of God that manifests itself in Jesus' ministry.[7]

We cannot but notice the contrast between the disciples' fearful reaction to Jesus' power in the first miracle story ("Why are you afraid? Have you still no faith?" 4:40) and the faithful reactions of the Gerasene demoniac, the hemorrhaging woman, and Jairus in the three miracle stories that follow. But then, when Jesus comes to his hometown in the subsection's concluding scene (6:1–6), he is rejected by his own townspeople. As a result, "he could do no deed of power there" and "he was amazed at their unbelief" (6:5, 6). Attention to context thus suggests that much is to be learned about the nature of faith as we draw near to these stories. As Mary Ann Tolbert observes, what this series of striking stories conveys is that "If faith is the response to hearing the word, the kingdom of God is revealed in transforming power that provides incredible results."[8] Let us turn, then, to the text before us and consider its testimony to Jesus and to faith.

Encountering the Text

The first four verses (vv. 21–24) narrate the "problem" presented by the first miracle story. Jesus has just been in Gentile territory, in the country of the Gerasenes (5:1–20), but has crossed again to the other side of the lake (v. 21). He is thus on the west side of the Sea of Galilee, back on Jewish soil, when he encounters a prominent Jewish official: "Then one of the leaders of the synagogue named Jairus came and, when he saw him, fell at his feet and begged him repeatedly, 'My little daughter is at the point of death. Come and lay your hands on her, so that she may be made well, and live.' So he went with him" (vv. 22–24). The mention of Jairus's name and office should give us pause, for they are important indicators of social class and status. Jairus, in fact, is as John Meier has observed, "the only individual (apart from the twelve disciples) who is directly named as the petitioner for a healing or exorcism of another person" in any of the Synoptic

Gospels.[9] It is an elite and noteworthy Jewish male, a prominent religious leader, who approaches Jesus. His behavior, however, is strikingly unconventional. He falls at Jesus' feet, indicating his sense of social inferiority. As Joanna Dewey observes, Jairus "does not maintain his public honor fitting his status as synagogue leader. This is the story of a man relinquishing status to seek healing for his daughter."[10] His poignant words and demeanor convey both his desperation and his confidence that Jesus can heal his daughter.

En route to Jairus's house, however, a second miracle story interrupts the first. A nameless woman emerges from the great crowd that follows Jesus, and a second "problem" is presented in graphic detail: "Now there was a woman who had been suffering from hemorrhages for twelve years. She had endured much under many physicians, and had spent all that she had; and she was no better, but rather grew worse" (vv. 25–26). What exactly is the woman's problem? It is hard to say for sure. The language describing the malady, found only here in the New Testament, translates literally as a "continuous flowing of blood." The NRSV explains that she has "been suffering from hemorrhages for twelve years." The location of the bleeding is not specified, though most commentators presume vaginal or uterine bleeding.[11] The Septuagint (the Greek translation of the Hebrew Scriptures) uses the same phrase in Leviticus in reference to bleeding that is presumably vaginal (Lev. 15:19, 25; 20:18), providing some slight support for this position. Certainty, however, is impossible in this matter. If we do understand the woman's problem to be vaginal bleeding, we should note that she suffers from an abnormal condition. Her problem is not menstruation, which is a normal, healthy condition, but a serious malady—perhaps a menstrual disorder of some sort, or chronic uterine hemorrhage. Whatever the diagnosis, Mark makes it clear that she is sick and every bit as desperate as Jairus. In fact, her problem is described in graphic detail, with a long series of participles indicating (1) the length of her problem; (2) the fact that she has suffered much under many physicians from whom she received no help; (3) that her condition has drained her finances, leaving her destitute, a victim of exploitation; and (4) that her condition has only grown worse. She apparently had, at one time, been a person of some wealth, for she had been able to afford the services of physicians. Their ineffectual treatment, however, has left her impoverished and debilitated. Indeed, the doctors have become part of her problem. As Ched Myers observes, "Mark spares no hyperbole" in describing her desperate situation.[12] These graphic details, shared from the perspective of the underside, are deleted in Matthew's and Luke's later versions of the story.

Many commentators observe that the woman's problem entails far more than physical and financial suffering; in a Jewish context, her continuous bleeding (if vaginal) also placed her in a state of perpetual cultic impurity. The purity laws in Leviticus 15 are referenced at this point (cf. Lev. 15:19–33). Mary Ann Tolbert, for example, articulates their implications in summary fashion, noting that her impurity "would not only have prevented her from participating in cultic activities but would also have infected anyone who touched her, lay on a bed in which she had slept, or sat on a chair she had vacated. It may be that this twelve-year curse of impurity, besides draining her finances, had also isolated her socially from friends and kin" and "placed her outside the religious community."[13] In sum, commentators often argue that her problem entails "physical, emotional, and spiritual pain," along with "failed trust, bitter disappointment and economic disaster."[14] (We examine the tenability of this interpretation below.)

Perhaps these factors explain the woman's covert, rather than direct, approach to Jesus, and the fact that she is alone. Unlike Jairus's daughter, she has no male kinsman to plead her case—at least, none is mentioned. Still, she is not without resource, for she has heard reports of the power at work in Jesus, and that has given birth to hope and faith: "She had heard about Jesus, and came up behind him in the crowd and touched his cloak, for she said, 'If I but touch his clothes, I will be made well'" (vv. 27–28). So desperate is her situation, and so great is her faith according to Mark, that she audaciously and courageously appears alone in public, works her way through the jostling crowd, approaches Jesus from behind, and touches his garments.

Herein lies one of the most extraordinary features of her story: her healing occurs at her own initiative.[15] She does not request healing. Instead, she violates social codes and perhaps even religious law to claim healing for herself, without permission from anyone—without even the compliance of Jesus. As Elizabeth Malbon points out, hers is the only healing in Mark "that occurs without the expressed intent of Jesus."[16] The evangelist Matthew emends this (presumably troubling) point in his later version of the story. In Matthew, the woman's healing occurs only after Jesus turns, sees her, and pronounces a saving word (cf. Matt. 9:22). In Mark, however, the healing takes place solely at the woman's initiative, and follows "immediately" upon her touching of Jesus' garments, before she and Jesus have exchanged a word: "Immediately her hemorrhage stopped; and she felt in her body that she was healed of her disease" (v. 29). The instantaneous nature of the healing that flows from Jesus stands in sharp contrast to the endless and ineffectual ministrations of the "many physicians" consulted over the course of twelve years. The woman has finally placed herself in the presence of one who has come as a truly great physician (see Mark 2:17).

So there we have it: problem, solution, proof—all the requisite elements of a miracle story. But the story does not end here. It is considerably expanded, for Jesus refuses to let the woman remain invisible. Mark continues: "Immediately aware that power had gone forth from him, Jesus turned about in the crowd and said, 'Who touched my clothes?' And his disciples said to him, 'You see the crowd pressing in on you; how can you say, "Who touched me?"'" (vv. 30–31). Jesus' clothes are clearly not possessed of magical properties, for Jesus is fully aware that power has gone forth "from him." That power is none other than the power of the Holy Spirit, which possessed and empowered Jesus for messianic ministry at the moment of his baptism (cf. Mark 1:9–11), God's own power at work in the world to heal and restore the creation. Moreover, clearly faith accessed that power. Indeed, the disciples' question serves as a second reminder that a large crowd presses in on Jesus (see also v. 24). The woman's touch, however, was different than that of others. Her touch was impelled by faith. Jesus immediately discerns that the touch of faith has summoned his power, and he insists on knowing the one who called it forth. The disciples are puzzled at his insistence. One cannot help but wonder what Jairus, too, is thinking at this moment, for in persisting in this matter Jesus puts a prominent religious official on hold and delays a very urgent mission.

Still, Jesus insists on personal contact and on drawing the woman into relationship: "He looked all around to see who had done it. But the woman, knowing what had happened to her, came in fear and trembling, fell down before him, and told him the whole truth. He said to her, 'Daughter, your faith has made you well; go in peace, and be healed of your disease'" (vv. 32–34). Two matters of interest and some import are obscured in many English translations of these verses. For one thing, an explicitly feminine participle in verse 32 specifies that Jesus "looked all around to see *the woman* who had done it" (italics added). Jesus is thus represented as knowing that the one who touched him was a woman (though some commentators would argue that this represents the evangelist's hindsight and should not be pressed). A significant translation issue appears also in verse 34, in regard to the verb *sōzein*, which connotes "healing" but can also mean "salvation." The NRSV translates this verb in terms of healing: "Daughter, your faith has made you well" (see also vv. 23 and 28). But, as Donald Juel notes, this translation of the key verb "fails to capture the sense in which the physical cure results in a more comprehensive restoration."[17] A translation much to be preferred is "Daughter, your faith has saved you." As we reach the conclusion of the inner story, we can discern that "the miracle involves far more than physical healing; it includes entry into a 'saving' relationship with Jesus himself."[18] The woman is no longer alone: Jesus calls her "Daughter," claims her as family, and restores her to community. Moreover, she is told to "go in peace"—*shalom*, wholeness, salvation—and to be healed of her disease (v. 34).

Jesus' response to the woman is startling when viewed within the honor-shame dynamics of the Greco-Roman world. As Wendy Cotter observes, "he disclaims public honor for the healing of the woman when she presents herself." Indeed, he grants to her the honor of the cure. In so doing, he "protects the woman's honor by affirming her bold action as an expression of deep faith. This removes her shame and accords her respect." Thus, in Cotter's view, this story presents Jesus as one who is "astonishingly free from the need for public honors, and also from the need to dominate women."[19]

Two further points represent important footnotes to the woman's story. First, many commentators view the exchange between Jesus and the woman as "correctional" in nature.[20] That is, they argue, Jesus insists on personal contact with the woman because she is motivated by superstitious, magical beliefs. He wishes to instruct and elevate her inadequate faith. The text itself, however, makes no such point. In fact, it makes precisely the opposite one. Jesus celebrates the woman's faith—her confidence that God's own power works through him. Indeed, that confidence is declared instrumental in her healing: "Daughter, your faith has saved you." Jesus does not denigrate the woman, and neither should we.

Second, a shift in nuance occurs in the woman's portrait. The one who so shamelessly and courageously fought her way through a jostling crowd to touch the Lord and claim her own healing is described at the conclusion of the encounter as one who fears, trembles, and falls down before him. There are perhaps two ways of reading this shift in her demeanor. One approach is that she is now under the protection of a male kinsman and consequently reverted to culturally prescribed submissive norms for women's behavior. Mary Ann Tolbert articulates this view: "Her earlier 'shameful' boldness in approaching Jesus was acceptable from one who was already banished from honorable society; but with her healing she may be reinstated in the religious and social community. Consequently, her timorous deference reflects her renewed conventional status as a woman in the male world of honor and shame."[21]

However, the shift in demeanor could also reflect the woman's spiritual awareness, for it is, after all, explicitly connected with her knowledge of "what had happened to her" (v. 33). Indeed, Mitzi Minor reads this action as an indication that the woman clearly understands the implications of her cure from so gripping a disease: "Only God has such power. Therefore, she knew that she must be in the presence of the holy!"[22] Are not fear and trembling frequent and appropriate expressions of awe in biblical encounters with the holy? Moreover, the woman does not run in the face of such holy power, as do the Gerasene swineherds in the immediately preceding scene (cf. 5:14). Instead, she comes out of hiding, breaks her silence, and finds her voice; she "told him the whole truth" (v. 33). Minor sees this as an important aspect of the wholeness to which she has been restored: "Women's silence betrays an attitude they often have toward themselves that they are unworthy of other persons' significant time or attention." Jesus, however, "refuses to accept the woman's attitude toward herself."[23] He draws her out of hiding, urges her to find her voice, and gives her the opportunity to tell her story. Moreover, he "acknowledges the significant role her own courageous action played in her healing."[24] Though we are not made privy to the exact words the woman speaks, the fact of her speaking, the telling of her story, and her naming of the reality that has transpired are significant. Jesus thereby "empowers" this woman in more ways than one—all of which are important aspects of the wholeness, the healing, and salvation with which he sends her on her way.

The story of Jairus's daughter resumes in verse 35. The problem has intensified, for during the delay occasioned by the hemorrhaging woman, the young girl has died: "While he was still speaking, some people came from the leader's house to say, 'Your daughter is dead. Why trouble the teacher any further?'" (v. 35). As John Meier observes, "The subliminal message here is that Jesus is only a teacher, and death marks the limit of whatever power he may have."[25] Jesus, however, ignores the messengers and encourages the leader of the synagogue to follow the woman's example, to emulate her faith: "Do not fear, only believe" (v. 36). The fact that the imperative appears in Greek in the present tense also suggests that Jairus is exhorted to "keep on believing." He is not to lose heart, but is to keep on believing as he does that God's power is at work in Jesus—power that transforms even the reality of death, as we will see.

Moreover, Jesus narrows the circle: "He allowed no one to follow him except Peter, James, and John, the brother of James" (v. 37). The fact that this same trio of disciples will also be present at the transfiguration (9:2) and in Gethsemane (14:33) indicates that something significant is now about to take place. When they reach Jairus's house, they find "a commotion, people weeping and wailing loudly" (v. 38). Mourning is already under way, the customary rituals of weeping and lamenting, though the mourning turns to ridicule and scornful laughter when Jesus insists that "The child is not dead but sleeping" (vv. 38–40). Jesus then quite literally takes hold of the mocking bystanders and "put them all outside" (*ekbalōn* in Greek).

At this point, Matthew and Luke's later versions of the story are different. Matthew, for example, strives to avoid depicting Christ acting like a nightclub bouncer (cf. Matt. 9:25).[26] Moreover, both Matthew and Luke make it clear that the child is dead—really dead—though Mark leaves this matter in the shadows. Perhaps Jesus, in Mark, employs a common euphemism for death when he insists that the child is sleeping. Given that he intends to restore her to life, she is not irrevocably dead. Her death has the nature of sleep. Perhaps, as some have noted, Jesus speaks ambiguously of the reality of death to protect himself, if in fact he is to be understood as transgressing purity regulations by contact with the dead. Or perhaps he is creating confusion over the real situation in order to avoid public acclaim over the stupendous miracle he is about to perform.[27] A theological point is also underscored. As Lamar Williamson observes: "The text intends to affirm that in the presence of Jesus and under his authority death itself, real death, is but a sleep."[28]

"Then he put them all outside, and took the child's father and mother and those who were with him, and went in where the child was" (v. 40). Interestingly, a mother is now included in the scene, though like her daughter and the hemorrhaging woman, she is unnamed—in contrast to all five of the men who make appearances: Jairus, Jesus, and three specified male disciples. A telltale grammatical shift can also be noted. Though previously the sick child has been referred to as her father's daughter in the patriarchal genitive—"My little daughter" in verse 23 and "your daughter" in verse 35—now she is in possession of a father and mother ("the child's father and mother," v. 40). Moreover, Jesus and now the narrator, following suit, speak to and of her as subject and not as object—as "the child" or as a "little girl," a person in her own right, and not as the property of a father:[29] "He took her by the hand and said to her, 'Talitha cum,' which means, 'Little girl, get up!' And immediately the girl got up and began to walk about (she was twelve years of age). At this they were overcome with amazement" (vv. 41–42). Again, as in the inner story of the hemorrhaging woman, restoration comes through a healing touch. Again,

Jesus speaks to the female before him. The immediacy of the girl's healing is likewise stressed, and verified by the fact that she rises and walks about, to the onlookers' amazement.

This point is an appropriate place for this second miracle story to conclude: problem, solution, and proof have all been narrated, as has an astonished reaction. But once again comes a departure from the standard pattern, for two odd, additional commands close the story. The first is to secrecy: "He strictly ordered them that no one should know this, and told them to give her something to eat" (v. 43). One has to wonder how the girl's restoration to life can possibly be kept a secret, for her death has been announced publicly before a crowd, mourners have gathered, and the deceased is now walking about and eating. There is also an odd contrast between the command of silence that concludes the young girl's story and the demand that the hemorrhaging woman's healing be brought out into the open. Still, secrecy is a favorite Markan theme, in service of Mark's insistence that Jesus cannot be fully understood on the basis of his miracle-working activity, but only in light of his death and resurrection. More than likely, the odd command to secrecy in this case pertains to the magnitude of the second miracle and to the fact that it precedes Jesus' own resurrection from the dead. As Morna Hooker observes, "The miracle of the resurrection can only be understood by those who believe in the one who has himself been raised from the dead."[30]

The second pointed command to give the girl something to eat may be taken as further confirmation of her restoration to bodily, everyday life. Ghosts may walk about, but they do not eat ordinary food. Thus in Luke 24 and John 21, the risen Lord eats to demonstrate his own corporeal nature. However, the command may also convey that the girl is to be restored to the family circle, as was the hemorrhaging woman—a sign perhaps that "reincorporation into community is the essence of Jesus' healing."[31]

Angles of Vision

Let us now consider several angles of vision that may help us delve more deeply into the significance of these interrelated stories.

Purity Regulations

The first angle of vision has to do with the extent to which purity regulations inform a reading of the story. Purity issues are not explicitly mentioned in the text, but a number of commentators maintain that they form an important backdrop to the story. The distinction between "clean" and "unclean" is an aspect of first-century Jewish consciousness that modern minds find difficult to grasp, though anthropologists have established that the distinction prevailed in most ancient religions. In fact, we should not assume "that purity was a Jewish concern of no real interest to either the Greeks or the Romans." As Mary Rose D'Angelo observes, "while purity regulations of Greek and Roman antiquity are less accessible than the holiness code in Leviticus, they exist, and appear to be rather symmetrical with those of Judaism of the same period."[32]

The biblical laws of purity, set forth in Leviticus and Numbers, sought to preserve the holiness of the Temple—the dwelling place of God on earth and the center of Israel's life—and laid out the conditions under which persons might approach the divine presence. Impurity—contracted chiefly through contact with a human corpse, certain unclean animals, or genital discharges—made one unacceptable for contact with the Temple and its religious practices. Observing such regulations preserved proper worship in the Temple, which was essential to the holiness that preserved the life of the nation.[33]

Certain sectarian groups within first-century Judaism sought to extend purity concerns beyond the life of the Temple into daily life. The Pharisees, for example, held that all Israel was a kingdom of priests, and believed that whenever they sat down at a table they were every bit as much in the presence of God as they were when in the Temple. Thus they promoted observance of the purity laws at all times and places in order to provide a living testimony to the faith. The Essenes exceeded even the Pharisees in their observance of purity concerns. In their view, an illegitimate priesthood had defiled the Temple and the whole land by their presence there, with the result that God had withdrawn. Consequently, they withdrew from the Temple, separated from all other Jews, and carried out the strictest holiness codes within a monastic community at Qumran, in order that one place on earth might be holy enough for God to dwell there. "Holiness" was thus a "core value of the society" and a shared concern among Jews; but first-century Judaism was a diverse phenomenon, and various Jewish sects in Palestine applied the purity regulations in different ways.[34]

Many interpreters have found this perspective helpful for reading the Gospels, and Mark's Gospel in particular, for in it Jesus engages repeatedly in activities and behaviors that would appear to transgress biblical purity regulations. For instance: Jesus touches a leper; he heals on the holy

Sabbath; he makes use of a bodily fluid such as spittle in acts of healing; his disciples eat with unwashed hands; he declares all foods clean; he eats with anyone under any circumstances. Jesus' engagements in the fifth chapter of Mark are particularly striking when viewed through this lens. In Mark 5, Jesus marches into Gentile (and therefore unclean) territory and enters a graveyard. There he encounters a demoniac with a legion of unclean spirits, whom he drives into a herd of two thousand pigs. (Can one get any more unclean than this?) But wait: on the heels of this episode, Jesus is touched by a woman with a continuous flow of blood and thereby rendered unclean. Then he takes a dead girl by the hand and renders himself unclean by touching a corpse.

It is hard to avoid the impression that much of Mark's story has to do with ritual uncleanness. Indeed, Markan scholar David Rhoads argues that "The issues of purity are writ large across the pages of Mark's story."[35] Rhoads maintains that Mark shares the notion that God is holy, but represents an alternative Jewish view: "In contrast to the view that people are to attain holiness by separation from the threatening force of impurity, Mark presents the view that people are to overcome uncleanness by spreading wholeness."[36] Through the agency of the Holy Spirit upon Jesus, God enters the arena of impurity without regard to the risk of defilement: "God's holiness is an active force that expands and invades in order to remove and to overcome uncleanness. Thus, in contrast to the view that God is to be protected within the confines of the Temple, the Markan God spreads the life-giving power of the kingdom through Jesus and his followers into the world wherever people are receptive to it."[37]

This perspective has been brought to bear on a reading of the stories in Mark 5:21–43. The biblical purity laws in Leviticus 15 relating to menstruation and other vaginal discharges are usually referenced as an important backdrop. Because they have figured so prominently in many interpretations of the story, it is important to revisit them:

> When a woman has a discharge of blood that is her regular discharge from her body, she shall be in her impurity for seven days, and whoever touches her shall be unclean until the evening. Everything upon which she lies during her impurity shall be unclean; everything also upon which she sits shall be unclean. Whoever touches her bed shall wash his clothes, and bathe in water, and be unclean until the evening. Whoever touches anything upon which she sits shall wash his clothes, and bathe in water, and be unclean until the evening; whether it is the bed or anything upon which she sits, when he

touches it he shall be unclean until the evening. If any man lies with her, and her impurity falls on him, he shall be unclean seven days; and every bed on which he lies shall be unclean.

If a woman has a discharge of blood for many days, not at the time of her impurity, or if she has a discharge beyond the time of her impurity, all the days of the discharge she shall continue in uncleanness; as in the days of her impurity, she shall be unclean. Every bed on which she lies during all the days of her discharge shall be treated as the bed of her impurity; and everything on which she sits shall be unclean, as in the uncleanness of her impurity. Whoever touches these things shall be unclean, and shall wash his clothes, and bathe in water, and be unclean until the evening. If she is cleansed of her discharge, she shall count seven days, and after that she shall be clean. On the eighth day she shall take two turtledoves or two pigeons and bring them to the priest at the entrance of the tent of meeting. The priest shall offer one for a sin offering and the other for a burnt offering; and the priest shall make atonement on her behalf before the LORD for her unclean discharge.

Thus you shall keep the people of Israel separate from their uncleanness, so that they do not die in their uncleanness by defiling my tabernacle that is in their midst.

This is the ritual for those who have a discharge: for him who has an emission of semen, becoming unclean thereby, for her who is in the infirmity of her period, for anyone, male or female, who has a discharge, and for the man who lies with a woman who is unclean. (Lev. 15:19–33)

Joanna Dewey articulates the significance of these Levitical laws for reading the story:

According to both the priestly regulations of Leviticus and the rabbinic rules of the Mishnah, a woman who is menstruating or has an irregular bloody discharge was considered a powerful source of pollution to men. She is unclean. Anyone who touches her or touches anything she has sat or lain on also becomes unclean. . . . The purity rules are clear. It is unclear to what extent Galilean peasant women at the time of Jesus observed the laws of menstrual purity. We may conjecture that unless they were the wife of a priest or a strict scribe or Pharisee, they probably did not feel strongly bound by the menstrual regulations. Yet popular culture internalizes much of the value system

of the dominant group, including here the understanding of menstruating women, or women with an irregular flow, as unclean. With
a disease as severe as a twelve-year nonmenstrual bleeding, almost
surely the society and the woman herself would consider her unclean
and a source of impurity to others. If she were maintaining proper
"shame" as the dominant male culture understood it, she should have
remained secluded.[38]

But what happens in this story? The woman shamelessly appears in
public, works her way through a crowd, and touches Jesus' garment. And
what does Jesus do? He does not rebuke her for her behavior; he ignores
it and welcomes her as kin, as "daughter." In the scene that follows, Jesus
himself takes the initiative and touches a dead girl, thereby rendering
himself unclean. In sum, in Mark 5:21–43, "what we find is clear rejection
of the purity regulations"—a "rejection of the purity code as it affected
women's bodies."[39] As Marcus Borg has summarized the matter, "The
politics of purity" are "replaced by a politics of compassion."[40]

Thus, a number of interpreters have argued that purity regulations
inform a reading of the story in significant ways. However, a second
important perspective to consider is whether these readings are misreadings of the text based on inaccurate stereotypes of Judaism and
women.[41] A number of Jewish scholars are raising this important question in pointed fashion. Amy-Jill Levine, for example, has observed that
"Students of Christian origins are obsessed with Levitical purity legislation: it may well be that scholars worry more about such matters, particularly as they concern women, than did many Jewish women in the first
century."[42]

Paula Fredriksen has, in addition, called attention to the ways in which
Christian interpreters often misconstrue Jewish purity laws by presuming
that such laws preserved unjust social distinctions. She makes three important points about the first-century Jewish understanding of impurity:

1. *Impurity was not sin* and was not prohibited, and thus no one erred in
contracting it. Indeed, Scripture assumes that people will contract impurity as a matter of course as they fulfill the more routine commandments
of the Torah, such as having marital intercourse, giving birth, and bury-
ing the dead. The remedy for impurity is not "forgiveness," but rather
purification.[43] This point is often obscured by a common mistranslation
of the "purification offering" (*hatta't* in Hebrew) as a "sin offering" (e.g.,
Lev. 15:30 in the NRSV).[44]

2. In Jewish tradition, *purity did not correspond to social class*: "Impurity is

a fact of life, but not of class. The lowliest peasant who has just completed the ritual of the red heifer is pure, whereas the most aristocratic priest, having just buried a parent, is not. The fussiest Pharisee, the highest high priest, is neither more nor less *tameh* [unclean] after marital intercourse than is the scruffiest Galilean fisherman."[45]

3. *Impurity was gender-blind*: "A healthy adult Jewish woman incurs impurity on a regular basis, through menses; but she is no more impure than is her husband, whose semen is a medium of impurity, after intercourse. . . . To erect on a foundation of Leviticus and Numbers a superstructure of supposed Jewish sexism is one way to enable Jesus to exorcise this modern demon; but it tendentiously misreads these texts."[46]

Remember that the Jerusalem Temple was the focal point of the purity system. Sin was involved when one took impurity into the sacred realm, and thus impurity of any kind had to be dissociated from the sacred space and the sacred objects of the Tabernacle or Temple (see Lev. 15:31). As Shaye Cohen, a historian of first-century Judaism, observes:

> *In the Temple and in proximity to persons and objects bound for the Temple, purity was an essential requirement; elsewhere the purity laws could be ignored.* During the latter part of the second Temple period (mid-second century B.C.E. to 70 C.E.) various sects and pietistic groups extended the limits of the sacred to include daily life outside the Temple, especially all matters connected with food. This perspective, however, had only a minimal impact on the *Jews at large, who continued to regard the Temple* as *the single locus of sanctity and the sole place that demanded ritual purity of its entrants.*[47]

This point is significant, for Mark 5:21–43 takes place in Galilee. Galilee is a three- or four-day journey from Jerusalem and the Temple precincts. Thus, if Jesus is rendered unclean by the touch of a hemorrhaging woman or by contact with a corpse, and thereby restricted from the distant central sanctuary, so what? It is unlikely that either Jesus or the woman would be in its vicinity anytime soon. As Cohen notes, "as long as those affected with impurity stayed away from the sacred precincts Jewish society did not care about their impurity."[48]

Readings of Mark 5 through the lens of purity regulations may also be based on an overreading of Leviticus 15, a text that Jewish legal scholar Judith Wegner refers to as "one of the most misconstrued passages in the entire Torah."[49] Amy-Jill Levine substantiates this point, commenting on the much-quoted Leviticus 15:19–33:

There is nothing here to prevent this woman from participating in "normal human social relations." She is not inhumanly restricted or socially ostracized. There is no prohibition against her touching anyone. Indeed, the concern in the Law for her bedding and anything on which she sits "can only mean that in fact her hands do not transmit impurity. . . . [T]he consequence is that she is not banished but remains at home. Neither is she isolated from her family.[50]

Charlotte Fonrobert also observes that "The difference between *being touched and touching* is more significant than it seems."[51] Leviticus 15 speaks of the former rather than the latter. In sum, interpreters of Mark 5 may be guilty of overstating the degree of social ostracism occasioned by Levitical legislation,[52] and of perpetuating an inaccurate picture of the world from which Jesus came.

A final point is also significant. Impurity is not mentioned in Mark 5:21–43, nor is there any explicit reference in it to Leviticus 15. Other Markan stories quite explicitly engage purity issues (e.g., 7:1–23; 1:40–44), but this one does not. As Shaye Cohen observes: "The Gospel story about the woman with a twelve-year discharge . . . does not give any indication that the woman was impure or suffered any degree of isolation as a result of her affliction."[53] Amy-Jill Levine concurs: "the laws are not mentioned, the crowd does not part from the woman or ever show any surprise at her public presence, and even the synagogue leader shows no hesitancy in asking Jesus to touch his child."[54] The arguments of those who maintain that the woman is "impure" (and consequently isolated or ostracized) are therefore based on what is not said. Perhaps we should attend more closely to what *is* mentioned. As Levine observes: "The woman is healed of her sickness; the girl is raised from the dead. The point is that those who were sick and dead are now alive and healthy, not that Jewish practices have been transgressed or overcome."[55]

How are we to reconcile these two perspectives? Do purity regulations inform a reading of the story, or do they not? Some readers may find it difficult to shake the impression that purity issues are at least a dimension of Mark's story, particularly in chapter 5, with its cumulative references to a graveyard, a legion of unclean spirits, two thousand pigs, a bleeding woman, and a dead girl. We may also wonder about the impact of a prolonged period of impurity resulting from an abnormal bleeding condition. Prolonged, abnormal bleeding would certainly prevent worship at the central sanctuary; would it not also have prevented the woman from either marrying (in light of prohibitions against intercourse with a menstruant;

cf. Lev. 18:19; 20:18) or giving birth? And to what extent might she have internalized society's values, as Dewey notes above? However, we are appropriately cautioned against overreading and overstating the case.

Moreover, all the characters in this story are presumably Jewish,[56] and what Jesus does in this story he does as a Jewish man for Jewish women. Interestingly, in Matthew's version of the story, the hemorrhaging woman attempts to touch not his garment, but rather the fringes of his garment (cf. Matt. 9:20)—that is, the fringes on his prayer shawl, worn in obedience to Numbers 15:37–41. In other words, Matthew presents Jesus as embodying in his clothing respect for the Jewish law. In the end, whatever one's final opinion in this matter, one must avoid teaching and preaching contempt for Judaism, and propagating inaccurate stereotypes—implying that Jesus was not thoroughly Jewish, or that he rescued women from a bad, oppressive religion. We must also attend closely to the more explicit dimensions of this text as we ponder its significance for our lives and ministries.

Prefiguring Jesus' Passion

An explicit but often overlooked dimension of the text is the striking connections between Mark 5:21–43 and Jesus' own passion. Feminist biblical scholarship has increasingly shed light on this point, noting that Jesus' suffering, death, and resurrection are prefigured in the experiences of the two women in Mark.[57]

Links between Jesus and the hemorrhaging woman are especially striking. The woman, for example, is described as "suffering" in 5:26: "She had suffered much under many physicians." The verb *paschein* ("to suffer"; translated by the NRSV as "to endure") is otherwise used only in reference to Jesus in Mark's Gospel (8:31; 9:12). Moreover, the woman's illness is twice referred to as an "affliction" (*mastigos*): in verse 29, "she felt in her body that she was healed of her affliction" (NRSV: disease); and in verse 34 Jesus sends her on her way with the words "be healed of your affliction" (NRSV: disease). In 10:34, Jesus employs the related verb *mastigein* ("to afflict" or "to flog") to describe his own torment in his third passion prediction. Also the only references to "blood" in Mark's Gospel are found in chapter 5 in reference to the woman's bleeding, and in 14:24 where Jesus speaks of the flowing of his own blood: "This is my blood of the covenant which is poured out for many." Finally, like Jesus in Mark 12:14 and 32, the woman is said to tell the truth (5:33). In all of these ways, as Hisako Kinukawa notes, Mark "dared to identify the woman's suffering with that of Jesus."[58] Susan Graham even claims, "Her illness enables her to understand 'the pain and outrage Jesus experiences before his death' in a way no one else shares."[59]

Connections can also be discerned between the experience of Jairus's daughter and that of Jesus. Her story features references to death, to weeping, to mocking, to raising, and to *ekstasis* or great astonishment. When Jairus's daughter rises, Mark tells us that the onlookers "were overcome with amazement" (v. 42). The word *ekstasis* appears only once again in Mark, in the last verse of the Gospel, to describe the terror and amazement that seizes the women at the empty tomb (cf. 16:8).

These connections between the experience of these women and Jesus' own passion are too profuse and too explicit to be ignored. As Amy-Jill Levine observes, "the bodies of women serve as figurations for Jesus' own body as it hangs on the cross and rises from the tomb."[60] In a day when women, Catholic and Protestant alike, continue to struggle for full inclusion in the church's ministry and against the perception that men more appropriately "image" Jesus, is it not fascinating that Mark presents the experience of two women as prefigurations of Jesus' own suffering, death, and resurrection?

Tactile Imagery

Other explicit dimensions of the story provide further food for thought and bear implications for life and ministry within the community of faith and for the daily life and ministry of every Christian. Tactile imagery, for example—the imagery of touch—appears prominently in the stories before us. As we have noted, the verb "to touch" appears four times (vv. 27, 28, 30, 31). Susan Graham highlights the significance of this imagery throughout Mark's Gospel as Jesus relates to women. As Graham notes, women are physically present to Jesus in Mark's Gospel, but that presence is a largely silent one, for their speech is rarely recorded. In fact, only two women in Mark actually address Jesus: the Syrophoenician woman (Matthew's Canaanite) in 7:24–30 and the woman with the flow of blood in 5:25–34—though in the latter case she is not accorded direct speech. The narrator relates that she "told him the whole truth" (5:33), but we are not privy to her words.[61]

Graham's point is that women in this Gospel have a relationship with Jesus that depends on a tactile means of communication, different from speech and hearing. In the story before us of the hemorrhaging woman, for example, the silence stands out: "[N]o word is spoken aloud in this healing; there is only touch. The narrative provides an image of a relationship which is both non-verbal and intimate, perceived internally by both people. . . . Jesus is present to the woman with the flow of blood in a non-linguistic way, for which the healing then becomes the sign."[62] To this I would add, however, that Jesus does then draw her into relationship and speech. Indeed, he insists on this, and provides the opportunity for her to tell her story. We have noted above that this, too, is an important aspect of the healing, wholeness, and salvation with which he sends her on her way.

Tactile imagery is also featured in the story of raising Jairus's daughter. Jairus seeks Jesus' healing touch for her: "Come and lay your hands on her, so that she may be made well, and live" (5:23). And "He took her by the hand and said to her . . . 'Little girl, get up!' And immediately the girl got up and began to walk about" (5:41–42). Though Jesus speaks to her, the girl does not speak to him; she receives the gift of life through touch.[63]

Graham observes that in Mark "Jesus nurtures in a physical way, as women do"[64] and that the Gospel conveys this as another way of being present to others.[65] Her point is further illustrated by two other stories of women that frame Mark's Gospel. The first woman to make an appearance in Mark is Simon's mother-in-law, who suffers from a fever in 1:29–31. As in the story of Jairus's daughter, Jesus heals her by touch: "He came and took her by the hand and lifted her up. Then the fever left her, and she began to serve them" (1:31). Connections between her experience and Jesus' own can again be discerned, for he "lifted" or "raised her up" (*ēgeiren*), just as he will be raised up at the end of Mark's story. And once raised, "she began to serve them." The verb "to serve" (*diakonein*) is used to describe her ministry—the same word Jesus uses to describe his own vocation in 10:45: "For the Son of Man came not to be served but to serve, and to give his life a ransom for many."[66]

At the Gospel's other end, the story of yet another silent woman precedes the passion. In chapter 14, an anonymous woman enters the house of Simon the leper where Jesus was at table, "with an alabaster jar of very costly ointment of nard," and without a word "she broke open the jar and poured the ointment on his head" (14:3). Her prophetic action prefigures Jesus' action of breaking and pouring, and anoints his body for burial. Graham observes:

> The touch of the woman with the flow of blood precedes the raising of Jairus's daughter. The touch of this woman precedes the flow of Jesus' own blood which in turn will precede his resurrection. She is

in touch with him, present to him in a way that no one else is, in one act both preparing his body for death and acknowledging him as the anointed one, the Messiah. And then she disappears; even her name is forgotten.[67]

Dualistic stereotyping is, to be sure, inherent in the tactile imagery, that is, stereotyping that assigns one set of characteristics to men and an opposite set of characteristics to women. This kind of stereotyping has often proved detrimental to women. Graham notes that she is merely making explicit what was previously an implicit stereotype, namely, that "women are associated with the body (here figured by touch), as opposed to men who are associated with the mind (speech and hearing)."[68] Nevertheless, Graham's fascinating study can help us further appreciate the important role that women play in Mark's story of Jesus' life and ministry, and the explicit connections that can be discerned between their experience and Jesus' own. Although their role is a largely silent one, they are present to Jesus, and Jesus is present to them, through touch. So also may we be present to others in significant and healing ways in communities of faith and in our daily lives and ministries. Perhaps Mark's story can help all of us—women and men—see and embody in appropriate ways this alternate means of being present to others.

Self-Care and the Struggle for Wholeness

One of the most extraordinary features of the hemorrhaging woman's story in Mark is that her healing occurs at her own initiative. She does not request healing. Instead, she violates social codes and perhaps even religious law to claim healing for herself, without permission from anyone—without even the compliance of Jesus. This feature of the story has implications for the spiritual development of women.

Karen Barta has highlighted the significance of the hemorrhaging woman's struggle for the full participation of Roman Catholic women within their community of faith. Her comments are relevant to the struggles that women commonly experience within male-dominated societies and churches. Barta maintains that the healing story in Mark 5 "offers a vivid example of a woman breaking the chains of paternalism."[69] Mark pointedly tells us that for twelve years the hemorrhaging woman "had [suffered greatly] under many physicians, and had spent all that she had; and she was no better, but rather grew worse" (5:26). Her illness drained her finances, leaving her destitute and in a deteriorated condition. Barta finds this "a poignant image of a woman's plight within a paternalistic system. To the already heavy burdens of physical, emotional, and spiritual pain are added a failed trust, bitter disappointment and economic disaster. She reached out to those with power within the system and they not only failed to help but contributed to her worsening condition until, at last, her illness defined her being."[70]

However, this word is not the last in the woman's story, for she hears of Jesus and recognizes him as one with healing power. Barta continues:

> The hemorrhaging woman approached Jesus. . . . The decision to reach out is her own; she takes matters into her own hands; she takes responsibility for her life. *She acts.* And through her bold and assertive act, she breaks out of the barriers imposed by her faith tradition, culture and society. She is healed.
>
> Following her cure, one barrier remained: to own up to her action, to claim her experience and name her reality. Jesus inquires who touched him. He refuses to let the woman remain invisible. His question calls her forth. . . . Jesus persists until the woman, overcoming her inner fear, comes before Jesus "and tells him the whole truth." She claims her new self and chances rejection. But instead of rejection, this bold, assertive, and courageous boundary-breaker receives affirmation with the words, "Daughter, your faith has made you whole. Go in peace and be cured of your affliction."[71]

The story is striking in its presentation of a woman who finds the courage and faith to care for herself, to act in her own behalf, and to strive for her wholeness. Barta notes:

> We never do find out whether she was a mother or even married. The focus of the story is rather on the great dignity of this person and her struggle toward wholeness. Her roles are not primary; she is. . . . After relying for many years on others to help her, she finally decides and acts on her own. Taking responsibility for her life, she identifies her need and finds someone who can truly help in her struggle toward wholeness. She is assertive, even bold, courageous, and honest. To claim herself, she has to cross boundaries that severely restricted her life and person.[72]

Similarly, Joanna Dewey observes that "the hemorrhaging woman acts in powerful nontraditional ways. She is depicted breaking out of her proper submissive role and daring to claim her own wholeness."[73] Indeed, the story is so strongly countercultural that it suggests to Dewey that it "might well have been told and retold by and among women before [it was] textualized in Mark."[74]

Mark's story invites those of us who continue to hear and retell it into the struggle for wholeness. It inspires us to break out of patterns of paternalism and dependency that may restrict our own circumstances and to take responsibility for our lives. In fact, the very form in which the story is narrated is intended to empower those who hear it. Antoinette Wire, who has classified miracle stories, identifies this particular miracle story as a "demand story":[75] "In the demand story the demanding party takes from the beginning an active role in the struggle and overcomes."[76] Moreover, "the teller seeks to draw the hearers into a demanding stance":[77] "the teller calls the hearer to break out of a closed world and to demand, struggle and realize miracle in human life. . . . Even in the stories where Jesus opposes the demand he is always drawn with respect as one who provokes people in their own cause and leaves them whole and in possession of their own story."[78] Demand stories thus direct our attention to the persons being healed, as well as to Jesus.[79]

To attend to the woman's courageous action in behalf of her own healing and wholeness scarcely diminishes the role or importance of Jesus in this story. He is, after all, the catalyst for her action, the one whose presence inspires her hope for healing and whose power makes her whole. Moreover, he "empowers" her in more ways than one, summoning her courage and her speech, and affirming the important role her own courageous faith has played in the securing of her healing.

But as Mary Rose D'Angelo observes, the story gives expression to "a christology of shared spiritual power, one in which Jesus' power is active through the participation of others."[80] Indeed, when Jesus visits his hometown synagogue in the following scene, "he could do no deed of power there" because of their unbelief (6:1–6). The Gospel of Matthew exhibits discomfort with this unique Markan perspective. Thus, in Matthew, the hemorrhaging woman no longer cures herself, and parents and disciples do not attend the raising of Jairus's daughter; and when Jesus arrives in his hometown he "did not do" (rather than "could not do") mighty works there because of their unbelief (see Matt. 9:22, 25; 13:58). In Mark, however, the power that resides in Jesus is active in response to the collaboration of others. D'Angelo's point "is not the 'low' character of Mark's christology, but the gospel's high estimation of the believer's and therefore the early Christian reader's share in the spirit."[81]

May the example of Jesus' empowering ministry shape our efforts to empower others in their own struggles for healing and wholeness. And may the example of this woman rouse us from our own despair or dependency to take responsibility for ourselves, to act courageously in our own behalf, to embrace the power of God that Jesus exercises on our behalf, and to claim our voices and full personhood in Christ.

Dealing with Interruptions

One final angle of vision emerges from the very structure of the story in Mark 5:21–43. As we have noted, two stories are intertwined. The sandwiching of two narratives provides a commentary on the way Jesus deals with interruptions.[82]

This incident is by no means the only occasion on which Jesus is interrupted in his work (cf. 1:35–39, 40–45; 2:2; 10:46–52). However, the contrasting social and economic positions of the petitioners make the interruption in Mark 5 a particularly striking one. Jesus allows himself to be interrupted by a nameless, destitute woman who deters his mission to a prominent religious official. Moreover, he insists on a more extended engagement than even she had in mind. During the delay occasioned by the interruption, the daughter of the synagogue leader dies.

We learn from this interruption that Jesus' compassion is indiscriminate. Could it not even be said that the story exhibits the priority of the poor in the ministry of Jesus? Ched Myers sees this priority as "the primary level of signification" in the episode:

> Jesus accepts the priority of the ("highly inappropriate") importunity of this woman over the ("correct") request of the synagogue leader. His mission to "lay his hands on" Jairus's daughter (5:23c) is interrupted by the "touch" of the doubly poor woman, and now she is the one who falls at the feet of Jesus (5:33). The most important symbolic reversal here is the status of the destitute woman. From the bottom of the honor scale she intrudes upon an important mission on behalf of the daughter of someone on the top of the honor scale—but by the story's conclusion *she* herself has become the "daughter" at the center of the story! "My daughter," proclaims Jesus, "your faith has saved you, go in peace and be in full health, free of your scourge" (5:34). Not only is her integrity restored, but she receives a grant of status superior to that of Jesus' male disciples, who are "without faith"

(4:40)! Such a profound reversal of dignity will occur only one other time in Mark: in the story of another destitute Jew, the blind beggar Bartimaeus (10:51).[83]

The dramatic reversal at the heart of the story embodies a truth that Jesus will affirm at a later point in Mark's story: "many who are first will be last, and the last will be first" (10:31).

Perhaps Jesus' example can inform our own engagement with interruptions. Henri Nouwen once said: "You know . . . my whole life I have been complaining that my work was constantly interrupted, until I discovered that my interruptions were my work."[84] William Willimon has likewise captured the inevitability of interruptions in the lives of busy pastors:

> Jesus will have none of our imposed order. He leads us down a road more circuitous than that toward Nazareth. He inserts into the journey those frightened parents and the suffering sick from whom we have averted our gaze. He assaults us with life and rebirth just when we had adjusted to death. A frequent complaint heard from laypeople is, "My pastor is so disorganized." Forgive the poor, disorganized pastor. Having had the day so often disrupted, the pastor long ago threw away the appointment book and decided just to tag along behind Jesus.
>
> Having witnessed a healing and a resurrection, I am dying to get back to my study and write a sermon. As I pack up my books, already composing the sermon outline in my mind, Jesus stops me and says, "Forget the sermon. Get in the kitchen. Give her something to eat" (Mark 5:43). When you're trying to keep up with Jesus, things never go quite as planned.[85]

Finally, Lamar Williamson provides an appropriate concluding observation: "Jesus' divine authority is placed at the service of desperately importunate people. His sensitivity can make us patient, just as his powerful care, working through our faith, can make us whole."[86]

Like the two women in Mark's story, may we know Jesus' healing touch, his empowering presence, and his indiscriminate mercy in the midst of our own desperate realities, summoning our faith and our voice, restoring us to wholeness and community, and raising us to new life. And may Jesus' tangible, empowering, and patient compassion shape our own daily ministries in conformity to his own.

Group Study Suggestions

Begin with a dramatic reading of Mark 5:21–43. Assign roles to a narrator, to Jesus, to Jairus, to a hemorrhaging woman. Ask the rest of the group to read collectively the lines of both the disciples and the mourners (and to provide sound effects called for by the narrative: "weeping and wailing loudly," "laughing," and "amazement").

Following the reading, ask participants: What impressions emerge as you hear the story and what questions does it raise for you?

Point out that two stories are sandwiched together in 5:21–43, and that the intertwining of the two stories invites us to compare them and to interpret them together. Ask group members to compare the two stories, and note parallels and contrasts that can be observed.

Proceed with any of the questions for discussion/reflection below.

Questions for Discussion or Reflection

Mark 5:21–43 contains a large cast of characters. With whom do you identify as you hear this story, and why? Where would you place yourself in the scene?

In what ways do you identify with Jairus? With his daughter? With her mother? With the hemorrhaging woman? With the disciples? With the mourners? With Jesus?

Where do realities reflected in the text intersect with your own experience? What word does the text address to the reality or experience you have identified?

In your view, do purity regulations inform a reading of this story in significant ways? Where do you come out on this disputed issue? Are distinctions between "clean" and "unclean" operative in our own contemporary experience? If so, how? What does this contribute to your reading of the story?

The woman in the inner story has traditionally been referred to as "the woman with a flow of blood." Can you imagine being referred to as such? Have you or persons you have known struggled with chronic illness? Have you or persons you have known felt "defined" by an illness? What does this contribute to your reading of the story?

To this day, women often struggle with health-care systems that fail them—as those whose lives have been adversely affected by the Dalkon Shield, DES, PMS, osteoporosis, menopause, breast implants, or estrogen replacement therapy can attest. What does this contribute to your reading of the story?

Have you or persons with whom you are acquainted ever been desperate over the condition of a seriously ill child? What does this contribute to your understanding of Jairus's situation?

What do you make of the explicit connections between the experience of the two women and Jesus' own passion, suffering, death, and resurrection? Are they significant for your reading of the text? If so, why?

The issue of "touching" is often an ambiguous one in our own Christian communities. On the one hand, people long to be touched and embraced. On the other hand, increased attention to boundary concerns and ethical issues has alerted us to the fact that there are both appropriate and inappropriate ways of "touching." Is this dimension of the text a significant one in your view? Why or why not? How does your own experience inform your interpretation of the tactile imagery in the story?

The hemorrhaging woman acts on her own behalf, takes responsibility for her life, and claims her own healing. How can her struggle toward wholeness inform your own?

What do you learn about Jesus in this story? Make a list of the impressions of him that emerge from the story. What is their significance for you?

Are "interruptions" a reality with which you struggle? How can the story of an interruption in Jesus' ministry inform your own engagement with interruptions?

What new insights have emerged for you from your engagement with this story?

Resources for Further Study

Barta, Karen A. "'She Spent All She Had . . . But Only Grew Worse': Paying the Price of Paternalism." In *Where Can We Find Her? Searching for Women's Identity in the New Church*, edited by Marie-Eloise Rosenblatt, 24–36. New York: Paulist, 1991.

Cohen, Shaye J. D. "Menstruants and the Sacred in Judaism and Christianity." In *Women's History and Ancient History*, edited by Sarah B. Pomeroy, 273–99. Chapel Hill: University of North Carolina Press, 1991.

———. "Purity and Piety: The Separation of Menstruants from the Sancta." In *Daughters of the King: Women and the Synagogue*, edited by Susan Grossman and Rivka Haut, 103–15. Philadelphia: The Jewish Publication Society, 1992.

Cotter, Wendy. "Mark's Hero of the Twelfth-Year Miracles: The Healing of the Woman with the Hemorrhage and the Raising of Jairus's Daughter (Mark 5.21–43)." In *A Feminist Companion to Mark*, edited by Amy-Jill Levine with Marianne Blickenstaff, 54–78. Sheffield: Sheffield Academic, 2001.

D'Angelo, Mary Rose. "Gender and Power in the Gospel of Mark: The Daughter of Jairus and the Woman with the Flow of Blood." In *Miracles in Jewish and Christian Antiquity*, edited by John C. Cavadini, 83–109. Notre Dame Studies in Theology 3. Notre Dame: University of Notre Dame Press, 1999.

Dewey, Joanna. "Jesus' Healings of Women: Conformity and Non-Conformity to Dominant Cultural Values as Clues for Historical Reconstruction." In *Society of Biblical Literature 1993 Seminar Papers* 32, edited by Eugene H. Lovering Jr., 178–93. Atlanta: Scholars, 1993.

Fonrobert, Charlotte. "The Woman with a Blood-Flow (Mark 5.24–34) Revisited: Menstrual Laws and Jewish Culture in Christian Feminist Hermeneutics." In *Early Christian Interpretation of the Scriptures of Israel: Investigations and Proposals*, edited by Craig A. Evans and James A. Sanders, 121–40. Journal for the Study of the New Testament Supplement Series 148. Sheffield: Sheffield Academic, 1997.

Fredriksen, Paula. "Did Jesus Oppose the Purity Laws?" *Bible Review* 11 (June 1995): 20–25, 42–45.

Graham, Susan Lochrie. "Silent Voices: Women in the Gospel of Mark." *Semeia* 54 (1991): 145–58.

Kinukawa, Hisako. *Women and Jesus in Mark: A Japanese Feminist Perspective*, 29–50. Maryknoll, N.Y.: Orbis, 1994.

———. "The Story of the Hemorrhaging Woman (Mark 5:24–35) Read from a Japanese Feminist Context." *Biblical Interpretation* 2 (1994): 283–93.

Levine, Amy-Jill. "Discharging Responsibility: Matthean Jesus, Biblical Law, and Hemorrhaging Woman." In *Treasures New and Old: Recent Contributions to Matthean Studies*, edited by David R. Bauer and Mark Allan Powell. 379–97. Atlanta: Scholars, 1996. Reprinted in *A Feminist Companion to Matthew*, edited by Amy-Jill Levine with Marianne Blickenstaff, 70–87. Sheffield: Sheffield Academic, 2001.

Minor, Mitzi. "Old Stories through New Eyes: Insights Gained from a Feminist Reading of Mark 5:25–34." *Memphis Theological Seminary Journal* 30 (Spring 1992): 2–14.

Myers, Ched. *Binding the Strong Man: A Political Reading of Mark's Story of Jesus*, 197–205. Maryknoll, N.Y.: Orbis, 1988.

Rhoads, David. "Social Criticism: Crossing Boundaries." In *Mark and Method: New Approaches in Biblical Studies*, edited by Janice Capel Anderson and Stephen D. Moore, 135–61. Minneapolis: Fortress, 1992.

Rosenblatt, Marie-Eloise. "Gender, Ethnicity, and Legal Considerations in the Haemorrhaging Woman's Story Mark 5:25–34." In *Transformative Encounters: Jesus and Women Re-viewed*, edited by Ingrid Rosa Kitzberger, 137–61. Leiden: Brill, 2000.

Selvidge, Marla J. *Woman, Cult, and Miracle Recital: A Redactional Critical Investigation of Mark 5:24–34*. Lewisburg, Pa.: Bucknell University Press, 1990.

Tolbert, Mary Ann. "Mark." In *The Women's Bible Commentary*, edited by Carol Newsom and Sharon Ringe, 263–74. Louisville, Ky.: Westminster/John Knox, 1992.

West, Gerald. "Constructing Critical and Contextual Readings with Ordinary Readers (Mark 5:21–6:1)." *Journal of Theology for Southern Africa* 92 (Spring 1995): 60–69.

Chapter Three

Martha and Mary

Luke 10:38–42

Now as they went on their way, he entered a certain village, where a woman named Martha welcomed him into her home. She had a sister named Mary, who sat at the Lord's feet and listened to what he was saying. But Martha was distracted by her many tasks; so she came to him and asked, "Lord, do you not care that my sister has left me to do all the work by myself? Tell her then to help me." But the Lord answered her, "Martha, Martha, you are worried and distracted by many things; there is need of only one thing. Mary has chosen the better part, which will not be taken away from her."

The story of Martha and Mary evokes strong reactions, both positive and negative. Some hail it as one of the most liberating texts for women in the Gospels, in that it reflects an opening for women within the circle of Jesus' disciples and challenges traditional expectations about women's roles. Others, however, find it oppressive, in that it pits sisters against each other, establishes a good woman/bad woman dualism, and presents a seemingly ungrateful Lord as devaluing the hospitality that a hardworking woman proffers. Indeed, whenever women gather to discuss it, at least one usually expresses the following sentiment: "I have always hated this story!"

If reactions to the story are strong, that may also be because its setting is so familiar to us, and as such immediately lures us into its dynamics, which is not always the case when we read the Gospels. Rarely do we personally see water turned into wine or witness miraculous physical healings. Few of us would have a successful Family Night Supper with five loaves and two fish. But all of us are familiar with the everyday setting of household living. Thus, as Luke takes us into the home of Martha and

Mary, we immediately recognize that we have been there and are keenly aware of the tensions apparent in the story.

Though Martha and Mary make an appearance in John's Gospel as well (John 11–12), this particular story is found only in Luke. Its literary context is that of Luke's distinctive travel narrative (9:51–19:27). The third evangelist turns the story of the life and ministry of Jesus largely into a story of Jesus' journey to Jerusalem and to his death. The journey begins in 9:51. Then, at the beginning of chapter 10, Jesus commissions seventy disciples. They are told to travel lightly, to expect food and shelter, and to eat and drink what is set before them (10:4–12). The theme of hospitality, which receives special emphasis throughout Luke's Gospel, is central here. The work of Jesus and his disciples clearly depended on the hospitality extended to them by people like Martha and Mary. Attention to this larger context sets the stage for consideration of the story.

The story's immediate context is equally noteworthy. It is part of a smaller unit that stretches from 10:25 through 10:42. In 10:25, a lawyer puts Jesus to the test, inquiring, "Teacher, what must I do to inherit eternal life?" In response, Jesus elicits from him the two great love commandments: "You shall love the Lord your God with all your heart, and with all your soul, and with all your strength, and with all your mind; and your neighbor as yourself" (10:27). Luke then explicates these two great commandments in reverse order in the two stories that follow. The parable of the Good Samaritan illumines the second commandment, providing a concrete illustration of what it means to love one's neighbor as oneself (10:29–37). The story of Martha and Mary then sheds light on the meaning of the first commandment, asserting that to love the Lord with all one's heart, soul, strength, and mind entails sitting at Jesus' feet and "listening to his word" (10:38–42). Devotion to God is implicit in this engagement, for Jesus is presented by Luke as God's own Son, conceived and empowered by God's own spirit, who knows God completely, obeys God perfectly, and reveals God to disciples.[1] Thus, to sit at Jesus' feet and listen to his word is in effect to know and love God more completely. In Luke's view the word of God and the word of Jesus are linked (see 5:1; 8:11, 21).

Although some commentators argue against reading the stories in tandem,[2] various similarities confirm that the stories of the Good Samaritan and Martha and Mary are linked. The parable of the Good Samaritan, for example, begins by directing attention to "a certain man" (*anthrōpos tis*) who was going down from Jerusalem to Jericho. The story that follows directs attention to "a certain woman" (*gynē tis*) named Martha who receives Jesus into her home. Thus, the evangelist pairs male and female figures in his interpretation of the two great commandments, as is his custom.[3] Moreover, both the story of the Good Samaritan and that of Martha and Mary are structured around contrasts. The first story emphasizes a contrast between the actions of a Samaritan, on the one hand, and those of a Jewish priest and Levite on the other. The second story paints a contrast between two sisters, emphasizing the distracted service of the one, and the undivided attention directed to Jesus' word by the other. At first glance, the juxtaposition of the two stories might appear odd, in that the first applauds action, and the second praises inaction. The lawyer is told to "go and do," whereas Martha is reprimanded for doing. The juxtaposition may well be deliberate on Luke's part, however. Indeed, the chief argument in favor of a tandem reading is the fact that the evangelist has arranged the narrative so that we hear the stories back-to-back. As we will see, it may be important to keep this juxtaposition in mind as we ponder the stories.

The story of Martha and Mary is short, simple, and to the point—indeed notable for its brevity. In terms of its genre, it is classified as a "pronouncement story." As such, it supplies a brief narrative context that sets the stage for a striking saying or pronouncement of Jesus that appears as its climax. The structure of the text is easily identified:

> Setting (v. 38)
> A contrast is drawn (vv. 39–40a)
>   Mary (positioned at the Lord's feet listening to his word)
>   Martha (distracted with much service)
> Martha reprimands/commands Jesus (v. 40b)
> The Lord's pronouncement (vv. 41–42)

The story invites us to consider a study in contrasts, and to attend closely to the Lord's pronouncement, which forms its climax.

Encountering the Text

Let us examine the scene more closely. The setting is provided in verse 38: "Now as they went on their way, he entered a certain village, where a woman named Martha welcomed him into her home." The opening words serve as a reminder that Luke's travel narrative is unfolding. Jesus and his disciples are "on [the] way" to Jerusalem (where he will be crucified) when Martha receives him into her home. Although the Gospel of

John locates Martha's home in Bethany, Luke does not specify the town through which Jesus passes on his journey, and although in John's Gospel Martha and Mary have a brother named Lazarus (see John 11–12), Luke's story mentions no brother, husband, or father. Jesus is welcomed into an autonomous female household. More than a pit stop is in view, for the hospitality extended entails more than simply the provision of food and drink. By "welcoming" or "receiving" him into her home, Martha embraces Jesus' eschatological mission and evinces her openness to the word and work of God.[4] Her welcome stands in stark contrast to the lack of reception accorded Jesus by a Samaritan village in 9:53: "they did not receive him, because his face was set toward Jerusalem." Indeed, her welcome exemplifies the positive response to the gospel blessed by Jesus in his mission instructions to the seventy: "Carry no purse, no bag, no sandals; and greet no one on the road. Whatever house you enter, first say, 'Peace to this house!' And if anyone is there who shares in peace, your peace will rest on that person. . . . Whenever you enter a town and its people welcome you, eat what is set before you; cure the sick who are there, and say to them, 'The kingdom of God has come near to you'" (10:4–9).

The contrast begins to be drawn in verse 39: "She had a sister named Mary, who sat at the Lord's feet and listened to what he was saying." The fact that Mary sits at Jesus' feet and listens to his word arrests attention and is variously interpreted. Many interpreters have been quick to note that Jewish women were typically excluded from study of the Torah, and therefore Jesus (and early Christianity) opened up liberating opportunities for women to engage in study and discipleship in company with men. A contrast between "Judaism" and "Christianity" is not, however, explicitly mentioned in the text; moreover, such a contrast rests on tenuous presuppositions about women's roles in Judaism and ignores the fact that both Mary and Jesus are Jewish.

Recently, in a study of women and meal customs in the broader context of Greco-Roman society, Kathleen Corley has reached an opposite conclusion concerning Mary's posture at Jesus' feet. In her view, Mary's stance is that of "a traditional, silent wife, who sits at the feet of her husband at the table":[5]

> Mary is quietly seated at the feet of Jesus and is not portrayed as reclining as his equal on the dinner couch. It is therefore not necessary to denigrate Judaism in order to make the point that Mary is here receiving instruction, particularly since there is ample evidence that certain rabbis did encourage the education of daughters, even in

Torah. Furthermore, the removal of the others from the narrative at this point underscores the private nature of the scene. Although it is true that such a scene of Jesus alone with two women might cause a scandal, to include a large host of other men and women in the scene would be worse. In the context of Greco-Roman social ideology governing women's behavior at meals, this text unmistakably extols the traditional, private role of a Hellenistic woman.[6]

Mary is not the only one to appear at Jesus' feet in Luke's larger narrative, however, and thus literary context also provides a clue as to how her demeanor is to be understood. Elsewhere in Luke's story, a weeping woman described as a forgiven sinner (7:36–50), a healed Gerasene demoniac (8:35), and a cleansed leper (17:16) all take up a position at Jesus' feet. In each case, their posture conveys discipleship, gratitude, and devotion.[7] Moreover, Luke repeatedly underlines the importance of listening, of hearing the word, as an essential characteristic of discipleship (cf. 2:19, 51; 6:46–49; 8:15, 21; 11:28). Those who "hear the word" and "hold it fast in an honest and good heart" represent the good soil in Jesus' parable of the sower (8:15); similarly, "those who hear the word of God and do it" constitute Jesus' true family (8:21). Luke tells us that Mary, seated at the Lord's feet, "listened to what he was saying." The imperfect verb tense of the original (*ēkouen:* "was listening") conveys her intense concentration. She is a portrait of a listening disciple. Like Martha, who received Jesus into her home, Mary demonstrates her openness to the word and work of God and her embrace of Jesus' mission. As Adele Reinhartz suggests, "we have come upon Martha and Mary in the very act of conversion."[8]

The other half of the contrast is sketched in verse 40a: "But Martha was distracted by her many tasks." Mary's intense concentration on Jesus' word stands in stark contrast to Martha's harried distraction with "many tasks"—or, translating more literally, with "much service" (*pollēn diakonian*). Interpreters have traditionally assumed that the Greek term *diakonia* refers to "waiting at table," and that Martha's distraction pertains to the supervising, organizing, and preparing of a meal. Thus, the scene is envisioned as follows: while Mary has her buns on the floor, so to speak, Martha has her biscuits in the oven and could use some help.

However, the text itself does not place Martha in a "kitchen"; nor is there specific reference to foodstuffs or a meal. Indeed, interpreters may have projected into the story their own assumptions about women's roles. Although *diakonia* can refer to table service, Elisabeth Schüssler Fiorenza has observed that *diakonia* is also the vocabulary of Christian ministry (cf.

Acts 6–8).[9] From this perspective, the *diakonia* in which Martha is engaged may well be eucharistic table service and proclamation of the word.[10] (This term and Schüssler Fiorenza's argument are examined below.) Whatever the case may be—whether she is involved in food preparation or ministry—Martha's engagement occasions "distraction." The verb *perispaomai* appears only here in the New Testament, but is thought to connote being "pulled away," "distracted," "quite busy," or "overburdened."[11] The imperfect verb tense suggests a continuous state of distraction. Martha's distraction with "much service" contrasts with Mary's single-minded concentration on one thing alone: the word of the Lord.

This contrast results in conflict, for overburdened as she is with "much service," Martha seeks the Lord's intervention to secure Mary's assistance: "so she came to him and asked, 'Lord, do you not care that my sister has left me to do all the work by myself? Tell her then to help me'" (v. 40b). Several things are striking about the words that Martha addresses to the Lord, not the least of which is the fact that Martha feels herself compelled both to reprimand and to command her distinguished guest! Moreover, attention to Greek grammar suggests that Martha expects the Lord to respond positively to her inquiry. In Greek, if a question begins with the negative particle *ou*, the speaker expects an affirmative answer; if it begins with the negative particle *mē*, the speaker expects a negative answer. Martha's question "do you not care . . ." begins with *ou* rather than *mē*, so the answer she clearly anticipates is "Yes, I care"—though it is not the answer she receives. Martha again here refers to her work as *diakonia*, and not specifically as food preparation and kitchen detail. Employing the related verb form, her complaint, translated literally, is that "my sister has left me to serve (*diakonein*) alone." Finally, Martha's words refer continually back to herself: "Lord, do you not care that *my* sister has left *me* to do all the work *by myself*? Tell her then to help *me*." As Turid Karlsen Seim notes, this "intensifies the contrast with Mary's concentration on Jesus' words."[12]

By this point in the story, the concerns and sympathies of those who read it or hear it are fully engaged. After all, we have been drawn into a story whose setting and tensions are entirely familiar, and we are made to eavesdrop on a family quarrel and an embarrassing social situation. Thus, we are in a position to hear and ponder all the more carefully, along with Martha, Jesus' response. His pronouncement in verses 41–42 is the climax and raison d'être of the entire story: "But the Lord answered her, 'Martha, Martha, you are worried and distracted by many things; there is need of only one thing. Mary has chosen the better part, which will not be taken away from her.'" Throughout the story, Jesus has been referred to consistently as "Lord": Mary sat at "the Lord's feet." Martha inquired, "Lord, do you not care . . . ," and now "the Lord answered her." Thus the risen Lord, whom Luke's community worships and confesses, now speaks an authoritative word. The word that he addresses to Martha is threefold.

First, he chides her: "Martha, Martha, you are worried and distracted by many things." The repetition of her name, a Lukan stylistic peculiarity, implies a gentle reprimand (cf. 6:46; 22:31; Acts 9:4; 22:7; 26:14). Moreover, two further descriptions provide a vivid portrait of Martha's mental state. If in verse 40 the narrator described Martha as "distracted," Jesus now provides further commentary on her demeanor, noting first that she is "anxious" or "worried" (*merimnas*). This point is not the only place at which this term surfaces in Luke's narrative. "Anxiety" or "worry" (*merimna*) is identified as an impediment to discipleship at several other points in the story. In his interpretation of the parable of the Sower, for example, Jesus observes that some who hear the word of God find themselves "choked by the cares (*merimnōn*) and riches and pleasure of life," with the result that "their fruit does not mature" (8:14). In 12:22–31, Jesus specifically admonishes disciples not to worry or be anxious: "Do not worry (*mē merimnate*) about your life, what you will eat, or about your body, what you will wear. For life is more than food, and the body more than clothing. . . . And can any of you by worrying (*merimnōn*) add a single hour to your span of life?" "Anxiety" or "worry" is clearly identified as a debilitating reality in the life of discipleship.[13]

Jesus describes Martha as "troubled" or "putting herself in an uproar" (*thorybazē*; the NRSV renders the verb less adequately in v. 41 as "distracted"). This verb appears only here in the New Testament and is quite colorful.[14] Moreover, Kathleen Corley makes a striking observation: cognates of this verb (such as *thorybeō* and *thorybos*) usually refer to groups and assemblies, rather than individuals, that are in a state of uproar or riot. At a later point, we consider the possibility, as Corley notes, "that the 'trouble' Martha causes concerns a community, not just an individual."[15]

Also apparent from Jesus' response is that Martha's anxiety and state of uproar are occasioned by the "muchness" of her task.[16] He describes her as anxious and troubled "by many things"; just as earlier the narrator had described her as distracted by "many tasks." The "muchness" of Martha's task is further underlined by the second part of Jesus' response to her, which emphasizes a contrasting point: "there is need of only one thing" (v. 42a).

This second part of Jesus' response to Martha (v. 42a) is plagued by textual difficulties. The Greek in the ancient manuscripts varies considerably, and contemporary readers are apparently not the first to experience discomfort with Jesus' words! The ancient scribes who copied the manuscripts by hand also squirmed and puzzled over the nature of Jesus' response to Martha. Six alternative readings emerge as a result. After sorting through the possibilities, however, scholars tend to agree that one of two readings is most likely to have been the original—that is, the one intended by the evangelist Luke: Jesus is represented as saying either (1) "few things are necessary, or only one" (*oligōn de estin chreia ē henos*), or (2) "there is need of only one thing" (*henos de estin chreia*).

What difference do these variants make for interpretation? The first, longer reading assumes a meal setting. If "few things are necessary, or only one," Jesus appears to suggest that a simpler meal would be fine: "that is, an olive or two will suffice."[17] The second, shorter reading ("there is need of only one thing") paints a sharper contrast between the activity of the two protagonists and more explicitly devalues Martha's service. The meaning in this case is that Mary (rather than Martha) has chosen the one necessary thing: discipleship and receiving from Jesus.

So which reading is the original one, intended by the evangelist? The situation is complicated, and certainty is impossible in this matter. As Turid Karlsen Seim observes: "For those who cannot bring themselves to sweep Martha aside completely, the variants with *oligōn* [the first option] are the most comfortable. They imply that something is said in Martha's favour; her mistake is simply that she bothers with much *more* than is necessary."[18] However, a majority of scholars incline toward the shorter reading as the best-attested, more "difficult," and thus more original one:[19] we are to understand that "there is need of only one thing." As Bruce Metzger notes, the absoluteness of *henos* ("one thing") appears to have been "softened" and thus made more palatable by copyists who replaced it with *oligōn* ("few things").[20]

Verse 42b, the third and concluding part of Jesus' response, further elevates Mary's choice over Martha's: "Mary has chosen the better part, which will not be taken away from her." Mary's choice (sitting at the Lord's feet and listening to his word) is described, literally, as "the good part" or "the good portion." It is a choice Jesus defends, insisting that it "will not be taken away from her."

Martha's choice of service is, by implication at least, not as good. But are her service and hospitality repudiated? In Luke the ministry of Jesus and his disciples depended to a great extent on the hospitality of people like Martha (10:4–12). Still, the Lukan Jesus explicitly states, "I am among you as one who serves" (22:27). Perhaps the point being made is that disciples learn from Jesus what it means to serve. Martha's mistake may then lie in supposing that she is the host, and in missing the opportunity to sit at his feet.

Is our discomfort with the text showing? Does a desire to defend and redeem Martha's choice betray deep uneasiness with the Lord's pronouncement? Perhaps attention to two angles of vision may help us understand the conflict the story evokes in many who hear it.

Angles of Vision

What is the evangelist Luke's attitude toward women, and how has it shaped the text? And what can we learn from the history of interpretation of this story? Attention to both of these questions helps us delve more deeply into the problems and possibilities the text presents.

Diakonia *and Luke's Portrayal of Women*

Elisabeth Schüssler Fiorenza has suggested that women often suspect that Martha received a "raw deal," because she did![21] Schüssler Fiorenza maintains that the story reflects "the struggle of early Christian women against patriarchal restrictions of their leadership and ministry at the turn of the first century."[22] Martha, she contends, should be viewed as the leader of a house-church who welcomes Jesus as an equal into her home. Moreover, she is engaged in *diakonia*, which (as noted above) is part of the vocabulary of Christian ministry.

This insight is confirmed by striking linguistic parallels between Luke 10:38–42 and Acts 6. Because Luke and Acts form a two-part work, authored by the same individual, such parallels merit close attention. In Luke 10, Martha complains that Mary has "left" (*katelipen*) her "to serve" (*diakonein*) alone in order to listen to the Lord's word (*logon*); in Acts 6:2 the twelve disciples argue that they cannot leave (*kataleipsantas*) the word (*logon*) of God in order to serve (*diakonein*) at tables, and seven "Hellenists" are then appointed to devote themselves to eucharistic ministry, in order that the twelve might devote themselves to the preaching of the word. The subsequent narrative indicates, however, that the two types of ministry cannot be rigidly distinguished. For example, one of the Hellenists, named Stephen, also performs signs and wonders (Acts 6:8) and proves to be a powerful preacher (Acts 6–7). This understanding of *diakonia* as ecclesial leadership clearly undermines the traditional, kitchen-bound view of Martha, and a number of interpreters have found it persuasive. For instance, in an article entitled "Getting Martha Out of the Kitchen," Warren Carter concurs that *diakonia* does not designate domestic or culinary activity but "refers, rather, to ministry and leadership in the Christian community and on its behalf."[23]

Martha, then, should be understood as engaged in eucharistic ministry in the house-church, which may well include proclamation of the word.[24] The evangelist Luke, however, seeking to restrict women's ministry and authority in his own community, as Schüssler Fiorenza observes, "appeals to the *Kyrios* and pits sister against sister in order to teach a lesson and make a point."[25] He approves of Mary, who sits silently at Jesus' feet; Martha, who argues for her interest, is silenced. Schüssler Fiorenza maintains that "The rhetorical interests of the Lukan text are to silence women leaders of house-churches who, like Martha, might have protested, and to simultaneously extol Mary's 'silent' and subordinate behavior."[26] As Mary Rose D'Angelo observes, Martha's complaint is that "My sister has left me to do all the ministry." Luke answers, "Women who have been discouraged from ministry have chosen the better part."[27]

Barbara E. Reid's reading of Luke 10:38–42 concurs with aspects of Schüssler Fiorenza's thesis, for she too maintains that Martha and Mary's story reflects disputes in Luke's community over women's involvement in certain ministries. Reid proposes, however, that "Martha's complaint to Jesus is not about having too much work to do, but rather that she is being denied her role in ministerial service."[28] Two striking translation issues in the phrase describing Martha as "burdened with much serving" (*periespato peri pollēn diakonian*) support this conclusion. First, since the preposition *peri* has the sense "about" or "concerning," Reid argues that "Martha is burdened *about* or *with reference to* her numerous ministerial works, not *by* or *with* them. Her distress *about* them is generated by the opposition of those who think she should be leaving them to men."[29] Second, while the verb *perispaō* can connote distraction or burden, its primary definition is "to be pulled or dragged away": "in Luke 10:40 the word alludes to Martha's being pulled away from her diaconal ministry by those who disapprove."[30] Reid further speculates that "part of Martha's anguish is that her sisters, former companions in ministry, have been persuaded that silent listening is the proper role for women disciples and have left her alone in the more visible ministries."[31]

Kathleen Corley's observation, noted earlier, concerning the verb "to trouble" or "to put in an uproar" (*thorybazein*) is also pertinent in this connection. Cognates of this verb usually refer to groups, rather than individuals, that are in a state of uproar, indicating that the "trouble" Martha causes concerns a whole community.[32] This perspective on the text (if regarded as persuasive) bears considerable import for interpretation of the text in teaching and preaching. For one thing, an immediate connection can be discerned between the ecclesial struggles reflected in the text and contemporary ones. Reid observes: "The real crux of disagreement, both in the early Church and today, is not the question of whether women can study theology, but rather the question of what ministries they may perform as a result of their theological education. It is around Martha that the controversies swirl, not Mary."[33]

Moreover, if a patriarchal perspective that seeks to limit women's engagement in ministry is in fact inscribed in the text, then contemporary interpreters must exercise caution lest they reinscribe patriarchal visions of women's roles within today's Christian community. Thus, Reid urges preachers and teachers to read against Luke's intent: "[T]he Lukan stories cannot be taught, preached, or passed on uncritically. . . . Unless their patriarchal framework is unmasked and addressed head-on, preachers and teachers will reinforce, rather than challenge, their inscribed gender role divisions."[34] By reinterpreting the text from a feminist perspective, the story "can be recontextualized to proclaim a message of good news for women and men called equally to share in the same discipleship and mission of Jesus."[35] Schüssler Fiorenza also urges interpreters to exercise their critical faculties, insisting that a patriarchal story such as Luke 10:38–42 should not be clothed with divine authority and proclaimed as the word of God: "Instead it must be proclaimed as the word of Luke!"[36]

Schüssler Fiorenza's historical reconstruction (and the related interpretations it has spawned) warrant careful reflection by all who would venture to preach or teach on Martha and Mary's complicated story. Indeed, it represents a landmark contribution to the study of Luke 10:38–42 and must be taken into account in all subsequent scholarly discussion of the story. Not all interpreters are convinced entirely by her reading, however, and various critiques warrant reflection as well. Some commentators take issue with the construal of *diakonia* as ecclesial leadership, and are unwilling to relieve Martha of housework. Robert Tannehill, for example, insists that "the verb *diakoneō* is consistently used in Luke of domestic service, such as providing food, something that women or slaves were expected to do."[37] Turid Karlsen Seim likewise contends that Luke's use of *diakon*-terminology connotes primarily the serving of food and waiting at table.[38] Examining all the appearances of these terms in Luke 4:39; 8:3; 10:40; 12:37; 17:8; and 22:26–27 shows, however, that explicit references to a meal situation appear in connection with only three out of six of these references (12:37; 17:8; 22:26–27). I am hard-pressed to concur with this position and wonder whether it can be sustained in light of the ministerial connotations so clearly associated with this vocabulary in Acts (see Acts 1:17, 25; 6–7; 11:29; 12:25; 19:22; 20:24; 21:19).[39] John N. Collins argues, however, that transpositions of sense (from Acts to Luke, for example) can never be valid: "The overriding principle of interpretation is to read words in their context. Because the *diakon*-words have no determinate or constant reference, the referent can be determined only within each particular context."[40] In his view, the scene sketched in Luke 10:38–42 entails a guest in the house of two women, and thus suggests (for reasons that are not altogether clear) that Martha is busying herself with delivering the courses of a meal. Collins insists, "It is the scene that has to be interpreted, not the words. The scene is not and never was about ecclesial ministry."[41]

Seim articulates an additional, noteworthy critique of Schüssler Fiorenza's position. She is not convinced that the role as patron or benefactor, assumed by Martha when she "receives" Jesus into her home, is necessarily linked with that of ecclesial leadership: "[T]here was not an obvious connection between the status of patron and active leadership, and . . . there is no terminological evidence that *diakonia* was especially associated with this kind of leadership. Thus, even if Martha is a house-holder exercising hospitality, she is not to be understood automatically, in a presupposed 'subtext', to have been the leader of a community."[42] This point bears reflection as we ponder the meaning of *diakonia* in Luke-Acts. Whether or not one is convinced by Schüssler Fiorenza's construal of the term, however, her reading should at the very least lead all interpreters (1) to scrutinize the extent to which they have projected their own assumptions about "women's roles" into Martha's story, and (2) to attend closely to how the text itself describes Martha's engagement.

Reservations have also been expressed about Schüssler Fiorenza's construal of Mary's role: is Mary in fact a silent, passive listener? Robert Tannehill, for example, counters: "The story does not require us to infer from the few words about Mary that she is only and always a listener. The scene itself suggests that she is not passive, for she has taken bold action in leaving her expected role of serving dinner in order to listen to Jesus."[43] Additionally, Herman Waetjen has noted that in the rabbinic tradition, those who sit at the feet of a teacher engage in lively discussion with the master.[44] However, though other teaching moments in Luke feature dialogue between Jesus and his disciples (cf. 5:1–11; 8:4–15; 9:10–11, 46–48, 54–56; 18:26–30; 22:24–30; 24:13–35),[45] no words are attributed to Mary in

Luke's depiction of this scene. Her presence in the story is a silent one, in contrast to that of her sister.

Differing hermeneutical convictions also enter into an evaluation of Schüssler Fiorenza's thesis. The canonical form of the text is accorded a certain authority by many interpreters of Scripture. Thus, some object to Schüssler Fiorenza's concluding contention that Luke 10:38–42 is not to be proclaimed as the word of God, but rather as the word of Luke.[46] In a related vein, some take issue with historical reconstruction that takes one "behind" the text, preferring a literary-critical approach that works with the text as it stands within its larger narrative context.[47] This latter approach has much to contribute to a reading of the story—a possibility we will continue to explore.

However, attention to narrative context and, in particular, to the depiction of women throughout Luke-Acts lends some support to Schüssler Fiorenza's construal of the story. This point may come as a surprise to many, for Luke has traditionally been hailed as "the Gospel of Women." Luke does evince special interest in women: this Gospel includes a larger number among its cast of characters, along with stories about women that are found in no other Gospel.[48] Women's lives and activities also figure prominently in several uniquely Lukan parables.[49] Moreover, Luke has a notable tendency to present gender pairs that include women in the narrative in an explicit way. The parable of the man searching for a lost sheep, for example, is paired with one about a woman searching for a lost coin (Luke 15:3–10; see also 13:18–21; 17:34–35). As a result, women are more visible in Luke's narrative than in any other Gospel. But does it follow that the evangelist is enhancing or promoting their status within the community of faith?

Such advocacy has often been held to be the case. Increasingly, however, feminist biblical scholars have asked: What's wrong with this picture?[50] Reevaluation has ensued, producing surprising and convincing results. Indeed, close attention to the depiction of women in Luke-Acts suggests that while women are more visible in Luke's narrative, they are in fact presented in carefully circumscribed roles, primarily as nurturers and benefactors, who support the ministry of Jesus and his disciples out of their means (cf. Luke 8:1–3), and as such are exemplary models of service. But they are never referred to in Luke as "disciples" or "apostles." Though they may sit at Jesus' feet and listen to his word, as does Mary, they do not go on to proclaim the word in public preaching and teaching ministries, as do their male counterparts in the new family of faith. To be sure, Mary the mother of Jesus is given a full speech of proclamation, the

Magnificat, in Luke 1:46–55. However, the context is a domestic one, and women such as Mary, Elizabeth, and Anna may have notable roles and speech in Luke's infancy narrative (Luke 1–2) simply because the context is the traditional women's role of bearing and raising children.[51] Elsewhere, they are recipients, but not bearers, of the word. Indeed, strikingly, in Luke's version of the empty tomb story, it is not to women that the risen Lord first appears, and they receive no word of commission, as Mary Magdalene does in Matthew 28 (along with "the other Mary") and John 20. Moreover, in Acts, female gender explicitly renders one ineligible for ecclesial leadership (cf. Acts 1:21–26; 6:3–6), and thus the role of women in the narrative is substantially reduced. An increasingly male perspective prevails in Acts as the (male) apostles move out from Jerusalem to take the gospel to all nations.

What accounts for this enigmatic presentation? The evangelist's restriction of women's roles may be directly attributed to apologetic interests; that is, Luke may seek to assure the Roman world that the new Christian movement is above reproach and represents no threat to conventional norms of decorum. Consequently, Luke's women rarely appear in the public domain—the domain of men—and are associated primarily with household settings and/or with groups of other women. Even within Luke's community of faith, women and men keep largely to segregated groups (cf. 8:1–3). As Seim has demonstrated, "Luke-Acts mediates a picture of a world divided by gender, of a culture and a mediation of tradition in which men and women within the same community keep each to their own sphere of life."[52] Is it any wonder, then, that an uppity woman such as Mark's Syrophoenician (Mark 7:24–30//Matt. 15:21–28), who dares to approach Jesus and argue with him in public, is discreetly omitted from the Lukan narrative? Or that when Martha seeks to argue her case with Jesus, she is silenced? Indeed, outside the infancy narrative (Luke 1–2), women who speak in Luke's story are either corrected or disbelieved (cf. 10:41–42; 11:27–28; 23:27–31).[53] Jane Schaberg aptly summarizes the matter: "Luke restricts the roles of women to what is acceptable to the conventions of the imperial world. . . . Motivated by the desire that Christian leaders and witnesses be acceptable in the public forum of the empire, the world of men, Luke blurs traditional and historical traces of women's leadership and exaggerates the leadership of men."[54]

Branding the evangelist Luke as either the "friend" or "enemy" of women would greatly oversimplify the matter, for the truth lies somewhere in between. Luke's presentation of women is decidedly ambiguous.

Indeed, in her study of gender patterns in Luke-Acts, Seim has demonstrated that the evangelist transmits a "double message": "The tension in Luke's narrative has indeed shown itself to be its ambivalent evidence both of strong traditions about women on the one hand, and of the social and ideological controls that brought women to silence and promoted male dominance in positions of leadership on the other."[55]

The tension and ambiguity that emerge from the whole of the narrative's portrayal of women are present in the Martha and Mary story in abundance, and account in no small part for the ambivalence the narrative evokes in many of its readers. On the one hand, Mary's right to sit at Jesus' feet and to listen to his word is defended. The expectations of others concerning her responsibilities for either hospitality or ministry are not to interfere with her choice. Mary's silence and the limitation of her role to "hearing" remain troubling aspects of the story, but in some respects her choice and Jesus' defense of it can be construed as good news. Schüssler Fiorenza, for example, notes that "when contextualized in the life of lower and working-class women, Mary's audacity in taking time out from work to sit idle and to relax in good company can have a liberating effect. . . . A homily stressing Mary's right to study and to read can . . . be liberating in a community where women's activity is restricted to caring and working for others in the family, on the job, or in the church."[56]

Still, even this line of interpretation runs certain risks that are articulated clearly by Loveday Alexander: "Mary is praised for refusing to conform to the cultural stereotype, for not accepting the traditional role assigned to women in her society. But how does she achieve this breakthrough? Not by challenging the patriarchal denigration of 'women's work,' but by accepting it: she can only achieve her own liberation by joining the men. It is a classic feminist dilemma."[57] Alexander further observes that "In affirming Mary's rights to pursue her own destiny, to leave the world of domestic tasks, we simultaneously condemn Martha to second-class status."[58]

Indeed, many readers find it hard to shake the impression that Martha is treated unfairly, and that either her hospitality or her ministry is devalued. This impression is enhanced when viewed in the context of Luke's larger narrative, which betrays careful circumscribing of women's roles. Martha's situation may well be instructive, reminding disciples who find themselves anxious and distracted by manifold tasks of service that the word of Jesus is the essential wellspring of all daily ministry. Even so, discomfort with the text often lingers.

Sharon Ringe captures well the ambivalent response that Luke 10:38–42 evokes in many women. She notes that "the story of Mary and Martha is a sad one for women," despite the fact that "a woman is praised for not fulfilling her prescribed social role":

> Martha, who welcomes Jesus and expends considerable energy in providing hospitality for him and those traveling with him, is called "distracted" and "worried." She is blamed for doing what she would have been expected to do in her society. Furthermore, she is portrayed as whining to the man Jesus about her sister's failure to help her, instead of resolving the matter herself, woman to woman. Instead of receiving a blessing as someone who welcomes Jesus and his followers (9:48; 10:8–9), she receives a scolding.
>
> Mary fares no better. She gets to sit at Jesus' feet and listen to his teaching, just as the male disciples do, and she is praised by Jesus for it. But she is a silent learner. She poses no questions to Jesus, and she does not interact with him as the male disciples do. Unlike male disciples who are described as learning from Jesus, and who then are charged to carry the message on to others, Mary gets no commission to preach, no speaking part whatsoever. Whatever may have been Jesus' relationship with women followers (8:2–3), Luke allots them carefully circumscribed roles. For them, the lifestyle of discipleship—at least in Luke's church—promises few real changes.[59]

What sadness or gladness does the story evoke in you? Each reader will answer this question differently, for responses to the story are as varied as the readers who engage it.

In fact, it should not be supposed that "feminist" biblical scholars speak with one voice or are of one mind on this story or any other single issue. Feminists represent a variety of perspectives, methodologies, and opinions, and in this connection, one final critique of Schüssler Fiorenza's position should be mentioned. A number of interpreters, feminists among them, deemphasize the gender dimension of Luke 10:38–42. Their point is that the story is not addressed to women per se, but to all disciples. Loveday Alexander, for example, maintains that the subject of the Martha and Mary story is not uniquely "women's business," but "the common experience of discipleship." Indeed, she cautions, "To insist that this is a story 'about women' is to risk confining it to the ghetto: 'women's stories,' notoriously, are felt to have nothing to teach men."[60] Adele Reinhartz concurs: "[T]he evangelist's purpose is not to describe the ideal female disciple in particular, but to illustrate his views on discipleship in general"[61] and "to deepen the theological understanding of all readers."[62] The fact that women (as well as men) serve illustrative and instructive purposes in the narrative conveys that they are fully eligible for discipleship, which is significant. The point, however—well taken and worth pondering—is that stories about women are not for women alone. This story is not the only Lukan narrative that features a contrast and conflict between two siblings. Luke's most memorable parable features a prodigal son and his resentful older brother (Luke 15:11–32), and are not the sympathies and concerns of both male and female readers engaged and addressed by it? Deemphasizing the gender dimension of Luke 10:38–42 does not necessarily eliminate the discomfort the story evokes in many who hear it, for another source of tension is at hand.

Dualism or Complementarity?

Conflicting reactions to Luke 10:38–42 are also frequently occasioned by the story's pronounced dualism, that is, by its sharp statement of opposing realities. Whether it contrasts two women or two aspects of discipleship, the text appears to present a stark choice between "good" and (by implication) "not as good" alternatives. Many readers find themselves uncomfortable with the choice and with the text's polarizing tendency.

Dualistic dynamics emerge from the text itself, as Schüssler Fiorenza observes:

> The text itself inscribes the oppositions: rest/movement; lowliness/ upright posture; listen/speak. Martha's intervention as a speaking subject reinforces this contrasting opposition:

Mary	Martha
student	householder
listening	speaking
rest	movement
receptiveness	argument
openness	purposefulness
passivity	agency
better choice	rejection[63]

Within the oppositions sketched by the text, Mary clearly functions as "the positive figure" and Martha as "the negative foil."[64]

The dualistic character of Luke's story has resulted in a long history of dualistic interpretations, in which the juxtaposed sisters exemplify varied abstract principles. Martha, for example, has often been held as a representative of Judaism, and Mary a representative of Christianity. Alternatively, when the Protestant Reformers got hold of Martha, she became a representative of "justification by works"—the negative foil for Mary's preferred choice of "justification by faith." Martha is thus exposed as either a Jew or Roman Catholic, and Mary as both Christian and Protestant. Such interpretations all too frequently have perpetuated distorted perceptions of both Judaism and Roman Catholicism, with Martha usually cast in the role of "fussy legalist."[65]

The story has most often been read as a commentary on two lifestyles, with Martha representing the active life of service and Mary the contemplative life of study and prayer. As Blake Heffner notes, "Traditionally, this passage is the *locus classicus* in Christian spirituality for comparing the ways of action and contemplation."[66] Viewed from this perspective, the text has often been interpreted as a commendation of the spiritual life over the active one.

In many respects, the history of dualistic readings is a showcase of interpretations to avoid, for it manifests both a tendency toward allegorizing the sisters and dangerous interpretive polemics. This approach has also inspired rampant defamation of Martha, for in dualistic comparisons Martha inevitably gets the short end of the stick. Indeed, she has been caricatured frequently in sermons and other interpretations of the text as a fussy, nagging, argumentative, legalistic busybody—in contrast to her tranquil, attentive, contemplative sister. Preachers are hard-pressed to deny the importance of the service Martha renders (dependent as they are on the voluntary service rendered by the many "Marthas" of their own congregations), but as Loveday Alexander observes, preachers often end up mired in the story's "all-too-familiar double-think, whereby a dominant social group simultaneously assigns certain necessary but unpopular tasks to a helot [slave] class and denigrates their importance": "Male preachers, in my own experience, rarely avoid falling into this patriarchal trap. Martha was 'fussing,' they say, looking down from the pulpit onto their predominantly female audience, about unnecessary female concerns: 'and we all know,' they add, before going home to their well-cooked Sunday dinners, 'how women do fuss.'"[67] Elisabeth Moltmann-Wendel confirms this interpretive tendency, as well as the long-standing exegetical preference for Mary: "If we are honest, Martha is presented to us as being useful and necessary. But when it comes to a model, a comfort or an ideal, it's Mary all the time."[68]

Within the history of interpretation, however, a tradition of resistance to dualistic readings may point a better way. Through the ages, a number of interpreters have refused to demonize Martha or to pit the sisters against each other in hierarchical opposition. Blake Heffner has highlighted their presence within the Christian tradition. In the earliest Christian centuries, he observes, John Chrysostom (347–407) represented a dissenting opinion on Martha and Mary:

> Like his namesake, John the Baptist, Chrysostom appeared as a voice crying in the wilderness, rejecting the "allegorical" interpretation of this story. He contends that Jesus' counsel to Martha implies neither wholesale reproof of work nor a categorical approval of leisure. Everything hinges, rather, on the significance of the moment. Christ does not praise Mary for her "contemplative life" but rather for her knowledge of "the time" (*kairos*). Likewise, he does not reprove Martha for her active hospitality; rather, it is her concern for peripheral matters (*merimna*) that is awry. When the Lord comes to one's house declaring the in-breaking of the kingdom, then it is time to drop everything and be attentive.[69]

Though allegorical interpretation long held sway, other interpreters also avoided dualistic readings, arguing that the sisters should be viewed as complements rather than polar opposites. Augustine of Hippo (354–430), for example, strove for a balanced picture in his preaching of Martha and Mary's story, lauding both women and arguing that they complement one another.[70] As Heffner, quoting Augustine, observes, Martha is not considered a second-rate disciple:

> On the contrary she "received him as pilgrims are customarily received; indeed, as a handmaid received her master, as a sick person her healer, as a creature her Creator." Indeed, Martha complements her sister Mary: "this one is disturbed [with feeding], so that the one may [simply] feast; this one orders many things, so the other may [simply] behold one." If these sisters are headed in different directions, they are for that very reason indispensably connected. And this connection is not so much hierarchical as dialectical. "Martha has to set sail in order that Mary can remain quietly in port."[71]

In his own preaching of Martha and Mary's story, Bernard of Clairvaux (1090?–1153) articulated the Cistercian ideal of a "mixed life," which includes both active charity and contemplative prayer. Heffner observes, "Bernard views the contemplative life as only the 'better part.' The best would comprehend both Martha's and Mary's portions."[72] Interestingly, Francis of Assisi (1182?–1226) "employed the story of Martha and Mary as his blueprint," organizing his fraternity into small groups of brothers who would assume and occasionally exchange Martha's and Mary's roles of service and contemplation. Thus, he too recognized the two ways represented by the sisters as "complementary and interdependent."[73]

Meister Eckhart (1260–1328) provided the most daring of interpretations, proposing that Martha was actually the more mature spiritually of the two sisters—one who "has learned through experience how to be active and still in essential communion with Christ." In other words, Martha successfully integrated action and contemplation, and pleaded for similar progress and maturation on the part of her contemplative sister.[74] Heffner suggests that in light of earlier resistant readings, Eckhart's interpretation "isn't so outlandish after all": "Eckhart seems to be gleaning his interpretation from the very fresh-flowing fountain of his received tradition."[75]

In addition to the resistant readings Heffner surveys, one other should be mentioned. The Protestant Reformer John Calvin (1500–1564) objected vigorously to allegorical interpretations of the story, urging a return to the literal sense of the text. Calvin's conviction that work was a positive human endeavor, ordained by God, did not permit a reading of the story as a commendation of the contemplative life over the active one. Moreover, he astutely critiqued the generalizing tendency of allegorical interpretation:

> Luke says that *Mary sat at the feet of Jesus*. Does he mean that she did nothing else throughout her whole life? On the contrary, the Lord enjoins his followers to make such a distribution of their time, that he who desires to make proficiency in the school of Christ shall not always be an idle hearer, but shall put in practice what he has learned; for there is a time to hear, and a time to act. It is, therefore, a foolish attempt of the monks to take hold of this passage, as if Christ were drawing a comparison between a contemplative and an active life, while Christ simply informs us for what end, and in what manner, he wishes to be received.[76]

In Calvin's view, the gist of Jesus' response to Martha is this:

> [W]hatever believers may undertake to do, and in whatever employments they may engage, there is one object to which every thing

ought to be referred. . . . The hospitality of Martha was faulty in this respect, that she neglected the main business, and devoted herself entirely to household affairs. And yet Christ does not mean that every thing else, with the exception of this *one thing*, is of no importance, but that we must pay a proper attention to order, lest what is *accessory*—as the phrase is—become our chief concern.[77]

Voices of dissent within the history of interpretation thus provide a variety of alternative perspectives from which to view the two sisters—perspectives that largely avoid setting them in dualistic opposition.

Several contemporary interpreters have also articulated alternative perspectives on Martha and Mary that avoid dualisms. Mary Rose D'Angelo, for example, makes a fascinating case for Martha and Mary as one of several missionary "women partners" in the New Testament (along with Tryphaena and Tryphosa in Rom. 16:12, and Euodia and Syntyche in Phil. 4:2). She calls attention to three features of the text that support the likelihood that Martha and Mary were a well-known missionary pair:[78] (1) the importance of the house in the stories about Martha and Mary in both Luke 10 and John 11–12, which suggests that these women were heads of a house-church; (2) an ancient and widespread text-critical variant in Luke 10:39, which translates: ". . . she [Martha] had a sister named Mary *who also* [*hē kai*] sat at the feet of Jesus"—thereby underlining that both women sat at his feet and were his disciples;[79] and (3) the use of the title "brother/sister" (*adelphos/adelphē*) elsewhere in the New Testament in reference to missionary partnerships. Paul repeatedly identifies Timothy, for example, as a "brother" and coworker (Phlm. 1; 2 Cor. 1:1; 1 Thess. 3:2; Rom. 16:21; Phil. 1:1), and D'Angelo notes, "the title is used to designate Timothy as Paul's partner in the mission in much the same way that 'sister' can be used to designate the women in a missionary pair."[80] Thus, she concludes: "Behind the stories in Luke and John lies a tradition about a famous missionary couple, Martha, the *diakonos*, and Mary, the *adelphē*. The references to Martha's house suggest that the women also gave hospitality and leadership to a house church."[81] Their presence in the New Testament attests to the participation of women in the early Christian practice of missionary pairs, and represents the tip of a very deeply submerged iceberg.[82]

Partnership also emerges as a central theme in Warren Carter's reading of the Martha and Mary story. Building on D'Angelo's analysis, Carter finds further support in the vocabulary and narrative context of the story for a reading of Martha and Mary as partners in ministry. "Sister" (*adelphē*), in his view, denotes physical as well as ecclesial relationship, and *diakonia* is the vocabulary of Christian ministry. Moreover, Carter notes that an emphasis on partnership with others in the acts of ministry pervades all eight texts in Acts in which the term *diakonia* appears.[83] These observations, he argues, bear significance for a reading of Luke 10:38–42:

> Given Luke-Acts' pervasive concern with partnership in ministry, Martha's question (her prayer) is an important one. It concerns a central aspect of the new community's style of ministry. It is the prayerful concern of a person committed to working out the Lucan model of leadership. It provides the occasion for instruction about this model. *One of the functions of this pericope, then, is to reinforce the gospel audience's understanding of ministry and leadership as an act of partnership.*[84]

Interestingly, in Carter's interpretation, the Lord's response instructs both Martha and Mary (Martha explicitly, and Mary implicitly) about how to maintain partnership in ministry, for both threaten the partnership in ministry in different ways. Some leaders "may be so energetically engaged in ministry that they, like Martha, are distracted from ministry's source." Others, like Mary here, may manifest a different danger: "that disciples may be so intently centered on the Lord's teaching that they do not *do* or *pass on* the teaching." Thus, Carter maintains that an "either-or" approach to the text will not do. Martha and Mary are partners in ministry, and their story provides significant instruction on "the dangers that attend all women and men who are engaged in the partnership of ministry and leadership."[85]

Another contemporary interpreter, Loveday Alexander, provides a variety of important insights that argue against dualistic construals of Martha and Mary's story. Alexander urges attention to the discourse of the text, noting that "in fact the tale is Martha's much more than it is Mary's: there is no syntactical pairing corresponding to the ideological duality in the minds of exegetes."[86] Grammatically speaking, Martha is foregrounded as the active partner with Jesus in the scene. Mary is a background character, of whom we are told the bare minimum.[87] As Alexander notes, "What we have, then, is not a three-cornered scene but, as so often in the gospels, a dialogue between two characters, Jesus and Martha: Mary's actions provoke the dialogue, but she does not herself speak or appear on stage."[88]

Alexander also urges attention to the discourse of "co-texts" in Luke that further diffuse dualistic readings. Three are particularly significant. First, she notes other scenes in Luke that feature disputes between siblings (6:41–42; 12:13–14; 15:11–32). In 12:13–14, an especially close parallel to Martha's story, Jesus is asked to intervene in a dispute between siblings, but refuses to be cast in the role of judge. Indeed, she notes, "Jesus in this Gospel shows himself remarkably unconcerned about who is in the right and who is in the wrong."[89] This fact, in addition to the tone in which the prodigal son's elder brother is addressed in 15:31–32 ("Son, you are always with me, and all that is mine is yours"), may "encourage us to look for gentle reproof rather than outright rejection in Jesus' reply to Martha."[90]

Second, Alexander reminds us that Luke is fond of dinner-party scenarios, scenes of hospitality (cf. 7:36–50; 11:37–52; 14:1–6, 7–11, 12–14, 15–24), many of which feature the element of surprise or reversal—sometimes for guests, as in 14:15–24, and sometimes for hosts, such as Simon the Pharisee in 7:36–50. This suggests that a story such as Martha and Mary's is "deliberately paradoxical," for "the behavior of Luke's Mary is contrasted not with a 'bad' course of action but with one which is in itself 'good,' namely, serving Jesus." Indeed, it highlights "a rather Pauline paradox, that 'good' behavior is not as important as devotion" to Jesus.[91]

Third, Alexander observes that Martha's "one-thing needful" echoes the "one thing" that a rich ruler lacks in 18:18–23, though he keeps all the commandments. Both texts pick up "the theme of single-mindedness" that "weaves in and out of Jesus' teaching in less explicit ways right through the central section of this Gospel: cf. 9:57–62; 11:33–36; 12:30–31."[92] In sum, what Alexander concludes from her observations is that Martha's story "is paradoxical rather than paradigmatic, deliberately overturning its auditors' expectations about 'good' and 'bad' behavior—which means that using the story to set up a new code of behavior is to repeat the mistake."[93]

Thus, a number of interpreters, ancient and contemporary, have provided nondualistic interpretations of Martha and Mary's story, and many readers will no doubt find these alternative perspectives appealing. However, given the wide variety of readings we have considered, bewilderment may also be in order. Indeed, one suspects that the many complex issues the story raises are not likely to be resolved by any single reading.

Still, for the sake of both discussion and closure, I should present my own view of the matter—tentative though it may be, and though it by no means resolves all the difficulties inherent in the story. I puzzle over the story of Martha and Mary, troubled by its ambiguities and deeply divided in my own response to it. However, the position toward which I incline is that: (1) the story instructs its readers (both male and female) in matters pertaining to the life of discipleship, and (2) the dualistic dynamics inscribed in the story are tempered considerably by attention to narrative context. Plucked out of its narrative context, the story would indeed appear to set the sisters in dualistic opposition and to present a stark choice between "good" and (by implication) "not as good" alternatives, however defined. But read within the context of Luke's larger narrative, the story can be said to offer a complementary picture. Several consider-ations nudge me in this direction.

First, "service" or *diakonia*, in which Martha is engaged, is depicted as a positive endeavor throughout Luke-Acts. Indeed, it is the model of Christian leadership and the very definition of Jesus' own ministry: "the greatest among you must become like the youngest, and the leader like one who serves [*ho diakonōn*]. . . . I am among you as one who serves [*ho diakonōn*]" (22:26–27). One cannot suppose, therefore, that in this one instance Martha's *diakonia* represents an inappropriate choice or regret-table endeavor—or that it is fairly represented in dualistic opposition as the short end of the stick. As Loveday Alexander observes, "Whatever Martha is doing wrong, it is surely not her *diakonia*."[94]

Second, the story's immediate literary context lends further support to a complementary understanding of "hearing" and "doing." As we noted earlier, the evangelist Luke has arranged his narrative so that readers encounter the parable of the Good Samaritan and the story of Martha and Mary back-to-back. At first glance, the juxtaposition of the two stories appears odd, in that the first applauds action and the second praises inac-tion. However, together they explicate the two great love commandments (10:27) in reverse order: the parable of the Good Samaritan provides a concrete illustration of loving one's neighbor as oneself (10:29–37), and the story of Martha and Mary provides an illustration of loving the Lord with all one's heart, soul, strength, and mind (10:38–42). Together, these stories suggest that both hearing and doing—contemplation and ser-vice—love of God and love of neighbor—are essential characteristics of the people of God. One does not exist apart from the other. The juxta-position of the Good Samaritan's story with that of Martha and Mary therefore cautions against any interpretation that would set Mary's "hear-ing" against Martha's "doing" in dualistic fashion.

Indeed, viewed within this larger narrative context, Martha and Mary's story can be said to underline the integral relationship between "hearing" and "doing." Martha (along with all disciples) is invited by Jesus to recognize that listening to his word is essential to service. Service is, after all, the very definition of his own person and ministry (cf. 22:26–27). Thus, as disciples sit at Jesus' feet, they learn what it means to serve. To sit at Jesus' feet is to make his word the touchstone of all our hearing and the wellspring of all our doing, and to be engaged by a word that gives perspective, context, and meaning to service. Indeed, in the immediately preceding chapter of Luke, at the moment of Jesus' transfiguration, the very voice of God urges undivided attention to the person and word by which all else is understood: "This is my Son, my Chosen; listen to him!" (9:35).

Without the touchstone and wellspring of his word—without this focal point for service—our work is enervated, and we are likely to find ourselves distracted, anxious, and depleted by too many tasks. This dilemma may well be Martha's (though admittedly, perhaps I find this conclusion likely because it is my own!). Turid Karlsen Seim has suggested that "Jesus' reply to Martha does not concern her serving, but the way it is done, with fuss and agitation. It can thus be claimed that the fundamental antithesis is not between hearing and serving, but between hearing and agitated toil."[95] I am persuaded by this point, for Jesus' response to Martha does not specifically make reference to Martha's *diakonia*, but rather to the fact that she is "worried" and "distracted" about "many things."

What is the antidote to agitated, anxious toil and the consequent burnout, which tasks of both daily and professional ministry may engender? The story of Martha and Mary holds up at least one essential: time spent in silence, listening at Jesus' feet, thereby engaging the person and word that empowers and centers our own service. One of the ways to listen is surely specified in the scene that follows Martha and Mary's story, in which Jesus teaches disciples how to pray (11:1–13). However, as John Calvin has noted, we should not imagine that Mary intends to sit at Jesus' feet forever! Her choice may be the "good *portion*," but it is not the *whole*.[96] Both hearing and doing together constitute the life of discipleship, for Jesus defines the members of his family as "those who hear the word of God and do it" (8:21; see also 11:28).

For all of these reasons, I lean toward a complementary reading of the realities in the life of discipleship that Martha and Mary together represent. In my view, their story instructs both male and female disciples on the centrality of Jesus' person and word in the life of discipleship. Both Martha's choice and Mary's choice cohere, ideally, in the life of every disciple, and discernment is needed as we relate the two. Fred Craddock captures this point in his own complementary reading of the text:

We must not cartoon the scene: Martha to her eyeballs in soapsuds, Mary pensively on a stool in the den, and Jesus giving scriptural warrant for letting dishes pile high in the sink. If we censure Martha too harshly, she may abandon serving altogether, and if we commend Mary too profusely, she may sit there forever. There is a time to go and do; there is a time to listen and reflect. Knowing which and when is a matter of spiritual discernment. If we were to ask Jesus which example applies to us, the Samaritan or Mary, his answer would probably be Yes.[97]

The fact that Martha's choice and Mary's choice cohere ideally in the life of every disciple may well explain why many who hear the story recognize themselves in both portraits. There are moments in our lives when we identify with Mary, and others in which we find ourselves in Martha's shoes. During my first year in seminary, I jumped at the chance to write one of my first exegetical papers on this story, for I perceived that Jesus' validation of Mary's choice legitimated my own right to engage in theological education! In later years, however, I have more often identified with Martha—anxious, distracted, overextended, and exhausted with "too much ministry"—and in need of the empowering word that gives focus, perspective, and meaning to service. Striking the appropriate balance between "hearing" and "doing" is a critical and ongoing struggle for all who engage in the life of discipleship. The fact that some readers immediately recognize this familiar struggle in the story of Martha and Mary suggests that this approach represents a valid perspective on the text, though by no means the only one that could be articulated.

Still, I confess that discomfort with the story lingers, as it may also for you. This short and deceptively simple narrative turns out to be far more complex than it appears at first glance, and no single reading is likely to resolve the many issues raised. Biblical texts, however, do not exist to make us comfortable. They exist to make us think, to be engaged by God, and to effect our transformation. Martha and Mary's story will no doubt continue to serve these ends as disciples wrestle both with and against its claims, and with the reactions, questions, and challenges it invariably evokes.

Group Study Suggestions

Begin with a dramatic reading of Luke 10:38–42. Assign roles to a narrator, to Martha, and to Jesus. (Mary has no speaking role!)

Following the reading, ask participants for their responses to the story—both positive and negative.

Alison Cheek recommends the following exercise: Designate a Martha group and a Mary group among participants, and have the groups discuss separately (and then share together) their responses to this statement: "If I were Martha (Mary) this is what I would have to say about the story Luke wrote about me. . . ."[98]

Proceed with any of the questions for discussion/reflection below.

Questions for Discussion or Reflection

What has been your experience with this story? What prior impressions do you bring to your study of it?

With whom do you identify when you hear the story, and why? Which sister are you most like, and why? Is there any sense in which you identify with both Martha and Mary?

What questions does the story raise for you?

Where do realities reflected in the text intersect with your own experience? What word does the text address to the reality or experience you have identified? What is your response to this word?

What would you like to say to Martha? To Mary? To Jesus?

How have you imagined the scene Luke depicts? Is Martha brandishing a frying pan? Is she in a kitchen? Does the text say anything about a meal? What do you think of Elisabeth Schüssler Fiorenza's reinterpretation of Martha's "service" (*diakonia*) as that of eucharistic ministry?

In your view, is the story relevant to debates in which contemporary Christians find themselves engaged concerning women's roles in ministry?

What is your reaction to the depiction of Jesus in this scene? What do you learn about him? How would you have wished him to respond to Martha?

If there are men in the study group, ask if their responses to the story differ in any way from those expressed by women in the group. Are the men equally engaged by the story? Why or why not? With whom do they identify?

A cartoon depicts a tombstone with the following inscription: "My Anxiety Is Cured!" Share your reflections on the reality of anxiety in your life of discipleship. What does this story contribute to your experience of this reality?

How can and do we sit at Jesus' feet and listen to his word? Are the ways identified important and regular aspects of your life of faith? Why or why not?

This chapter surveyed a wide variety of interpretations of the story. Which have provided perspectives you appreciate? Which do you find most persuasive?

What new insights have emerged for you from your engagement with this story? What questions linger?

Resources for Further Study

Alexander, Loveday. "Sisters in Adversity: Retelling Martha's Story." In *Women in the Biblical Tradition*, edited by George J. Brooke, 167–86. Studies in Women and Religion 31. Lewiston, N.Y.: Edwin Mellen, 1992. Reprinted in *A Feminist Companion to Luke*, edited by Amy-Jill Levine with Marianne Blickenstaff, 197–213. Sheffield: Sheffield Academic, 2002.

Carter, Warren. "Getting Martha Out of the Kitchen: Luke 10:38–42 Again." *Catholic Biblical Quarterly* 58 (1996). Reprinted in *A Feminist Companion to Luke*, edited by Amy-Jill Levine with Marianne Blickenstaff, 214–31. Sheffield: Sheffield Academic, 2002.

Collins, John N. "Did Luke Intend a Disservice to Women in the Martha and Mary Story?" *Biblical Theology Bulletin* 28 (1998): 104–11.

Corley, Kathleen E. *Private Women, Public Meals: Social Conflict in the Synoptic Tradition*, 133–46. Peabody, Mass.: Hendrickson, 1993.

D'Angelo, Mary Rose. "Women in Luke-Acts: A Redactional View." *Journal of Biblical Literature* 109 (1990): 441–61.

———. "Women Partners in the New Testament." *Journal of Feminist Studies in Religion* 6 (1990): 65–86.

Heffner, Blake R. "Meister Eckhart and a Millennium with Mary and Martha." *The Lutheran Quarterly* 5 (1991): 171–85.

Koperski, Veronica. "Women and Discipleship in Luke 10.38–42 and Acts 6.1–7: The Literary Context of Luke-Acts." In *A Feminist Companion to Luke*, edited by Amy-Jill Levine with Marianne Blickenstaff, 161–96. Sheffield: Sheffield Academic, 2002.

Reid, Barbara E. *Choosing the Better Part? Women in the Gospel of Luke*, 144–62. Collegeville, Minn.: Liturgical, 1996.

Reinhartz, Adele. "From Narrative to History: The Resurrection of Mary and Martha." In *"Women Like This": New Perspectives on Jewish Women in the Greco-Roman World*, edited by Amy-Jill Levine, 161–84. Atlanta: Scholars, 1991.

Schaberg, Jane. "Luke." In *The Women's Bible Commentary*, edited by Carol Newsom and Sharon Ringe, 275–92. Louisville, Ky.: Westminster/John Knox, 1992.

Schüssler Fiorenza, Elisabeth. *But She Said: Feminist Practices of Biblical Interpretation*, 51–76. Boston: Beacon, 1992.

Seim, Turid Karlsen. *The Double Message: Patterns of Gender in Luke-Acts*. Nashville: Abingdon, 1994.

———. "The Gospel of Luke." In *Searching the Scriptures*, vol. 2, *A Feminist Commentary*, edited by E. Schüssler Fiorenza, 728–62. New York: Crossroad, 1994.

Chapter Four

A Bent Woman, Daughter of Abraham

Luke 13:10–17

Now he was teaching in one of the synagogues on the sabbath. And just then there appeared a woman with a spirit that had crippled her for eighteen years. She was bent over and was quite unable to stand up straight. When Jesus saw her, he called her over and said, "Woman, you are set free from your ailment." When he laid his hands on her, immediately she stood up straight and began praising God. But the leader of the synagogue, indignant because Jesus had cured on the sabbath, kept saying to the crowd, "There are six days on which work ought to be done; come on those days and be cured, and not on the sabbath day." But the Lord answered him and said, "You hypocrites! Does not each of you on the sabbath untie his ox or his donkey from the manger, and lead it away to give it water? And ought not this woman, a daughter of Abraham whom Satan bound for eighteen long years, be set free from this bondage on the sabbath day?" When he said this, all his opponents were put to shame; and the entire crowd was rejoicing at all the wonderful things that he was doing.

Only Luke among the evangelists tells the story of Jesus' encounter with a bent woman in a synagogue on the sabbath. The passage represents both a "healing story" and a "controversy story," a hybrid form in which the two are intertwined. It begins as a healing story, for verses 10–13 describe a miraculous event, following the sequence of problem, solution, and proof. In verses 14–17, a controversy story then unfolds, as Jesus engages in a confrontation with an adversary that climaxes in a significant pronouncement from Jesus. Some would argue that the two should be read separately in order to do justice to the woman, for her story

84

quickly becomes the occasion for a religious conflict among men.[1] Others, however, argue for the unity of the passage, noting many connecting links that integrate the two: location and temporal setting, repeated use of the language of binding and loosing, and repeated reference to the woman and her suffering for "eighteen years."[2] In Luke as in much of life, male voices take up most of the air space, and we wish we knew more of the woman and her story—what she had to say, for example, and what became of her, how she spent her next eighteen years! Still, we may be grateful that a snapshot of her is at least included in our biblical family album, and in eavesdropping on the debate her healing evoked, we may discern ways in which her story may bear upon our own.

Encountering the Text

Let us examine the scene more closely. The story is located in the midst of Luke's distinctive travel narrative (9:51–19:27), in which Jesus is presented as steadily making his way toward Jerusalem and his destiny on the cross. En route, "he was teaching in one of the synagogues on the sabbath" (13:10). Both the location (the synagogue) and the day (the sabbath, noted five times) are significant for the story that unfolds; both situate Jesus within the heart of his native Judaism. Indeed, his presence in the synagogue is a demonstration of God's faithfulness and ongoing commitment to Israel. This time is not the first that Jesus has appeared in a synagogue in Luke, for such "was his custom" (according to 4:16). In fact, Jesus' public ministry began in Luke with a rather dramatic appearance in his hometown synagogue in Nazareth, in which he articulated a programmatic statement of the nature and course of the ministry that would unfold: "The Spirit of the Lord is upon me, because he has anointed me to bring good news to the poor. He has sent me to proclaim release to the captives and recovery of sight to the blind, to let the oppressed go free, to proclaim the year of the Lord's favor" (4:18–19). That inaugural appearance in a synagogue is followed by subsequent visits (4:44; 6:6). In 13:10–17, we have the first time Jesus has entered a synagogue since he set his face toward Jerusalem, and it will also be his last. The scene that unfolds embodies one of the key themes of his ministry announced on that opening day in Nazareth, for during this final visit he encounters a "captive" desperately in need of "release": "[J]ust then there appeared a woman with a spirit that had crippled her for eighteen years. She was bent over and was quite unable to stand up straight" (v. 11).

The bent woman is not identified by name, but only by her chronic illness. Her malady is supposed by some to be ankylosing spondylitis, an inflammatory disease affecting joints between the vertebrae of the spine, and the joints between the spine and the pelvis, which in time can cause the affected vertebrae to fuse or grow together, leading to permanent stiffness, limitation of motion, and curvature of the spine.[3] However, Luke provides no such clinical diagnosis. Her malady is attributed simply to (translating literally) "a spirit of weakness" (*pneuma astheneias* in Greek; v. 11). *Astheneia* is a word used widely in the New Testament to signify "weakness" or "powerlessness" of various kinds, sickness being one of its manifestations.[4] The woman's malady is further attributed to satanic bondage ("And ought not this woman, a daughter of Abraham whom Satan bound for eighteen long years, be set free from this bondage on the sabbath day?" v. 16). The woman is not necessarily "demon-possessed," for the passage does not bear the marks of an exorcism story, but Luke 13 offers a way of conveying an apocalyptic view of reality—that is, a view that holds that the world and humans are caught up in struggle between the life-destroying powers of evil and the life-giving power of God.[5] Forces in the world disfigure and diminish human life, contrary to God's intentions, and such forces are thus appropriately described as "demonic." Indeed, almost every act of healing in Luke is portrayed as an encounter with diabolic forces (see Acts 10:38).[6] Luke presents Jesus as the divine agent of "salvation" (2:11; 19:10), which denotes participation in the reign of God—a present possibility that involves liberation or rescue from anything that prevents one from living life as God intends (Luke 4:18–19).[7] In his ministry the reign of God is made present and the domain of Satan is rolled back.[8] Make no mistake about it: a cosmic battle is engaged on this woman's back.

Her bondage is described in vivid, poignant detail: "She was bent over and was quite unable to stand up straight" (v. 11). Imagine the effect of such crippled posture. She would be rendered unable to meet another person face-to-face, and confined "to a world defined by the piece of ground around her own toes or looked at always on a slant."[9] Moreover, she has been captive to restricted movement for a protracted period—"for eighteen years" (v. 11), evoking memories of Israel's eighteen years of bondage to Moab (Judg. 3:14) and again to the Philistines and the Ammonites (Judg. 10:8). As Sharon Ringe observes, given the short life expectancy of women in the first century, eighteen years of bondage is likely also to have been about half of her adult life.[10] Interestingly, her eighteen years of suffering have not enervated her spirituality,[11] for she makes her way to the synagogue on the sabbath. We are not told that she has come in search of miraculous healing, and we must presume that she has come simply to worship God.

Indeed, Jesus takes all the initiative in her restoration: "When Jesus saw her, he called her over and said, 'Woman, you are set free from your ailment'" (v. 12). Given the woman's restricted field of vision, one wonders if she would have been aware of his presence. Jesus is represented as taking note of *her* presence, interrupting his teaching, and calling her forward from the margins to the center of the worshiping community. Moreover, he announces that the very power of God has released her from her sickness, declaring it an already-established fact, which is pointedly underlined by the perfect tense and passive voice of "you have been set free" (*apolelysai*). The perfect tense denotes a present state resulting from a past action, and Jesus' use of the passive voice ("you have been set free" rather than "God has freed you") reverentially avoids direct reference to the holy name of God.

Clearly, however, Jesus is the very agent and channel of God's saving power, for "When he laid his hands on her, immediately she stood up straight and began praising God" (v. 13). Her praise is described as continuous in nature ("she began praising God" or "kept praising God," imperfect tense), and acknowledges God as the source of her healing. Her voice is thus now heard in the midst of the sanctuary as she gives audible expression to her praise—praise which she had no doubt also been offering silently from the margins of the sanctuary just moments before, for she had come to the synagogue that day to worship God. She adds her voice to the swelling chorus of praise resounding throughout the Gospel of Luke, joining Mary, angels, and shepherds in glad recognition of God's merciful benefactions through the savior Jesus Christ. Moreover, in "standing up straight," the woman assumes an eschatological posture appropriate to the coming of the Son of Man and God's new age, for the Lukan Jesus, in foretelling the final days in 21:28, says, "Now when these things begin to take place, stand up and raise your heads, because your redemption is drawing near."

Not everyone present in the synagogue that day, however, recognized the cosmic significance of the events taking place. Not everyone discerned the presence of the very reign of God in Jesus' ministry, manifest in the release of a captive woman, for the miraculous healing quickly gives way to controversy: "But the leader of the synagogue, indignant because Jesus had cured on the sabbath, kept saying to the crowd, 'There are six days on which work ought to be done; come on those days and be cured, and not on the sabbath day'" (v. 14).

A "leader of the synagogue" (*archisynagōgos*) performed various duties involving both practical and spiritual leadership, among them regulating worship and thus maintaining the reading and faithful teaching of the law.[12] He ought not to be caricatured as legalistic and picayune in his insistence upon proper observance of the sabbath, for as we note later, sabbath observance was a matter of utmost import for Jews, essential to the preservation of their identity and integrity in a culture that threatened to engulf them. Anything that undermined this important mark of identity was taken very seriously. In his view, Jesus' action in behalf of a crippled woman constitutes "work" and thus is in violation of the principles enunciated in Deuteronomy 5:12–15 and Exodus 20:8–11, which prohibit work on the sabbath. Deuteronomy 5:12–15, for example, commands:

> Observe the sabbath day and keep it holy, as the LORD your God commanded you. Six days you shall labor and do all your work. But the seventh day is a sabbath to the LORD your God; you shall not do any work—you, or your son or your daughter, or your male or female slave, or your ox or your donkey, or any of your livestock, or the resident alien in your towns, so that your male and female slave may rest as well as you. Remember that you were a slave in the land of Egypt, and the LORD your God brought you out from there with a mighty hand and an outstretched arm; therefore the LORD your God commanded you to keep the sabbath day.

Though the leader of the synagogue does not cite these texts, their prohibition against work is clearly presumed in his complaint as self-evident. There are indeed six days on which "work" can be done, and the woman's ailment is chronic, not life-threatening. Could not Jesus have waited a few hours, until sundown at least, to heal her?

The peculiar aspect about the leader's complaint is that it is addressed not to the one who in his view has violated the sabbath but to the crowds, who are (1) reminded that there are six other days on which healing can be procured and (2) reprimanded for seeking it on the sabbath. As the text says nothing at all about why the woman or the crowds came to the synagogue, and indicates that Jesus took all the initiative in the healing, the leader is, curiously, "blaming the victim" and "accessories" rather than the perpetrator of the crime.[13] In so doing, he opens a public discussion of the matter.

Jesus responds in kind, in a public manner, addressing not only the leader of the synagogue but anyone present who would share his view. He takes both his objector(s) and the objection seriously. As elsewhere in Luke (e.g., 7:36–50), his response reflects genuine, if harsh, engagement with a religious authority and a substantive attempt to persuade another through his own careful interpretation of Scripture: "But the Lord answered him and said, 'You hypocrites! Does not each of you on the sabbath untie his ox or his donkey from the manger, and lead it away to give it water? And ought not this woman, a daughter of Abraham whom Satan bound for eighteen long years, be set free from this bondage on the sabbath day?" (vv. 15–16). This response is delivered as from "the Lord," as one with authority to interpret God's will.

Several points in his authoritative response are noteworthy. First, Jesus by no means questions the principle of sabbath observance, for his very presence in the synagogue testifies to his commitment to it. The matter at stake in his debate with the synagogue leader is rather the application of sabbath regulations, and Jesus argues his point in good rabbinic fashion, moving from a "lesser" example to the "greater." He, too, alludes to the Scriptures, reminding the synagogue leader that animals fall within the purview of the sabbath commandment (Deut. 5:14), and noting a reasonable accommodation to their need, the commonly accepted practice of untethering them so that they may get water to drink on the sabbath. If it is appropriate to "untie" a farm animal bound for a few hours, would it not be even more appropriate to "untie" a human being—a daughter of Abraham, no less, who has been bound for eighteen years?

Jesus' response also reflects attention to another essential feature of the sabbath commandment—that the sabbath is, above all, an occasion to commemorate Israel's release from bondage: "Remember that you were a slave in the land of Egypt, and the LORD your God brought you out from there with a mighty hand and an outstretched arm; therefore the LORD your God commanded you to keep the sabbath day" (Deut. 5:15). "Freedom" and "liberation" are the very essence of the sabbath celebration. The release of a captive woman, then, is a highly appropriate way to make the day holy, representing the very fulfillment, rather than a violation, of the sabbath. It is also the fulfillment of covenant promises to Abraham.

Second, the woman is pointedly referred to as a "daughter of Abraham" (*thygatera Abraam*), a phrase located emphatically at the beginning of the sentence (13:16). This striking expression appears only here in the New Testament, and it identifies the woman as a child of the covenant promise. While "Abraham's son" is a traditional Jewish designation, the term "Abraham's daughter" does not appear in earlier and contemporary Jewish literature and thus is a striking and in some sense original designation. Turid

Karlsen Seim has demonstrated, though, that it is not entirely unique to Luke. Abrahamic categories are applied to the mother of seven sons in 4 Maccabees (14:20; 15:28; 17:6; 18:20), who appears in this apocryphal writing as a strong and exemplary God-fearing martyr; scattered use of the expression "Abraham's daughter" also occurs in later Jewish sources.[14]

Seim notes, however, a surprising element in Luke's use of the phrase, though it is not the fact that a Jewish woman is called Abraham's daughter. "The surprising element is rather that the woman about whom this is said, is not a paragon of piety, but a woman who has been possessed for a great part of her life. She is not given any attributes that might legitimate a special likeness or relationship to Abraham." She is "quite simply confirmed as Abraham's daughter."[15] As such, she has the right to share in the community of the people of God and salvation, and is thus appropriately set free on the sabbath, the day of rest which was an essential sign of the covenant.[16] Her masculine counterpart is none other than Zacchaeus, the despised chief tax collector and only male character in Luke designated specifically as a "son of Abraham" (19:9). He is "short in stature" (19:3) and of ignominious reputation, as she is "crippled" and "bent over," of ignominious posture, but the true stature and dignity of both are confirmed: They are Abraham's own children and are to share in the blessing promised to Abraham's progeny, and thus are claimed and liberated by the one in whose ministry God's covenant promises to Abraham are fulfilled (1:55, 73; Acts 3:25). In Christ, God "raise[s] up children to Abraham," as John the Baptist had foretold (Luke 3:8), affirming their place within the people of God. Jesus' action on the sabbath thus represents not only the fulfillment of the sabbath, but also the fulfillment of God's covenant promises to the children of Abraham.

Finally, Jesus' response also highlights, in noteworthy fashion, the importance of discernment. He castigates the leader of the synagogue and any present who share the leader's views as "hypocrites" (13:15), an epithet used sparingly in Luke (only three times, in 6:42; 12:56; 13:15) to refer to willful blindness.[17] In 12:54–56, for example, Jesus castigates others for failing to see what is self-evident:

> He also said to the crowds, "When you see a cloud rising in the west, you immediately say, 'It is going to rain'; and so it happens. And when you see the south wind blowing, you say, 'There will be scorching heat'; and it happens. You hypocrites! You know how to interpret the appearance of earth and sky, but why do you not know how to interpret the present time?"

In the same way, in the very next chapter when the epithet appears one last time, the leader of the synagogue is castigated for refusing to see the fittingness of the release of a crippled daughter of Abraham on the sabbath—that is, for failing to perceive the significance of "the present time."[18] He perceives only human necessity, "there are six days on which work ought (*dei*) to be done," overlooking divine necessity: "ought (*edei*) not this woman, a daughter of Abraham whom Satan bound for eighteen long years, be set free from this bondage on the sabbath day?" Ironically, he employs the same Greek word (*dei*) that the Lukan Jesus uses repeatedly to express his own commitment to the divine purpose. The leader cannot see that God's saving activity is unfolding right before his eyes in Jesus' ministry when a bent woman, a daughter of Abraham, stands up straight. He fails to perceive it as the fulfillment of the sabbath and of the covenant promises to Abraham, and indeed a sign of the dawning of the reign of God. As Jesus himself had said earlier of his healing ministry, "If it is by the finger of God that I cast out the demons, then the kingdom of God has come to you" (11:20).

Lest we miss this point, Luke sees to it that his first two parables of the kingdom of God follow on the heels of our story in 13:18–21:

> He said therefore, "What is the kingdom of God like? And to what should I compare it? It is like a mustard seed that someone took and sowed in the garden; it grew and became a tree, and the birds of the air made nests in its branches."
>
> And again he said, "To what should I compare the kingdom of God? It is like yeast that a woman took and mixed in with three measures of flour until all of it was leavened."

With the word "therefore" (*oun*) in verse 18, Luke clearly attaches these parables as commentary on the story of the bent woman and the controversy in the synagogue. In so doing, he directs our attention to ordinary persons, circumstances, and places of our lives where the reign of God may be drawing near in seemingly small acts of restoration, as forces that disfigure and diminish human life are overcome by the power of God in Christ, and captives are released from whatever keeps them from living as God intends. What does the kingdom of God look like? For those with eyes to see, it looks like a woman standing up straight in the midst of the community of faith, praising God. Though she may be perceived as seemingly small and insignificant, and her restoration inconsequential, her cure and response to what God has done for her in Christ "reveal her as full of hope and potential as are the seed and leaven."[19] Like them, she conveys "the capacity of each to be changed or change something for the better," and thus her encounter with Jesus is an apt image of the kingdom of God.[20]

Luke's parables resound with confidence in what God is accomplishing in Jesus' ministry, but clearly not all will perceive in that ministry the dawning of God's reign. Indeed our story ends with a house divided, as both Simeon (2:34–35) and Jesus himself (12:49–53) had predicted: "all his opponents were put to shame," while "the entire crowd was rejoicing at all the wonderful things that he was doing" (13:17). As many commentators have noted, the unusual noun "wonderful things" or "marvels" (*endoxois*) appears only here in the New Testament—a word that in the Septuagint (the Greek translation of the Hebrew Scriptures) is associated with the mighty deeds of the Lord during the Exodus (Deut. 10:21; Exod. 34:10). Thus it is also appropriately associated with the one in whose ministry the liberating reign of God draws near. The story concludes on this note of both division and wonder. Soon thereafter Jesus exits the synagogue for the final time and continues on his journey to Jerusalem, and to the cross that is so inextricably related to his divine mission of setting people free.

Angles of Vision

As we ponder the import of this story for our own lives and daily ministries, problems and possibilities both emerge. Let us first consider two problems that bear on interpretation of the text for our own context: its anti-Judaic potential and Luke's ambiguous presentation of women. Then we consider points of contact between the text and the experience of contemporary communities of faith, noting three significant areas for further reflection: the spirit of weakness, the reality of physical disability, and the perennial communal question of timing.

Anti-Judaic Potential

One of the decided problems of the text is its potential to generate anti-Jewish interpretation and sentiment. Both the location of the miracle in the synagogue and its timing, on the sabbath, establish Jewish concerns as an integral feature of the story. That the healing evokes a "controversy" in which a leader of the synagogue objects to the timing opens the door for anti-Jewish perceptions that have far too often characterized the history of interpretation. Elisabeth Schüssler Fiorenza highlights the potential for such a response in her perceptive reading of the text, describing the impact the story can have on Christian readers: "Claiming for ourselves the biblical authority of Jesus, Christians read these passages in an anti-Jewish way, get angry with the leader of the synagogue, and feel religiously and morally superior to Judaism."[21] Indeed, in the history of interpretation of the text, Christian preachers and teachers have found it an occasion to promote contempt for Judaism as legalistic, inhumane, and oppressive of women.

Feminist interpretation has often unwittingly enhanced this dangerous potential interpretation of the text, as has the homiletical airing of many popular misconceptions about the role of women in Judaism. Frequently, for example, it is assumed that women were not allowed to participate in Jewish worship life and that the woman's very presence in the synagogue would have been unusual, although the text itself does not suggest that the woman's presence was in any way surprising. In this connection, purity concerns have also been invoked, and it is supposed that the woman's malady would have rendered her impure and a source of contagion to others, or that Jesus deliberately transgressed purity laws when he touched her. (As one popular reading would have it, Jesus overcomes a "politics of purity" with a "politics of compassion."[22]) However, these frequently aired misconceptions fly in the face of evidence to the contrary. Bernadette Brooten's impressive study of synagogue inscriptions, for example, has convincingly demonstrated that Jewish women were not only active, but even played significant leadership roles in the life of the ancient synagogue.[23] Moreover, purity concerns are not mentioned in this text (see chap. 2, pp. 38–45, for further discussion of purity matters). To make an issue of them in Luke 13, one must import them into the text and construct an argument on silence.

How then should interpretation proceed? How can we defuse the dangerous anti-Judaic potential of the text and avoid conveying the impression that a feminist Jesus "liberated" women from a bad, oppressive religion? Three ways of tackling this dilemma suggest themselves. First, we need to acknowledge, and to mourn, the fact that anti-Judaic rhetoric is embedded in Christian Scripture, and also to recognize that it emerges from a time and place in which Jews and Christians found themselves engaged in a difficult process of self-differentiation. Christianity emerged from the womb of Judaism and, in establishing its own distinctive identity and claims, found it necessary to distinguish itself from its mother faith. Like many adolescents, it did not always do so gracefully! Luke-Acts, for example, includes both pro-Jewish material (insisting, for example, that the ministry of Jesus is the continuation of the story of God and God's people in the Old Testament) and anti-Jewish material (for example, subtly transferring much of the blame for Jesus' death from Roman to Jewish authorities). Scholars themselves hotly debate what to make of the place of the Jewish people in Luke-Acts, though most would agree that Luke's position is decidedly ambivalent.[24] Moreover, New Testament scholars suspect that the sabbath controversy stories recorded in the Gospels in all likelihood reflect matters of ongoing debate among the communities to whom the Gospels are addressed and their Jewish neighbors. We stand far removed from the evangelists' historical context and have no need in our own historical context to engage in further debate, apologetics, or differentiation. Indeed, we should make a concerted attempt to avoid reinscribing ancient anti-Jewish rhetoric in contemporary interpretation.

Second, we need to avoid caricaturing or trivializing as legalistic or picayune the issue of sabbath observance expressed by the synagogue leader. Indeed, it may be important to acknowledge that the concern he articulated was a significant one. For one thing, sabbath observance was an important mark of identity for Jewish people, who, from the time of the Babylonian exile in 587 B.C.E. until 1948, lived almost exclusively under foreign domination. The importance of identity markers and identity preservation may escape us if we have not ourselves experienced the reality of foreign overlords and military occupation. Sabbath observance was, and is, a visible, regular discipline that distinguished members of the faith community from the general culture in which it lived.[25] Furthermore, sabbath observance honored important humanitarian concerns, as well as theological ones, providing rest from work and a reminder that human life is not defined by productivity but rather by God's sovereign will and purpose. So, perhaps, trying to appreciate the question the synagogue leader raises is important. The woman's condition was chronic, but not life threatening. Why could Jesus not have waited until the next day, until sundown at least, to heal her?

Third, and most important, we must remember and acknowledge that Jesus was a first-century Jew! In Luke 13, he by no means questions the principle of sabbath observance, for it was clearly "his custom" (4:16). As noted, the matter at stake in his debate with the synagogue leader is rather the application of sabbath regulations, and debate and argument over matters such as this played an important part in communal discernment. Moreover, Jesus should not be seen as standing over against Judaism. What he does for the bent woman in Luke 13, he does as a Jewish man for a Jewish woman. As Judith Plaskow reminds us, Jesus' attitudes toward women "represent not a victory *over* early Judaism but a possibility *within* it."[26]

Insights we gain from engagement with the story might best be applied within our own contexts of communal discernment. In other words, our reflection on the text ought not to elevate "Christian" views over against those of another religious group such as "Jews," but ought rather to inform realities of debate and argument within our own Christian groups as we engage in equally difficult and divisive processes of communal discernment.

Luke's Ambiguous Presentation of Women

In chapter 3, on the story of Martha and Mary in Luke 10:38–42, we discussed the evangelist's decidedly ambiguous presentation of women (see pp. 64–72). As we noted, Luke transmits a "double message,"[27] for while women are more visible in the Gospel narrative, they are presented in carefully circumscribed roles. We also noted that the evangelist's restriction of women's roles may be directly attributed to apologetic interests. Luke seeks to assure the Roman world that the new Christian movement is above reproach and represents no threat to conventional norms of decorum.

Ambiguities surface in the story of the bent woman as they do elsewhere in Luke's presentation of women, and by being alert to their presence we can hope to avoid perpetuating them in our own interpretations. For example, the role attributed to the bent woman is a passive one. Unlike the feisty Canaanite woman in Matthew 15 who demands crumbs from the table of the Lord for her daughter (whom Luke omits from his narrative), or the woman with the hemorrhage in Mark 5 who claims her own healing, the bent woman simply appears in the synagogue while Jesus takes all the initiative in her restoration. As Turid Karlsen Seim observes, "On the whole, the role of the women in the miracle stories [in Luke] remains remarkably respectful to common conventions regarding women's behavior. . . . The message of liberation is expressed with due consideration to possible public offense."[28] Elisabeth Schüssler Fiorenza articulates a problematic result: "Read in an androcentric way that privileges the healing power of Jesus as male gendered . . . the miracle story of the woman freed from her infirmity both reinscribes female religious dependency and self-alienation and augments male self-affirmation and importance."[29] The story does not have to be read this way, but it bears this potential. Barbara E. Reid concurs that this dimension of the story represents a danger: "If Christian women identify with the woman as victim, the story can reinforce a dependency on males for well-being. . . . Women must take an active part in the work of liberation. They cannot wait for men with power to notice their burden and lift it. Nor can they allow the work for equality to degenerate into a controversy by men over women, as happens in this text."[30]

To be sure, the woman responds to her restoration by praising God, thereby modeling an appropriate response to God's merciful benefactions in Christ, which is echoed by the crowd four verses later in verse 17. But that is the end of her story. We do not know if she joins the movement surrounding Jesus. Like other women in Luke, she is not described as a disciple or follower. As Schüssler Fiorenza notes, "Her story is cut off and forever lost in historical silence. We know of her at all only because she has become the occasion for theological debate. Like so many other women, she remains nameless, faceless, and forgotten."[31]

In noting these ambivalent points in Luke's presentation, I am not suggesting that the story must be read in this way. But they do represent points at which Luke's presentation of women is notably circumscribed in comparison to that of other evangelists, and thus points at which to exercise caution in order to avoid perpetuating ambivalence and circumscription in contemporary interpretation. To be sure, we may celebrate the ways in which Luke renders women more visible in the narrative. We can be glad that Luke has included the bent woman's story, thereby explicitly noting that both women (13:10–17) and men (14:1–6) are healed by Jesus on the sabbath, and that Abraham has daughters (13:16) as well as sons (19:9). Moreover, the story of the bent woman also has liberating potential, and to these more positive emphases we now turn.

The Spirit of Weakness

One of the most intriguing aspects of the story is the description of the bent woman's malady. For years, she has been crippled by "a spirit of weakness" (v. 11, *pneuma astheneias* in Greek). As we have noted, "salvation," in which Luke is vitally interested, denotes participation in the reign of God—a present possibility that involves liberation from anything that prevents one from living life as God intends, whether it be demonic influences, disease, hunger, poverty, ostracism, or attachment to wealth.[32] Interestingly, we have today become increasingly aware that low self-esteem, which diminishes and deforms the lives of many young girls and women, can also be described as a spirit of weakness.

Diminishment and deformation by a spirit of weakness apparently afflicts many women early in their development, with lasting impact. In 1994, journalist Peggy Orenstein published a landmark study, *SchoolGirls*, prompted by an extensive and disturbing national survey on gender and self-esteem conducted by the American Association of University Women in 1991. Orenstein describes and investigates what the results of the AAUW survey confirmed:

> For a girl, the passage into adolescence is not just marked by menar-che or a few new curves. It is marked by a loss of confidence in her-self and her abilities, especially in math and science. It is marked by a scathingly critical attitude toward her body and a blossoming sense of personal inadequacy.
>
> In spite of the changes in women's roles in society, in spite of the changes in their own mothers' lives, many of today's girls fall into tra-ditional patterns of low self-image, self-doubt, and self-censorship of their creative and intellectual potential. . . . They emerge from their teenage years with reduced expectations and have less confidence in themselves and their abilities than do boys. Teenage girls are more vulnerable to feelings of depression and hopelessness and are four times more likely to attempt suicide.[33]

As many women know, the adolescent free fall in self-esteem can inflict wounds from which some never fully recover.

Feminist theologians have incorporated this experience into reflection on the nature of sin and salvation. Sin, they observe, has traditionally been defined as self-assertion, self-centeredness, and pride, which speak out of and to the experience of powerful men and may be appropriately addressed by a theology that emphasizes the importance of self-sacrifice. This traditional overemphasis on pride may encourage a woman "to con-fess the wrong sin," thereby failing "to judge her in her actual sin" and "to call her into her full humanity."[34] Women's true "sin" is often lack of self, self-abnegation, and irresponsibility.[35] Feminist theologian Elizabeth Johnson describes many women's predicament:

> Within patriarchal systems women's primordial temptation is not to pride and self-assertion but rather to the lack of it, to diffuseness of personal center, overdependence on others for self-identity, drifting, and fear of recognizing one's own competence. . . . In this situation grace comes . . . not as the call to loss of self but as empowerment

toward discovery of self and affirmation of one's strength, giftedness, and responsibility.[36]

Many women may recognize this as an apt description of their spiritual reality and mental health history—and also of their experience of God's grace in Christ.

Some men may identify with this reality as well, especially those who occupy marginal positions in society that restrict their choices and limit their destinies. Indeed, in more recent feminist theological work, the line dividing male and female sins has been blurring, as it is increasingly acknowledged, as Mary Elise Lowe has observed, that "all humans experience powerlessness and pride, fear and arrogance, irregardless of gender."[37] In other words, women as well as men can be tempted to pride and self-centeredness, if given the opportunity; men, as well as women, can find themselves bound by a crippling spirit of weakness. The spirit of weakness, in whomever it appears, diminishes and deforms human life, preventing us from living life fully as God intends. This spirit is appropriately described as contrary to God's will for us, and thus as "demonic." We cannot fully heal ourselves of such a wound, which is one of the liberating emphases of this story: There is another party present to our lives, one with divine power who sees us, calls us, moves us "from margin to center, from invisibility to presence, and from silence to the praise of God"[38]—one who lays healing hands upon us, releasing us from a crippling spirit, and empowering us with God's own spirit to stand up straight, to find our voices, and to embrace our strength, gifts, and responsibility as trusted children of a covenant God.

Physical Disability

The physical disability represented in the text also bears on human experience in significant ways. We ought not to ignore it, for the language of the text vividly emphasizes the difficult physical reality with which the woman lives: "She was bent over and was quite unable to stand up straight" (v. 11). In this connection, let us consider two further interpretive matters.

First, the woman's spinal disorder is often assumed to be occasioned by a crippling disease, but is this assumption appropriate? The text itself does not provide a medical diagnosis, and our assumptions may expose blind spots in our imaginations. Megan McKenna raises one such blind spot when she observes, "Maybe it was not a disease at all, but a condition brought on by a lifestyle, by back-breaking work, by being stooped over for so many hours in a day that eventually her body revolted and she could not straighten up. Had she been no more than a slave, a farmworker, a beast of burden?"[39] To illustrate the relevance of this question, McKenna narrates the following experience:

> On my first trip to Japan, I noticed older men and women so stooped and bent that they were unable to stand up. They were given seats in the trains and deferred to by those who were middle-aged. But it wasn't until I traveled to the countryside that I realized these were farmers who had grown up in the rice fields, bent over and hand-sowing, weeding and reaping the rice harvest. They had spent their lives standing in wet fields raising the staple food of a densely packed nation.[40]

She goes on to remind us of the shameful conditions under which many poor, often migrant, workers labor in our own midst:

> In our own country, those who do the back-breaking work of picking grapes, lettuce, and other produce are young, the women, and those most in need of work. They work long hours for the meagerest wages, suffering from conditions brought on by the weather, malnutrition, pesticides, lack of decent housing, and lack of health care. They constitute a lower caste that provides the undergirding of a society of wealth that depends upon them, yet ignores and oppresses them.[41]

Political and economic realities can have a detrimental impact on mental and physical health. In this connection, we need to look at the Roman imperial context of the Gospel stories, which decisively determined the conditions of life in Palestine. By Jesus' day, Rome had established "a new world order," as Richard Horsley observes, "with itself as the only remaining superpower." But as he goes on to note, the new world order was experienced as a devastating "new world disorder" by many of the subject peoples, for imperial political-military power enforced an economic system in which goods flowed from the borders of the empire toward Rome.[42] Judeans and Galileans faced both military occupation and escalating economic demands. Thus, the Gospel narratives are filled with indebted, hungry, broken, damaged human beings suffering from the effects of empire.

To be sure, Luke 13 is silent on the specific cause of the bent woman's malady, though it is described as demonic in nature. She is "Satan bound," in the grip of a reality that disfigures human life, distorting God's intentions. As our imaginations are stretched to consider the variety of realities that may quite literally burden and cripple the bodies and spirits of our human companions, this story may call us to reflect on our complicity in human suffering and to work for justice. As Walter Rauschenbusch once prayed:

> May we not unknowingly inflict suffering through selfish indifference or the willful ignorance of a callous heart. . . . May the time come when we need wear and use nothing that is wet in your sight with human tears, or cheapened by wearing down the lives of the weak. Speak to our souls and bid us strive for the coming of your realm of justice when your merciful and saving will shall be done on earth.[43]

The snapshot that Luke 13 provides of Jesus' ministry is a blueprint for our own ministries in Jesus' name, for in Luke's view, the church is the continuation of everything that Jesus began to do and teach. Luke-Acts, a unique two-volume work in the New Testament, combines the story of Jesus with that of the church, describes discipleship repeatedly in terms of "following Jesus" (e.g., 9:23; 14:27), and is the only New Testament witness to refer to the church as "the Way" (Acts 9:2; 18:25; 19:9, 23; 22:4; 24:14, 22). Our glimpse of Jesus' ministry in Luke 13 is thus also a glimpse of our own, a glimpse that calls us to interrupt our discourse if need be and notice the crippled among us, to bring them from the margins of visibility to the center of the church's attention, to lay healing hands upon them and engage in ministries of release. Luke's Jesus cared deeply about those who did not have good health, and the implication is that we should care too.

A second issue is how those who live daily with physical disability might engage this text, and how those of us not disabled can interpret it in appropriate ways in their presence. The Scriptures are filled with healing stories in which the deaf, the mute, the blind, the paralyzed, the demonically possessed, the chronically ill are restored to physical health and wholeness. What must it be like for those who live with disabilities (43 million Americans, for example—one out of six persons—and 600 million people worldwide) to hear these stories read in worship and expounded upon in Christian preaching? What is it like for the 8 million American women who live with severe osteoporosis or arthritis to hear the story of the bent woman in Luke 13? How can those with special responsibility for preaching and teaching such texts do so in ways that are healing rather than hurtful to their hearers?

Hermeneutical hazards abound, as Kathy Black has observed. On one end of the theological spectrum Black identifies those who interpret the New Testament healing stories literally, focusing on the need of persons with disabilities to be "cured," to be returned to "wholeness." Something is wrong with the person that needs fixing, and the faith or lack thereof of the person with the disability is often highlighted as playing a decisive role in healing. On the other end of the theological spectrum are those who do not believe in miracles and avoid addressing them, who try to explain the healings scientifically, or who relegate them to the realm of mystery and unexplained phenomena.

Many in mainline denominations probably fall somewhere in between, wanting to avoid both literal and dismissive postures, and thus approach these texts metaphorically: "Metaphorical interpretations identify the disability of a few with the sins of many: for example, 'We are all *deaf* to the word of God.'"[44] (The interpretive possibility highlighted above in connection with the "spirit of weakness" no doubt falls into this category!) Surely it is important to acknowledge the disability represented in the text, rather than to ignore it, but Black highlights pitfalls:

> Both literal and metaphorical interpretations result in identifying the person with the disability in the text with sin in some way. On the one hand, the person either is being punished for sin or is lacking in faith; on the other hand, the physical reality of a few is equated with the disobedience and sin of many. Neither method treats the persons with disabilities in the texts as subjects in their own right. They are often used as objects or object lessons.[45]

One finds no easy answers in Black's analysis, and unfortunately no treatment of Luke 13 to guide us, but perhaps these tentative suggestions highlight some of the ways in which the text may appropriately engage the reality of persons with disabilities. One strategy Black recommends in the preaching of healing narratives is to "emphasize the actions of the person with the disability in the text," for disabled persons, often on the margins of society, are typically "expected to be passive and out of sight."[46] One of the significant things about the story is the woman's very presence in the worshiping community, which, as I have noted, is not described as surprising in any way. Indeed, Simon Horne has observed, "Archaeology and literature from the ancient world show that people with impairments were present and active at all levels of society. They were widely seen and known in the cultures from which the Christian scriptures emerged."[47] The snapshot in Luke 13 thus calls us to reflect on any absence of such persons in our own worshiping communities and the circumstances that may account for it, for persons with impairments are widely denied access to the full life of the church. They need to be there if the whole body of Christ is to be present and if the range of human experience and diversity is to be represented and available as a resource for communal reflection. As Horne observes, "Their experience as people living [with] impairment is a requirement for the life of the church to be full."[48]

Several important distinctions may also be helpful. Disabled Peoples International distinguishes between impairment and disability: "Impairment is the lack of part of or all of a limb, or having a defective limb, organ or mechanism of the body; Disability is the loss or limitation of opportunities that prevents people who have impairments from taking part in the normal life of the community on an equal level with others due to physical and social barriers."[49] As Horne notes, "This distinction is useful for people who experience their impairment as not outside God's will, in contrast to their experience of disability."[50]

A related distinction between "curing a disease" and "healing an illness" is found in the work of medical anthropologists. John Dominic Crossan, a biblical scholar whose work engages social-science research, explains, "A disease, is, to put it bluntly, between me, my doctor, and a bug." "Illness," in contrast, involves the broader psychological and social dimensions of the physical reality and forces us to ask, "How does my dysfunction involve my family, my job, or in some cases, wider and wider levels of society?"[51] As Crossan observes, a cure for a disease is absolutely desirable, "but in its absence, we can still heal the illness by refusing to ostracize those who have it, by empathizing with their anguish, and by enveloping their sufferings with both respect and love."[52] Black also highlights this important distinction between "cure" and "healing," challenging Christian communities to participate with God in offering possibilities of well-being to one another, asking,

> Will the community be one that brings healing through acceptance,
> support, and encouragement. . . ? Will our preaching imply that one
> has to be physically and mentally "whole" . . . through miracle or
> medicine in order to be an active participant in the life of the church,

or will difference be honored and accepted? Will our preaching nurture an interdependent community where we are agents of the daily miraculous transformations God wills for each of our lives?[53]

In Luke 13, Jesus notices the bent woman, calls her over, and lays hands upon her. Nancy Eiesland, a theologian who lives with a disability, suggests that the practice of laying on of hands can become a ritual of inclusion for disabled people: "Our bodies have too often been touched by hands that have forgotten our humanity and attend only to curing us."[54] More importantly, Eiesland reminds us all that a disabled God lies at the very center of Christian theological reflection—a resurrected one who presents impaired hands and feet and a pierced side to his companions, calling them "to recognize in the marks of impairment their own connection with God, their own salvation." Eiesland goes on to note: "In so doing, this disabled God is also the revealer of a new humanity. The disabled God is not only the One from heaven but the revelation of true personhood, underscoring the reality that full personhood is fully compatible with the experience of disability."[55] Surely these observations are significant in connection with Luke 13, a story that enfolds during the journey Jesus makes toward the cross, where his body will be broken. Perhaps all of these reflections may provide important food for thought as we wrestle with the challenge of engaging New Testament healing narratives in ways that are helpful and healing, rather than hurtful, to persons who live with disabilities.

The Question of Timing

As we observed above when discussing the anti-Judaic potential of Luke 13:10–17, the insights we gain from engagement with the story might best be applied within our own contexts of communal discernment. All the participants in the story are Jewish, and surely their location is significant: the story unfolds in the midst of a worshiping community. Thus, perhaps our engagement with the story can inform debate and argument within our own religious groups as we too engage in difficult and divisive processes of communal discernment. Surely, a matter of perennial import and divisiveness in many religious groups is that of "timing." As we have noted, timing is the objection of the synagogue leader to Jesus' healing activity as he articulates his indignation before those gathered for worship: "There are six days on which work ought to be done; come on those days and be cured, and not on the sabbath day" (v. 14). As we have also noted, Jesus does not question the principle of sabbath observance but rather its application, arguing that the sabbath is a highly appropriate time for releasing from bondage a daughter of Abraham.

In each new age as communities of faith struggle together to discern what God is calling them to be and do, debates over appropriate timing continue to surface. In 1963 Rev. Dr. Martin Luther King Jr., for example, composed his famous "Letter from Birmingham Jail" as a reply to an open letter published by eight Alabama clergymen who regarded his nonviolent demonstration in Birmingham to be "unwise and untimely" because it provoked violent reactions by those opposed to King's call for justice. In his response to the clergymen, King defended his presence and actions in Birmingham ("Injustice anywhere is a threat to justice everywhere. We are caught in an inescapable network of mutuality, tied in a single garment of destiny"[56]) and expressed his grave disappointment in the white moderate "who constantly advises the Negro to wait for a 'more convenient season'":

> For years now I have heard the word "Wait!" It rings in the ear of every Negro with piercing familiarity. This "Wait!" has almost always meant "Never." We must come to see . . . that "justice too long delayed is justice denied."
>
> We have waited for more than 340 years for our constitutional and God-given rights. . . . Perhaps it is easy for those who have never felt the stinging darts of segregation to say "Wait."[57]

King also debunked a tragic misconception about time, "the strangely irrational notion that there is something in the very flow of time that will inevitably cure all ills":

> Actually, time itself is neutral; it can be used either destructively or constructively. . . . Human progress never rolls in on wheels of inevitability; it comes through the tireless efforts of men willing to be co-workers with God, and without this hard work, time itself becomes an ally of the forces of social stagnation. We must use time creatively, in the knowledge that the time is always ripe to do right.[58]

Many persons who have struggled for justice share the concerns King articulates.

Women who long for equal rights, for example, have also found themselves advised to "wait" for a more convenient season. Indeed, women who have struggled for full inclusion in the life and leadership of the church may feel a special bond with the woman in Luke 13. As Barbara Reid notes, "This woman's eighteen years of suffering have become symbolic of the more than eighteen centuries of patriarchal burdens that women have carried. . . . Not unlike the synagogue official, there are many voices today that advocate patient endurance, assuring women that if they wait long enough the day of equality will come."[59] She also notes:

> Many women, like the woman bent double, have learned to live with the burdens of sexism. They have found a way to accommodate themselves to the system so that they can still hobble their way in to give praise to God. Although they know that the range of what can be seen from a bent over position is very limited, this is a familiar world, and one not readily relinquished.[60]

But Luke 13, she says, can move us to realize "the urgency of acting for liberation now": "In it the voice of Christ can be heard to insist upon the necessity of setting free all the daughters of Abraham and Sarah today. In this way all God's people have fuller range of vision and glorify God standing erect. There will always be objections to the timing. Is there ever a convenient time for liberation?"[61]

That very question is currently being raised in another arena of the church's life. Many mainline denominations are presently engaged in debates over sexuality, as gay and lesbian Christians struggle for the full rights of membership, including ordination. Once again, the airwaves are filled with objections that the "time is not right" and admonitions to "patience," and some voices insist that the church ought to disengage from "social issues" and "get back to the gospel."

We can recognize this complaint as one that surfaces repeatedly in the life of the church: Can we not get off the civil rights kick, or the women's rights kick, or the gay rights kick, and get back to the fundamental teachings of Christianity? Luke reminds us, however, that nothing is more fundamental to Christianity than liberation, release of the captives. Luke insists that Jesus defined his ministry and commitment to the divine purpose in those terms: "The Spirit of the Lord is upon me, because he has anointed me to bring good news to the poor. He has sent me to proclaim release to the captives and recovery of sight to the blind, to let the oppressed go free, to proclaim the year of the Lord's favor" (Luke 4:18–19).

Luke also underlines the presence of salvation with repeated use of one of his favorite words: "today" (*sēmeron*, in Greek)! "Today this scripture has been fulfilled in your hearing" (4:21). Think of the song of the angels:

"to you is born this day [today] in the city of David a Savior, who is the Messiah, the Lord" (2:11). Remember Jesus' words to Zacchaeus ("Today salvation has come to this house" [19:9]) and to the penitent thief on the cross ("Truly I tell you, today you will be with me in Paradise" [23:43]). Luke shifts the emphasis from "eschaton" to "*sēmeron*"—to the presence of salvation in encounter with Jesus today.

Luke's vision can perhaps help us grasp the urgency of the difficult processes of communal discernment in which the church finds itself engaged in each new age. Clearly, the healing and liberating reign of God does not come without objection and conflict, but we must persist in discerning what God is calling us to be and do in our day and time. At stake is the healing and restoration of daughters and sons of Abraham, bound by demonic realities that prevent them from living life as God intends.

The snapshot that Luke 13 provides of Jesus' ministry is a blueprint for our own ministries in Jesus' name, for in Luke's view, the church is the continuation of everything that Jesus began to do and teach. As the church engages ministries of "release to the captives," it continues to embody "the Way." As those who are bound by crippling spirits and realities are liberated and empowered by God to stand up straight in the midst of the congregation and find their voices, the life of the church itself is also blessed with expanded vision and praise. Like the bent woman, they are yeast in the community of faith who leaven the whole group and extend it beyond its boundaries. Indeed, this is what the kingdom of God looks like, as God's liberating, saving purposes are manifest in our presence today.

Group Study Suggestions

Begin with a dramatic reading of Luke 13:10–17 in which participants not only read the text, but act it out. Assign roles to a narrator, to Jesus, to a leader of the synagogue, and to a bent woman. Ask the rest of the group to assume the role of the crowd.

Following the reading, ask participants: What impressions emerge as you hear the story and what questions does it raise for you?

Proceed with any of the questions for discussion/reflection below.

Questions for Discussion or Reflection

The story in Luke 13:10–17 contains a number of characters. With whom do you identify as you hear this story, and why? Where would you place yourself in the scene?

In what ways do you identify with the bent woman? With the leader of the synagogue? With the crowd? With Jesus?

Where do realities reflected in the text intersect with your own experience? What word does the text address to the reality or experience you have identified?

Have you or persons with whom you are acquainted lived with the reality of chronic illness and physical disability? What does this contribute to your understanding of the story?

Share your reactions to Luke's presentation of the woman. What positive features do you appreciate? What ambiguous features concern you? What do you imagine the woman would have said? How do you imagine she spent the next eighteen years of her life?

Share your reactions to the discussion of the anti-Jewish interpretive potential the text bears, and your way of handling this problem. What anti-Judaic assumptions have you brought, perhaps unconsciously, to a reading of this story?

Have you ever been crippled by "a spirit of weakness"? How so? Why do you think so many young girls and women are afflicted with a disabling lack of self-esteem? What good news does this text address to this reality?

What do you learn about Jesus in this story? Make a list of the impressions of him that emerge from the story. What is their significance for you?

Has the question of timing emerged in your own experience of Christian communal discernment? If so, how? What does the story contribute to your reflection on contemporary processes of discernment in which the church is engaged?

We have mentioned three points of contact between the text and contemporary communities of faith (the spirit of weakness, the reality of physical disability, and the question of timing). What other points of contact come to mind? What other realities reflected in the text engage your experience?

What new insights have emerged for you from your engagement with this story?

Resources for Further Study

Black, Kathy. *A Healing Homiletic: Preaching and Disability.* Nashville: Abingdon, 1996.

Eiesland, Nancy. *The Disabled God: Toward a Liberatory Theology of Disability.* Nashville: Abingdon, 1994.

Green, Joel B. "Jesus and a Daughter of Abraham (Luke 13:10–17): Test Case for a Lucan Perspective on Jesus' Miracles." *Catholic Biblical Quarterly* 51 (1989): 643–54.

Hamm, M. Dennis. "The Freeing of the Bent Woman and the Restoration of Israel: Luke 13.10–17 as Narrative Theology." *Journal for the Study of the New Testament* 31 (1987): 23–44.

McKenna, Megan. In *Leave Her Alone*, 51–70. Maryknoll, N.Y.: Orbis, 2000.

O'Toole, Robert. "Some Exegetical Reflections on Luke 13, 10–17." *Biblica* 73 (1992): 84–107.

Reid, Barbara E. *Choosing the Better Part? Women in the Gospel of Luke*, 163–68. Collegeville, Minn.: Liturgical, 1996.

Schüssler Fiorenza, Elisabeth. In *But She Said: Feminist Practices of Biblical Interpretation*, 196–217. Boston: Beacon, 1992.

Seim, Turid Karlsen. *The Double Message: Patterns of Gender in Luke and Acts.* Nashville: Abingdon, 1994.

———. "The Gospel of Luke." In *Searching the Scriptures*, vol. 2, *A Feminist Commentary*, edited by Elisabeth Schüssler Fiorenza, 728–62. New York: Crossroad, 1994.

Chapter Five

The Samaritan Woman

John 4:1–42

Now when Jesus learned that the Pharisees had heard, "Jesus is making and baptizing more disciples than John"—although it was not Jesus himself but his disciples who baptized—he left Judea and started back to Galilee. But he had to go through Samaria. So he came to a Samaritan city called Sychar, near the plot of ground that Jacob had given to his son Joseph. Jacob's well was there, and Jesus, tired out by his journey, was sitting by the well. It was about noon.

A Samaritan woman came to draw water, and Jesus said to her, "Give me a drink." (His disciples had gone to the city to buy food.) The Samaritan woman said to him, "How is it that you, a Jew, ask a drink of me, a woman of Samaria?" (Jews do not share things in common with Samaritans.) Jesus answered her, "If you knew the gift of God, and who it is that is saying to you, 'Give me a drink,' you would have asked him, and he would have given you living water." The woman said to him, "Sir, you have no bucket, and the well is deep. Where do you get that living water? Are you greater than our ancestor Jacob, who gave us the well, and with his sons and his flocks drank from it?" Jesus said to her, "Everyone who drinks of this water will be thirsty again, but those who drink of the water that I will give them will never be thirsty. The water that I will give will become in them a spring of water gushing up to eternal life." The woman said to him, "Sir, give me this water, so that I may never be thirsty or have to keep coming here to draw water."

Jesus said to her, "Go, call your husband, and come back." The woman answered him, "I have no husband." Jesus said to her, "You are right in saying, 'I have no husband'; for you have had five husbands, and the one you have now is not your husband. What you have said is true!" The woman said to him, "Sir, I see that you are a prophet. Our ancestors worshiped on this mountain, but you say that the place where people must worship is in Jerusalem." Jesus said to her, "Woman, believe me, the hour is coming when you will worship the Father neither on this mountain nor in Jerusalem. You worship what you do not know; we worship what we know, for salvation is from the Jews. But the hour is coming, and is now here, when the true worshipers will worship the Father in spirit and truth, for the Father seeks such as these to worship him. God is spirit, and those who worship him must worship in spirit and truth." The woman said to him, "I know that Messiah is coming" (who is called Christ). "When he comes, he will proclaim all things to us." Jesus said to her, "I am he, the one who is speaking to you."

Just then his disciples came. They were astonished that he was speaking with a woman, but no one said, "What do you want?" or, "Why are you speaking with her?" Then the woman left her water jar and went back to the city. She said to the people, "Come and see a man who told me everything I have ever done! He cannot be the Messiah, can he?" They left the city and were on their way to him.

Meanwhile the disciples were urging him, "Rabbi, eat something." But he said to them, "I have food to eat that you do not know about." So the disciples said to one another, "Surely no one has brought him something to eat?" Jesus said to them, "My food is to do the will of him who sent me and to complete his work. Do you not say, 'Four months more, then comes the harvest'? But I tell you, look around you, and see how the fields are ripe for harvesting. The reaper is already receiving wages and is gathering fruit for eternal life, so that sower and reaper may rejoice together. For here the saying holds true, 'One sows and another reaps.' I sent you to reap that for which you did not labor. Others have labored, and you have entered into their labor."

Many Samaritans from that city believed in him because of the woman's testimony, "He told me everything I have ever done." So when the Samaritans came to him, they asked him to stay with them; and he stayed there two days. And many more believed because of his word. They said to the woman, "It is no longer because of what you said that we believe, for we have heard for ourselves, and we know that this is truly the Savior of the world."

John's portrait of the Samaritan woman who encounters Jesus at a well deserves special attention, for at least two reasons. For one thing, their conversation is Jesus' longest recorded conversation. This is noteworthy in itself, but especially so in John's Gospel, where Jesus is given to extensive monologue. (Wordy is the Lamb!) Few others get a word in edgewise. The Samaritan woman, however, finds herself engaged with Jesus in a genuine and extended conversation in which she holds her own quite well.

For another thing, her portrait has been clouded by considerable interpretive litter. The details of her marital history (narrated briefly in 4:16–18) have proved overly fascinating for generations of preachers and teachers, evoking imaginative (and often prurient) speculation about her circumstances and character. As Fred Craddock observes, "Evangelists aplenty have assumed that the brighter her nails, the darker her mascara and the shorter her skirt, the greater the testimony to the power of the converting word."[1] Consequently, much has been read into her portrait, while notable features of it unrelated to her sexual history have, sadly, been overlooked. Attend closely then to the way that John describes her, and to her remarkable encounter with Jesus, in hopes of recovering a more accurate portrait.

Encountering the Text

Several literary and historical contextual issues are noteworthy as we begin to examine this portrait.

Contextual Considerations

In terms of historical context, John 4 departs from what we know of Jesus' ministry in the other Gospels, for only John mentions a ministry of Jesus in Samaria. Because this is not corroborated anywhere else in the New Testament, that the historical Jesus carried out a mission in Samaria is perhaps unlikely. This scene probably represents the experience of Johannine Christians, who embraced Samaritan converts as brothers and sisters in Christ.[2] Therefore, as we read the story, we should keep in mind that the woman Jesus encounters at the well has a symbolic function: she represents the Samaritan presence within the Johannine Christian community. Indeed, as she appears on the scene in verses 7–9, she is described three times as a "Samaritan woman." Rather than stating her name, her national identity is underlined. Moreover, in the course of her extended conversation with Jesus, she raises a variety of religious and theological issues that were key matters of dispute between Jews and Samaritans (see vv. 9, 12, 20). She functions in the story as a spokesperson for the Samaritan people.

For additional historical context, first-century Jews and Samaritans had been divided by centuries of hostility and deep prejudice. They shared a common heritage, each maintaining they were the bearers of the true faith of ancient Israel. However, they differed radically in regard to the relative sanctity of Jerusalem and Mount Gerizim (see 4:20), and also held different legal and scriptural traditions. Samaritans were considered heretics, foreigners, and unclean by Jews, who avoided contact with them—as is reflected in the first words out of the woman's mouth in 4:9: "How is it that you, a Jew, ask a drink of me, a woman of Samaria?" The narrator also emphasizes this point with a parenthetical aside: "(Jews do not share things in common with Samaritans)." However, Jesus is presented as deliberately crossing this ethnic and religious boundary. Indeed, as the story opens, the narrator whispers to us that "he had to go through Samaria" (4:4; or translating more literally, "it was necessary" for him to pass through Samaria). Though the main route from Judea to Galilee was through Samaria, Jesus could easily have avoided it; most Jews did. The narrator thus speaks not of geographical necessity, but of theological necessity—the divine imperative of Jesus' presence among the Samaritan people.[3]

In terms of literary context, the woman Jesus encounters in chapter 4 is the mirror opposite of Nicodemus, whom he engages in chapter 3. They are at opposite ends of the social, political, and religious spectrum.[4] One is named and male; the other is an unnamed female. One is a distinguished religious leader, a pillar of the community; the other is a despised foreigner with an irregular marital history. Nicodemus comes to Jesus by night; the Samaritan woman encounters Jesus at noon, in the fullest light of day.[5] Moreover, the dialogue between Jesus and Nicodemus quickly shifts into one of Jesus' monologues, and Nicodemus fades into the shadows. We have no idea how he responds to Jesus or if he responds at all, for his subsequent appearances in 7:50–51 and 19:39 are ambiguous in nature.[6]

The conversation between Jesus and the Samaritan woman, by contrast, is characterized by lively give-and-take. The exchange is, in fact, as Adele Reinhartz notes, "one of the few occasions in this Gospel in which a dialogue between Jesus and another character does not become a monologue for Jesus alone."[7] Moreover, at the conclusion of her story, the Samaritan woman does something very important that Nicodemus did not do: she bears witness to Jesus. As a result, a whole village comes to faith!

Finally, an Old Testament literary connection is significant, for in John 4 we hear echoes of an old familiar story: boy meets girl at a well! Consider how Isaac met Rebecca, Jacob met Rachel, and Moses met Zipporah (Gen. 24, 29; Exod. 2). The recognized biblical pattern (known as a "betrothal type-scene") unfolds in this manner: The future bridegroom journeys to a foreign land, where he encounters a girl at a well, and one of them draws water. Afterward, the girl rushes to bring home the news of the stranger's arrival. Finally, but only after he has been invited to a meal, a betrothal is concluded between the stranger and the girl.[8]

John clearly follows this pattern, but with a few wrinkles! Jesus travels to a foreign country, and like his biblical predecessors meets a woman at a well. In fact, like Jacob, he meets her there in broad daylight, at noon. However, Jesus meets not a maiden, but a five-time-married woman. Also, rather than looking for a wife, he is looking for worshipers in spirit and truth. The woman does rush home to share the news, but no betrothal meal takes place. In fact, Jesus declares that his food is to do the will of the one who sent him and complete God's work. However, he does visit her home and accepts the hospitality extended to him by the Samaritan community, staying two days. There is joy all around, though the story ends not with betrothal, but the conversion of the whole Samaritan community to faith in Jesus as "Savior of the world."

The echoes deepen when we take note of the marital motif that runs throughout John 2–4: Jesus' public ministry begins, in John 2, with a wedding at Cana, and in 3:29 he is pointedly referred to as "the bridegroom." On the heels of this, a boy meets a girl at a well in John 4. What is one to make of this narrative?

As strange as it seems, the scene in John 4 has been interpreted as an attempted seduction on the part of the woman. Lyle Eslinger, for example, discerns sexual innuendoes throughout the conversation, noting the sexual orientation of the imagery of living water, springs, wells, and cisterns in the Old Testament. Proverbs 5:15–18ff., for example: "Drink water from your own cistern, flowing water from your own well . . . and rejoice in the wife of your youth."[9] I cannot endorse Eslinger's reading, but it does illustrate what can happen if one completely sexualizes the scene and runs wild with this line of interpretation. Sandra Schneiders suggests a fascinating alternative and plausible interpretation: she calls attention to the use of marital imagery in Israel's prophetic literature to describe the relationship between Yahweh and the covenant people. In this scene, "Jesus, the new Bridegroom who assumes the role of Yahweh, bridegroom of ancient Israel, comes to claim Samaria as an integral part of the New Israel"—that is, the Christian community.[10]

Another Old Testament connection sheds further light, for the woman's personal history parallels the Samaritan national history as detailed in 2 Kings 17:24ff. In that account, we learn that when the Assyrians conquered the region in 721 B.C.E., they brought colonists from five foreign nations into Samaria. Thus, the woman's five previous husbands may well be symbolic of Samaria's intermarriage with foreign peoples and the acceptance of their false gods. What about the sixth man? Perhaps the current man is Rome, for colonization continued under first-century Roman rule, though the Samaritans did not intermarry with the Roman colonists as extensively as they did with the Assyrians.[11] Alternatively, cohabitation with a sixth man might refer to the Samaritans' syncretistic worship of Yahweh in the New Testament era, which lacked the full integrity of the covenant relationship.[12] Whichever the case may be, the woman's personal history of marriage to five husbands and cohabitation with a sixth may well symbolize the colonial history of Samaria.[13] Indeed, Schneiders suggests that "the entire dialogue between Jesus and the woman is the 'wooing' of Samaria to full covenant fidelity in the New Israel by Jesus, the New Bridegroom."[14]

To be sure, many will resist any such symbolic reading, smacking as it does of allegorical interpretation. However, a number of issues suggest that it is worthy of serious consideration. The symbolic nature of John's distinctive language points in this direction, as does the pointed use, in a dialogue between two lone individuals, of plural forms of speech:

> "Are you greater than **our** ancestor Jacob, who gave **us** the well, and with his sons and his flocks drank from it?" (v. 12)

> **"Our** ancestors worshiped on this mountain, but **you (pl.)** say that the place where people must worship is in Jerusalem." (v. 20)

> Jesus said to her, "Woman, believe me, the hour is coming when **you (pl.)** will worship the Father neither on this mountain nor in Jerusalem. **You (pl.)** worship what **you (pl.)** do not know; **we** worship what **we** know, for salvation is from the Jews." (vv. 21–22)

> The woman said to him, "I know that Messiah is coming" (who is called Christ). "When he comes, he will proclaim all things to **us**." (v. 25)

The use of plural forms of speech (obscured by English translation but evident in the Greek) emphasizes a point we noted earlier: the Samaritan woman functions as a spokesperson for her people.

Indeed, commentators note that many characters in the Gospel of John serve as representative figures (e.g., Nicodemus, in John 3, who is thought to be representative of "closet-" or "crypto-Christians," and who also speaks alone with Jesus in the middle of the night, but in plural forms of speech; or the man born blind in John 9, who embodies the story of the Johannine community in his confrontation with religious authorities and subsequent expulsion from the synagogue for his confession of faith).[15] Moreover, if the woman's personal history symbolizes the colonial history of Samaria, with its syncretistic religious tendencies (2 Kgs. 17:24–41), then it would appear that she clearly catches the drift of Jesus' point about five husbands and stays with the problem of religious infidelity when she raises the question of true worship. The second part of the conversation in verses 16–26 is then tightly unified, from beginning to end, by the theme of "true worship."

Finally, Stephen Moore calls attention to a curious circumstance— indeed, an interpretive "double standard" on the part of those who insist on a literal interpretation of "five husbands":

> The majority of Johannine commentators have preferred the literal reading of 4:18 to the figurative one. . . . At the same time, these commentators have scrupulously noted the repeated failure of the woman to grasp the nonliteral nature of Jesus' discourse. In opting to take Jesus' statement in 4:18 at face value, then, they effectively trade places with the woman. They reenact what they purport to be describing. They mimic the literal-mindedness that marks her as inferior in their eyes. The standard reading of 4:18 conceals a double standard, then. To interpret Jesus literally is a failing when the woman does it, but not when the commentators follow suit.[16]

So are the "five husbands" to be taken literally or symbolically?[17] Here as elsewhere in the Gospel of John, certainty in this matter eludes us, though the varied interpretations stretch us to embrace multivalent possibilities.

The Point of the Conversation

The Samaritan woman's marital history has more often been interpreted along literal, rather than symbolic, lines. Indeed, much has been made of her sinfulness, her shady past, her dubious morals, her promiscuity, her aberrant sexual behavior. John Calvin serves as an instructive example. Consider his explanation for the five marriages: "The reason of this probably was, that, being a froward and disobedient wife, she constrained her husbands to divorce her. I interpret the words thus: 'Though God joined thee to lawful husbands, thou didst not cease to sin, until, rendered infamous by numerous divorces, thou prostitutedst thyself to fornication.'" Moreover, Calvin speculates, "Christ, *in order to repress the woman's talkativeness,* brought forward her former and present life."[18] No comment!

Let us be clear about one fact. The text tells us that the Samaritan woman had five husbands, but it does not tell us why. We do not know whether she has been divorced or widowed. Perhaps, like Tamar in Genesis 38, she is trapped in the custom of levirate marriage, and the last male in the family line has refused to marry her, as Gail O'Day suggests.[19] Moreover, we should bear in mind that divorce (which is not mentioned in the text) was an exclusively male privilege. As Linda McKinnish Bridges observes, "Maybe her five husbands found her lacking, unsuitable, unlovely, unfit for their desires, and they simply rid themselves of responsibility and relationship. . . . What if this woman with no name needed redemption not from the excesses of sexual promiscuity but from a series of injustices from five husbands in a culture programmed for male domination?"[20]

Is she guilty of sin? Maybe—maybe not! We may discern that she has had a tragic personal history of some sort, but the details of it are not available to us. In fact, to focus single-mindedly on these issues may well be to miss the main point of the conversation. Gail O'Day makes an important observation in this regard:

> When we read verses 16–19 carefully, we notice that *the history of the woman's five husbands is presented quite disinterestedly, with no suggestion or coloring of moral outrage or judgment.* How or why the woman has had five husbands and what the quality of those marriages was is not a concern of the Evangelist as he tells the story. More importantly, those questions are also unimportant to Jesus. One searches in vain for any words of judgment about the woman's character uttered by Jesus in these verses.[21]

O'Day insists that "The conversation is intended to show the reader something about Jesus, not primarily about the woman."[22]

What do we learn about Jesus in the course of their conversation? A number of important things. In the first round of their conversation (vv. 7–15), we learn that he crosses boundaries between male and female, and between chosen and rejected people, demonstrating that the grace of God is available to all. Indeed, he makes that gift available to all as he offers the Samaritan woman living water—a symbol of the gift of God that he represents (3:16), and also of the new life or the spirit that God gives to humans in Christ (7:37–39).[23] People who drink of it will never be thirsty, for the gift of God fills our whole being and runs over, penetrating every part of human existence. Though the Samaritan woman does not fully grasp what he offers, she is open to Jesus and asks him to give her this water, as he has invited her to do.

In the second round of their conversation (vv. 16–26), Jesus continues to draw the Samaritan woman to faith, with a reference to her marital history that illustrates his ability to see and know all things. Stunned by Jesus' extraordinary knowledge of her life, the woman is now able to see him with new eyes: "I see that you are a prophet" (v. 19). This being the case, she sets before him what was at that time the most pressing theological question separating Jews and Samaritans: Is God to be worshiped in Jerusalem (as Jews maintained) or on the Samaritan mountain of Gerizim (v. 20)? Unfortunately, many commentators see this not as a serious theological query on her part, but rather as a smokescreen, a diversionary tactic—a "desperate" attempt to change the topic and extricate herself from an embarrassing conversation. Others cannot imagine that she would be capable of theological inquiry. (One distinguished Johannine scholar, for example, says this in his otherwise magnificent commentary: "We may still wonder if a Samaritan woman would have been expected to understand even the most basic ideas of the discourse."[24])

She ought not to be devalued as a legitimate conversation partner. In the circumstances of that time, the question she asks is risky, courageous, and deeply theological. (And, if the Samaritan history of syncretistic worship is in view in 4:18 when five husbands are mentioned, then her question about true worship hardly represents a "shift" in the conversation, but rather a probing continuation of it.) In Jesus' answer, we learn that the spirit he gives is not bound to any location and enables believers to worship God properly, "in spirit and truth." Moreover, as their conversation concludes, he discloses that he is the expected Messiah and more—for the words "I AM" ("I am he" in many translations; see 4:26) link his very being with the one revealed to Moses in the burning bush (Exod. 3:14). This is the first time these striking words appear in the Fourth Gospel, and the Samaritan woman is the first to hear them.

Bearing Witness

Older lectionaries amputated the Samaritan woman's story, concluding with verse 26. The Revised Common Lectionary is an improvement, encouraging us to continue through verse 42. Doing so is important, for three concluding scenes in verses 27–42 are essential to a complete portrait.

First, in a fascinating transitional scene (vv. 27–30), Jesus' disciples return and the Samaritan woman temporarily exits. Upon their return, the disciples are "astonished that he was speaking with a woman" (v. 27), though a more literal translation of the Greek (*ethaumazon*) suggests a continuing state of shock rather than mere "astonishment." Curiously, they are shocked not because he is talking with a Samaritan, but because he is talking with a woman. They, however, in marked contrast to the woman's straightforward questioning of Jesus, do not openly question and challenge Jesus' purposes in doing so (v. 27).

At this point, the woman leaves her water jar and returns to the city, saying to the people: "Come and see a man who told me everything I have ever done! He cannot be the Messiah, can he?" The abandoned water jar, an intriguing detail, teases our imaginations and is open to varied interpretations. Perhaps it conveys the woman's enthusiasm and haste to share her news; perhaps she has no further need for it as she is now in possession of living water and will never thirst again (4:14); maybe even she herself has become a vessel for the gospel. Alternatively, some see it as the Johannine feminine counterpart to the Synoptic presentation of male disciples leaving their nets and boats behind to follow Jesus,[25] or more simply, as an indication that the woman intends to return to the well. Her story is not finished yet.[26]

Whatever the case may be, we would also do well to attend to her words of witness before her compatriots. "Come and see a man who told me everything I have ever done!" (v. 29), as Fred Craddock observes, is "not exactly a recitation of the Apostles' Creed."[27] We should also note the question mark in her voice: "He cannot be the Messiah, can he?"[28] Her faith is tentative, not yet mature, but she is moved by the presence of Jesus and eager to share the news, wanting her friends to encounter him too. This response on her part is a critical dimension of her portrait, not to be overlooked. Here she embodies one of the primary marks of discipleship in John: bearing witness to Jesus. Moreover, faith that is tentative, full of questions, and not yet mature can bear witness and do so effectively.

Following the transitional scene in verses 27–30, a conversational interlude with the disciples in verses 31–38 addresses their skepticism and vindicates the Samaritan woman. The disciples are told to lift their eyes and see the fields already ripe for harvest as the Samaritans pour out of their city and make their way toward Jesus. The Samaritan woman has sown the seed, and they may now reap. She has labored, and they may enter into her labor. What the disciples learn is that mission is shared labor and responsibility that includes both women and men—a fact that may be hard for them to swallow. Indeed, Sandra Schneiders observes:

> The brief episode of the return of the disciples, looked at from a feminist perspective, reveals the all-too-familiar uneasiness of men when one of their number takes a woman too seriously, especially in an area of men's primary concern. Jesus' discourse about his mission and its extension into Samaria only serves to confirm their worst fears, that they are neither the originators nor the controllers of the Church's mission. The effectiveness of the woman's evangelization of her town caps this scene in which any male claim to a privileged or exclusive role in the work of Jesus is definitely undermined by Jesus' own words and deeds.[29]

Finally, the conclusion to the story in verses 39–42 emphasizes the effectiveness of the Samaritan woman's ministry: "Many Samaritans from that city believed in him because of the woman's testimony" (v. 39). She is a success in spite of herself, in spite of her own tentative faith. And though the story began with a notation that "Jews do not share things in common with Samaritans" (v. 9), it ends on a note of reversal, as the Samaritans invite Jesus to stay. As Jesus accepts their hospitality and remains (or "abides") with them two days, "many more believed because of his word. They said to the woman, 'It is no longer because of what you said that we believe, for we have heard for ourselves, and we know that this is truly the Savior of the world'" (vv. 41–42).

Some interpreters have viewed this closing comment as denigration of the woman and dismissal of her role in bringing the Samaritans to faith. (John Calvin, for example, notes: "The Samaritans appear to boast that they have now a stronger foundation than a woman's tongue, which is, for the most part, light and trivial."[30]) However, this conclusion represents the Johannine pattern of faith development and discipleship. Faith has powerful results when it is shared with others, but faith based on the witness of others must move on to a firsthand experience of Jesus. The

Samaritan woman's missionary task is fulfilled when the Samaritans make this transition and their own confession of faith in Jesus as Savior of the world.

In sum, revisions of the Samaritan woman's portrait seem to be in order. In the history of interpretation, much has been made of her irregular marital history but very little of her witness, her missionary endeavor, or Jesus' vindication of her role against the disapproval of male disciples. She is much more than a woman with an interesting love life or a model of sin. She is the first character in John to engage Jesus in serious theological conversation. Moreover, she is the most effective evangelist in this whole Gospel—hence a model for Christian faith and witness. As Robert Kysar observes, "Because of her the reader of this Gospel knows that no matter who you are—no matter what your status in society may be—the revelation of God in Christ is for you!"[31]

Angles of Vision

One of the most intriguing things about biblical narratives is their ability to generate more than one reading. Texts are multivalent, containing within themselves diverse interpretive possibilities and meanings. Readers, too, are diverse, rooted as they are in different historical and social locations, which affect not only what they see in a given text, but even the questions they think to ask of it. Perhaps nowhere is this as apparent as in John 4. As Gary Phillips observes: "The widespread and conflicting readings of this passage suggest something important about the way this text resists any confident critical handling and closure. Indeed, John 4 invites us back repeatedly to wrestle with its aporias, tensions and points of textual undecidability. Like the well itself, the text draws readers back for further reading."[32] Let us consider two areas in which ever-evolving readings leave the text ajar, and leave interpreters with the suspicion that they might not have grasped it completely after all. First we consider once again the Samaritan woman's portrait, and then we attend to the theology and practice of mission that finds expression in the text, both of which have generated varied angles of vision.

The Samaritan Woman's Portrait

As noted earlier, the portrait of the Samaritan woman has been clouded by considerable interpretive litter. Sandra Schneiders states the case more bluntly, "The treatment of the Samaritan woman in the history of interpretation is a textbook case of the trivialization, marginalization and even sexual demonization of biblical women."[33] Even so, the woman's portrait has evolved through the years, acquiring distinctive nuances in different generations.

Church historian Craig S. Farmer has examined this evolution. Ancient and medieval commentators, he observes, portray the Samaritan woman in largely flattering terms, as a "well-meaning" if "dim-witted" woman whose intellect is gradually enlightened to an understanding of Jesus' divine status. John Chrysostom, for example, repeatedly emphasized the great respect and patience that she showed to a man who was not only unknown to her, but also a foreigner, thereby allowing Jesus to enlighten her feeble understanding. Chrysostom lavished praise on her exemplary evangelistic work: "In a certain sense, she is even superior to the apostles, who left their fishing nets only after being commanded by Jesus; in contrast, she leaves her water jar of her own accord and performs apostolic work with a zeal and fervor worthy of emulation."[34] Augustine also praised her admirable zeal in bearing witness to Christ, urging those who desire to preach the gospel to learn from her example. Medieval commentators followed the lead of these two ancient Christian theologians. "In general," Farmer observes, "ancient and medieval commentators present her as polite, friendly in her dealings with Jesus, and eager to be taught, hindered simply by a lack of understanding rooted in a rather dull, slow-witted intellect."[35]

In the sixteenth century, Farmer notes, a different portrait of the Samaritan woman began to emerge in the exegesis of Protestant Reformers. She was no longer described as polite and sweet-spirited, but in unflattering terms as "brash, saucy, and practically insolent in her conversation with Jesus"—indeed, as "a hussy who ridicules Jesus."[36] As Farmer surveys the commentary of early Reformed theologians such as Johannes Oecolampadius, Heinrich Bullinger, Martin Bucer, Wolfgang Musculus, and John Calvin, one is startled to hear the Samaritan woman described variously as one who spurns and resists Jesus' gentle attempts to begin a conversation, who speaks rashly "with womanly temerity," who is "garrulous and impertinent," even proud, sassy, and eager for a fight. Clearly, most of them discern a caustic and flippant tone in her voice. She is presented as "jeering" at Christ, mocking and taunting him.

Moreover, while all of the Reformed commentators admire the zeal with which the repentant sinner subsequently proclaims Christ before her compatriots, they variously assess her role and status as a witness to Christ. Oecolampadius and Bullinger follow their ancient and medieval predecessors in presenting her as an apostle who leads others to eternal life, but Musculus insists that she is not an apostle:

> [T]he Samaritans, he writes, "did not believe through the word of the apostles, who were chosen by Christ and sent to preach the Gospel, but through the word of a woman, a person of the inferior sex, and a private citizen not called to the ministry of the word." She thus does not represent the normal mode of preaching the word through the ordained ministry; her witness merely shows that "from time to time" a lay person, even a woman, may be useful in establishing the kingdom of Christ "among acquaintances and friends."[37]

For Calvin, too, her role is strictly limited to alerting her townsfolk to Christ's presence: "If she had presumed to teach or preach, she would have acted recklessly, since she hardly knew anything about Christ or heavenly doctrine. But Calvin assures us that she merely functioned as 'a trumpet or bell to invite others to Christ.'"[38]

What accounts for these striking sixteenth-century shifts in the Samaritan woman's portrait? Two theological emphases: self-knowledge and election. Farmer explains:

> This new exegetical portrait can be explained partly by the Reformed emphasis on self-understanding as the *sine qua non* for the experience of divine grace; in the economy of salvation, self-knowledge is the absolute precondition for a living faith that seizes the benefits of gracious forgiveness found in Christ. The Reformed commentators hear the Samaritan woman speaking with self-assured bravado because they are convinced she has not come to grips with her sinful condition.[39]

By directing attention to the woman's irregular marital history, Jesus brings her face-to-face with her sin and guilt, and this self-knowledge prepares her for salvation.

But the Reformed emphasis on self-knowledge alone does not account for the new, negative portrayal of the woman's personality. Farmer suggests that the driving force at work in Reformed interpretations of the Samaritan woman is the doctrine of election: "The Samaritan woman has been elected to salvation not on the basis of her pleasing disposition, not on the basis of her meritorious response to Jesus, but solely on the basis of God's goodness and mercy."[40] In other words, the more obstinate and reprobate the sinner, the more beautifully the story serves as an illustration of divine mercy: "All the Reformed commentators make this point, accenting the Samaritan woman's petulance in order to exhibit the unconditional grace of God."[41]

Negative portrayals of the Samaritan woman persist in Christian preaching and teaching to this day. One wonders, in fact, if the increasing frequency with which sexuality is featured on public airwaves has impacted homiletical airwaves as well, permitting preachers to go to even bolder lengths in eroticizing her portrait. Recently, for example, I heard a sermon on John 4 in which the preacher burst into country-and-western song—"Looking for love in all the wrong places"—lyrics that he took as appropriate commentary on the Samaritan woman's personal history. What accounts for her continued deprecation and sexualization? The theological concerns that emerged in Reformation exegesis may continue to wield their influence, but prurient interests no doubt also play a role, as does the puzzling and persistent tendency to equate women, sexuality, and sin.

Fortunately, in recent years feminist biblical scholars have made significant contributions to our understanding of John 4 and have begun to rehabilitate the Samaritan woman's portrait. Sandra Schneiders, for example, observes,

> I will interpret the passage as a feminist who does not assume that most women (insofar as they are interesting at all) are whores and that Jesus' paradigmatic relationship with women is centered on saving them from sexual sins, and who does not accept the assumption that Jesus called only males to apostleship or that all missionary activity in the early Church was done by men.[42]

Thus, feminist scholars such as Schneiders, Gail O'Day, Linda McKinnish Bridges, and many others have helped us attend to many overlooked features of the Samaritan woman's portrait, such as her astute theological discourse, her missionary endeavor, and Jesus' vindication of her role against the disapproval of male disciples. Neither a "dimwit" nor insolent, she engages Jesus in extended, serious theological conversation,[43] subsequent to which she appears as the Fourth Gospel's most effective evangelist. Moreover, while commentators continue to debate whether the woman's marital history is to be understood literally or symbolically, feminist scholarship has reminded us that the specific circumstances of the woman's marital history, sparely noted in 4:16–18 yet so often the focus of elaborate imaginative, prurient, and moralistic speculation, are not available to us. All such contributions have advanced interpretive litter control, and we can only hope that litter reduction will increasingly characterize Christian preaching and teaching of John 4.

Feminist work has also directed critical attention to the text's androcentric and patriarchal features. Sandra Schneiders, for example, while recovering many positive features of the text, also calls attention to the underlying sexism of a prominent metaphor in the dialogue of John 4—the prophetic tradition's marital metaphor for the covenant relationship: "Not only is it based on the model of patriarchal marriage to which male domination and female subordination are intrinsic, but it always casts God as the faithful and forgiving husband and Israel as the faithless and adulterous wife, thus consolidating the entrenched tendency to divinize men and demonize women."[44] Others have pressed a hermeneutics of suspicion further, discerning much more problematic androcentric and patriarchal assumptions embedded in the narrative.

Most notably, Adeline Fehribach, in a work entitled *The Women in the Life of the Bridegroom*, investigates how a first-century reader would have heard and understood the text in relation to its cultural and literary milieu—particularly in its use of a variety of patriarchal tendencies in the Hebrew Bible—and in so doing attends to ambiguous elements in the portrayal of the Samaritan woman. Her thesis is that women in the Fourth Gospel function to reveal Jesus as the messianic bridegroom, who is sent to give people the power to become children of God. A bridegroom needs a bride, which is the function of the Samaritan woman in John 4:

> As betrothed and bride of the messianic bridegroom on behalf of the Samaritan people, the Samaritan woman represents the Samaritan people with whom God desires to reestablish familial relations. The Samaritan woman is never named because she is not important in her own right. She is important only to the extent that she is "woman" and "Samaritan," the two aspects of her character that are essential for her to fulfill her role.[45]

In short, she would have been perceived by first-century readers as a symbolic wife, and as such, her role in the narrative is a largely passive one: she is a foil for Jesus' self-revelation, a passive recipient of water, and a passive recipient of the seeds of faith that Jesus sows in her. Indeed, Fehribach maintains that it was common in ancient cultures for a woman (or a nation characterized as female) to be symbolized as a field that a man (or God characterized as a man) plows with seed (e.g., Jer. 2:2–3; 3:1; Hos. 2:2–23). Thus, first-century readers would have equated the Samaritan woman with one of the fields that Jesus had sown, and not as the sower of the seeds of faith in the Samaritan people, as some scholars have suggested.

In other ways, too, her role is diminished. As Fehribach notes,

> there is no real marriage through which she could physically give birth to male children and receive status (cf. Gen 30:20). The offspring of this divine union are to be born "from above" and of the spirit, not of flesh (cf. 3:6–7). Her womb is not needed. Because the Samaritan woman only symbolically fulfills her role as betrothed, bride and "mother," she is betrothed, bride, and mother in word (text) only.[46]

For this reason, the townspeople minimize her witness in 4:42: "It is no longer because of what you said that we believe. . . ." According to Fehribach, these words

> would have communicated to the reader that the woman has no real place of honor in the familial relationship that Jesus establishes between God and the Samaritan people. . . . Once the Samaritan woman has fulfilled her role as a symbol for her people, as betrothed/bride of the messianic bridegroom, and as spiritual mother, her significance is put into patriarchal perspective and she falls out of the story never to be seen or heard from again.[47]

In subsequent chapters, other women characters usurp the role of betrothed/bride of the messianic bridegroom. In sum, "the important point for this gospel is that Jesus is portrayed as the messianic bridegroom. As far as the implied author is concerned, any woman can function as the betrothed/bride of the bridegroom. The woman is not important in and of herself; she is only important to the extent that she represents some community of faith. For such a task, any woman will do."[48]

Not all will be persuaded that this reading does justice to John's distinctive presentation of women characters, or to the full integrity of the Samaritan woman's encounter with Jesus. Sandra Schneiders, for example, writes in response to Fehribach's monograph, "While it is obviously true that the Fourth Evangelist was not, and could not have been, free of cultural assumptions and patterns of thought to which there was no alternative, much less critique, in the first century, denying the originality and power of John's contribution to Christian reflection on women in church and society on these grounds seems to me somewhat anachronistic and overly historicist."[49]

One also wonders how such a reading could serve Christian proclamation. Yet what Fehribach calls for is "intellectual honesty": "I do not maintain that equality for women in the Church and society today is dependent upon proving that such equality existed in the past. . . . [N]either do I believe it to be helpful for feminists to uphold equality where it did not historically exist. Where patriarchy existed in the past, I believe that we should acknowledge it, mourn it, and move beyond it."[50] Christian feminists will no doubt continue to debate these matters, and readings of the Samaritan woman will continue to evolve!

Theology and Practice of Mission

John 4 is doubtlessly a key text for any consideration of what the Fourth Gospel has to teach us about mission, but what one discerns in this regard has been variously assessed. We consider here this matter from three different perspectives: what we learn about the theology and practice of mission from Jesus, from the Samaritan woman, and from a postcolonial reading.

The central mission portrayed in John 4 is clearly that of Jesus, who initiates contact with despised Samaritans in order that they, too, might come to belief and receive power to become children of God (1:12). Though the main route from Judea to Galilee was through Samaria, Jesus could easily have avoided it; most Jews did. But as we noted earlier, "he had to go through Samaria" (4:4), for divine necessity dictated his presence among the Samaritan people. Indeed, the story in John 4 gives expression to Jesus' "thirst" and "hunger" to carry out his Father's mission and will. This thirst, which initiates his engagement with the Samaritan woman ("Give me a drink"; 4:7) is not mentioned again in John 4; apparently his thirst is assuaged by his encounter with her. And his hunger, as the disciples learn, is not one they can satisfy: "I have food to eat that you do not know about. . . . My food is to do the will of him who sent me and to complete this work" (4:32, 34). In the final moments of his life, Jesus speaks again of his need from the cross, giving final expression to his thirst to drink his cup of suffering to the full and thereby fulfill the plan of God set forth in the Scriptures: "After this, when Jesus knew that all was now finished, he said (in order to fulfill the scripture), 'I am thirsty'" (19:28).

African scholar Teresa Okure has highlighted John's decidedly theological (God-centered) and christological (Christ-centered) understanding of mission, which she views as the leitmotif of the whole Gospel. Indeed, her central thesis is that "fundamentally, the Gospel knows of only one mission, that of Jesus; all other missions portrayed in the Gospel are in function of his one saving mission from the Father. Once completed, his mission stands completed such that the disciples do no more than reap its fruit."[51] Jesus thus, she argues, plays a unique and exclusive role in the missionary enterprise; indeed, he remains the primary and abiding evangelizer and teacher of the community.[52] As the disciples, who are pointedly absent when Jesus engages the Samaritan woman, learn in 4:38: "I sent you to reap that for which you did not labor. Others have labored, and you have entered into their labor." In Okure's view, those "others" who have labored are the Father and Jesus (not the Samaritan woman). As disciples engage in their work of harvesting this mission, they remain completely dependent on Jesus, the vine who sustains them and the shepherd of the sheep: "in the Johannine model Jesus is never replaced and he personally continues his mission in history and in the Church itself, working through believers to draw others to himself."[53]

What accounts for this decidedly christocentric vision of mission? Okure suspects that the community to which the Fourth Gospel was first addressed needed to be reminded of Jesus' unique and exclusive role as God's agent of salvation and of their resulting need for total dependence on him: "The missionary emphases in the Gospel suggested that an attitude of boasting, a tendency to behave as if they owned the mission, and pride in a variety of forms must have constituted a special weakness of the Johannine audience."[54] Okure's pointed christological reading of mission in John is an important resource for contemporary Christian reflection, lest we too find ourselves tempted to the hubris of "ownership" attitudes toward mission. Also significant is Okure's insight that missionary activity, in John, embraces both believers and unbelievers: "to the New Testament authors, to John certainly, initial conversion marked the beginning, not the end, of missionary activity, since believers had constantly to be urged to live out their belief practically. Moreover, given the constant threat to faith from an unbelieving majority, the world, believers needed to be constantly sustained in their belief and held personally responsible for it."[55] This insight can help guard against restricted visions of mission.

Finally, Okure helpfully highlights how Jesus models appropriate method in mission. For one thing, he engages in genuine dialogue. Indeed, she argues, the story shows

> to what lengths Jesus went out of his way to meet the situation of the woman, using her immediate concerns (water-fetching, Jacob's well, the issue of worship) as well as his own physical predicament as a thirsty traveler as the starting point. Not only did the conversation develop along lines in which the woman understood Jesus' initial request for a drink, but the woman herself determined throughout the conversation the categories used in communicating the revelation.[56]

(The same can be said of his subsequent exchange with the disciples.) Jesus thus models genuine dialogue and appropriate method with "his humble approach which gives the advantage to the dialogue partner, in his deep respect for the woman, in his deference for her views and that of the disciples, in his gracious acceptance of the invitation of the Samaritans, and in his leading both the woman and the disciples each in her/their own way through a process of discovery."[57]

The story also illustrates, Okure observes, the difficulty of missionary undertaking. This reality is underscored "by the difficulty Jesus experiences in convincing the woman; the disciples, too, stand in need of his reorientation, and it took two days before the Samaritans ventured a personal confession of Jesus (v. 42)."[58] In all of these respects, Okure's reading of John 4 provides important resources for contemporary reflection on mission. But does she do full justice to what we may also learn from the Samaritan woman about the theology and practice of mission?

As we have seen, many commentators, ancient and modern, would give further weight to this second angle of vision, noting that the Samaritan woman's example is also instructive. Does she not embody one of the primary marks of discipleship in John: bearing witness to Jesus? When one finds the Christ, the natural reaction for the true disciple is to share him with others. Thus, like Andrew who enlisted Simon, and Philip who finds Nathanael in John 1, the Samaritan woman is also eager to share the news of her encounter with Jesus. Ironically, she brings not her husband, but a whole Samaritan village to Jesus, and as a result of her testimony, they come to faith in Christ as "Savior of the world." As many commentators have noted, in so doing she proleptically fulfills Jesus' final prayer for his disciples and those who "will believe in me through their word" (John 17:20), for the story concludes by noting that "Many Samaritans from that city believed in him" (translating literally) "because of the word of the woman bearing witness" (John 4:39).

Moreover, we have also had occasion to note the tentative nature of her witness ("Come and see a man who told me everything I have ever done! He cannot be the Messiah, can he?" [4:29]), for this statement too is instructive. Her example reminds us, as noted earlier, that faith that is tentative, full of questions, and not yet mature can bear witness and do so effectively. As Robert Kysar has observed, "John honors the power of a faith which is not yet immature. Witness to such a faith has results far beyond itself. With this narrative he invites Christians to put aside timidity and reluctance and to share their stories of faith, however minimal they may be!"[59] Furthermore, Fred Craddock insightfully highlights ways in which the Samaritan woman, too, is a refreshing model of genuine dialogue:

> Her witness . . . is invitational (come and see), not judgmental; it is within the range permitted by her experience; it is honest with its own uncertainty; it is for everyone who will hear. How refreshing. Her witness avoids triumphalism, hawking someone else's conclusions, packaged answers to unasked questions, thinly veiled ultimatums and threats of hell, and assumptions of certainty on theological matters. She does convey, however, her willingness to let her hearers arrive at their own affirmations about Jesus, and they do: "This is indeed the Savior of the world."[60]

In all of these ways, the Samaritan woman models effective method in mission.

Another important point to note is Jesus' vindication of her role, against the disapproval of male disciples. Sandra Schneiders is persuasive on this aspect of the story:

> The note that the disciples are shocked but do not dare to question what Jesus seeks (*zēteō*) with a woman [4:27] does not in any way further the action of the narrative, which suggests that this one-verse vignette is a deliberate attempt by the Fourth Evangelist to reflect a real tension in the Johannine community over women exercising roles men consider reserved to themselves, namely, theological exploration and evangelization.[61]

What the disciples learn is that mission is shared labor and responsibility that includes both women and men—a fact that may be hard for them to swallow. The Samaritan woman would appear to be presented as a partner in mission.

Finally, Schneiders has proposed that the Samaritan woman is the most likely candidate for the evangelist's textual alter ego and literary self-portrait. Though we will never know with certainty the identity of the evangelist (because, as Schneiders observes, the evangelist does not want us to know and is a good enough writer to keep us from finding out), she marshals compelling evidence for her proposal:

> The Samaritan woman in chapter 4 is certainly the most theologically sophisticated interlocutor of Jesus in the Fourth Gospel and is deliberately contrasted with the theologically obtuse "teacher of Israel," Nicodemus in chapter 3. She knows both Jewish and Samaritan law and theology (e.g., about the role of the patriarchs in Samaritan theology, the appropriate place of worship, and relations between Jews and Samaritans) and requires of Jesus some reconciliation of their differences before she accepts his revelation (cf. 4:9–12, 20–24). She receives the first "*egō eimi*" (I am) revelation of Jesus' identity in the Fourth Gospel (4:26), understands that he is the messianic prophet like Moses "who will tell us all things" (4:25) awaited by the Samaritans and the "messiah" expected by Jews, which together constitute the way that Jesus' identity is presented in the Fourth Gospel by the evangelist. And despite the fact that she obviously correctly identifies Jesus and must, therefore, believe in him since she goes off to bring her fellow townspeople to "come and see," she does not simply tell them who Jesus is but poses the question, "Can this be the Messiah?" (4:29). This, in fact, is exactly what the evangelist does in the Gospel, that is, presents the words and works—that is, the signs—of Jesus and leaves the readers with the challenge to come and see, to decide whether to believe that this is indeed the Messiah, the Son of God, the Savior of the World, so that believing they may have life in his name (cf. 20:30–31).[62]

Famed director Alfred Hitchcock made a fleeting cameo appearance in virtually all of his films, for which audiences were always alert. Schneiders is suggesting that John 4 may be the Fourth Evangelist's Alfred Hitchcock moment! Whatever the case may be, the Samaritan woman has much to teach us about discipleship and the practice of mission.

However, lest we rest too comfortably with positive contributions that John 4 may make to the theology and practice of mission, yet a third angle of vision—a postcolonial reading—raises troubling questions about ways in which the text may subscribe to and promote the ideology of imperialism. As Botswanan scholar Musa W. Dube explains, "Imperialism is . . . about controlling foreign geographical spaces and their inhabitants. By its practice and its goals, imperialism is a relationship of subordination and domination between different nations and lands, which actively suppresses diversity and promotes a few universal standards for the benefit of those in power."[63] Literary texts, she notes (including biblical ones), can propound imperialistic values, authorizing "expansionist tendencies grounded on unequal international/racial relations."[64] Dube maintains that imperial domination is central to the story of the Samaritan woman in John 4: "the story authorizes the Christian disciples/readers/believers to travel, to enter, to educate, and to harvest other foreign lands for the Christian nations in a literary fashion that is openly modelled on imperialist values."[65]

In illustration, she observes, "Imperialism as an ideology of expansion involves superior travelers who represent the superiority of their origin." (There is no doubt that Jesus is presented in John as of divine origin.) Moreover, she observes, "Imperialism expounds an ideology of inferior knowledge and invalid religious faith of those who must be colonized."[66]

> There is a sharp division between those who know, the colonizers, and those who know nothing, the colonized. Thus the Samaritan woman is characterized as an ignorant native (v. 10) and in need of help (v. 10). She is constructed as morally/religiously lacking, that is, she has had five husbands, and the one she has is not her own (vv. 17–18), and she does not know what she worships (v. 22). On the contrary, Jesus, a superior traveller, is knowledgeable (vv. 10, 22); powerful (vv. 14, 25, 42); sees everything about her past (vv. 17–18, 29); knows and offers answers for her society (vv. 21–26); and teaches her and her people (vv. 21–23).[67]

Interestingly, postcolonial critics have demonstrated that one of the strategies of imperializing texts is the use of female gender to validate relationships of subordination and domination.[68] Thus, that a Samaritan woman becomes a first point of contact in John 4 is significant, for "Like the woman who represents them, the foreign land must be entered, won, and domesticated."[69]

An imperialist ideology of expansion also devalues, replaces, and suppresses diversity, using a strategy of massive inclusivity but not equality.

Thus, when Jesus declares the cultural centers of Jerusalem and Gerizim as inadequate and replaces them with spirit and truth, "the transcendence of both Jewish and Samaritan cultural spaces by the realm of Spirit and truth (vv. 23–24), is, in fact, an installation of the superiority of Christianity—which, as we now know, proceeds by discrediting all other religious cultures for its own interests."[70]

Finally, an ideology of imperialism conceals its interests by portraying the colonized themselves as people who require and ask for domination. The Samaritan villagers beg Jesus to enter the village and stay with them, and they themselves proclaim Jesus as "Savior of the world," a title used in the first century to refer to the Roman emperor. As Dube notes, "Surprise, surprise—the Johannine Jesus emerges fully clothed in the emperor's titles. Thus Jesus too lays claim to unlimited access to all geographical spaces and foreigners."[71]

Dube's searing reading exposes the complicity of biblical texts in colonial projects, and she urges readers "to interrogate the biblical ideology of travel, expansion, representations of differences, and their function."[72] Moreover, she insists that "biblical critical practice must be dedicated to an ethical task of promoting decolonization, fostering diversity, and imagining liberating ways of interdependence."[73]

One can hardly reconcile this third perspective with the other two. However, too much rings true for it to be easily dismissed. All three perspectives highlight significant resources, problems, and possibilities for our reflection, despite their incompatibility. As we continue to wrestle with the text's varied contributions to contemporary theology and practice of mission, may diverse perspectives expand our reflection, compelling us back to the well again and again for ever-evolving readings.

Group Study Suggestions

Before beginning your study of John 4, share: What impressions of the Samaritan woman do you bring with you to your present study of her portrait? What comes to mind when you think of her, and why? How do you remember hearing her described?

Do a dramatic reading of John 4:4–42. Assign roles to a narrator, to Jesus, and to the Samaritan woman. Have the rest of the group read collectively the lines of both the disciples and the Samaritan townspeople. Following the reading, share briefly: What most captures your attention as you hear the story? What questions does the story raise for you?

Proceed with any of the questions for discussion/reflection below.

Questions for Discussion or Reflection

What do the historical and literary contextual observations noted at the beginning of this chapter contribute to your reading of the story? Any new insights or surprises?

Are you inclined to take the reference to the woman's five husbands literally or symbolically? Why?

Much has been made of the fact that the woman appeared at the well at noon—at the hottest hour of the day. How have you heard this fact interpreted? What do you make of it? Often when this story is conveyed in preaching or teaching, the hour is said to convey the contempt in which the woman is held by others. She comes to the well at noon, when it is deserted, to avoid any public humiliation. However, (1) isn't "light" a central, positive image throughout the Gospel of John, from beginning to end? (2) Isn't the hour in which she appears one of the many striking contrasts between the woman and Nicodemus? (Nicodemus came to see Jesus by night, under the cover of darkness, whereas the Samaritan woman encounters Jesus at noon, in the fullest light of day.) (3) What of the echoes of the old familiar story: boy meets girl at a well? Do they not also caution us against imputing moral significance to the noon hour? Jesus meets the woman at the well at noon, just like Jacob, who met Rachel at a well at noon, in broad daylight. But do we ever say "O Rachel—what a slut—she was there at noon because no one wanted to have anything to do with her"? Do you run errands at time when places of business are likely to be more or less crowded? Is it possible that the Samaritan woman's workload might have required multiple trips to the well?[74] In sum, is this yet another point at which we are reading a lot of trash into the story?

Gossip, sexual innuendoes, and tragic marital circumstances are often allowed to "define" people completely—clouding our perception of their gifts and achievements and dignity as children of God. Would you agree? Do other examples come to mind, in addition to that of the Samaritan woman?

Water is one of the central images in John. Throughout, there are conversations about water, water pots, rivers, wells, springs, the sea, pools, basins, thirst, and drink.[75] What is the significance of water in human life? What does this suggest about Jesus, who in John 4 uses living water as the symbol for the gift he represents and for the new life or the spirit of which he is the giver and source?

In the first-century world, Jews and Samaritans were divided by centuries of hostility and deep prejudice. Though they shared a common heritage, Samaritans were considered heretics, foreigners, and unclean by Jews, who avoided contact with them (this history is reflected in John 4:9). Who are the "Samaritans" in our world? How might we follow Jesus' example and cross boundaries that separate us from such persons? Should we?

Verse 28 provides a fascinating detail: "the woman left her water jar" as she went back to the city. What do you make of this detail? In your view, what does it convey?

In what ways do you identify with the Samaritan woman?

How can the Samaritan woman's tentative witness inform your own discipleship? Who are the persons in your life who risked sharing their own faith stories, thereby drawing you into relationship with Jesus Christ?

What is your reaction to the depiction of the Samaritan woman in the history of interpretation?

What does your study of John 4 contribute to contemporary reflection on the theology and practice of mission? What resources, problems, and possibilities do you discern?

What new insights have emerged for you from your engagement with this story? What questions remain?

Resources for Further Study

Bridges, Linda McKinnish. "John 4:5–42." *Interpretation* (April 1994): 173–76.

Brown, Raymond. *The Community of the Beloved Disciple: The Life, Loves, and Hates of an Individual Church in New Testament Times.* New York: Paulist, 1979.

Dube, Musa W. "Reading for Decolonization (John 4:1–42)." *Semeia* 75 (1996): 37–59.

Eslinger, Lyle. "The Wooing of the Woman at the Well: Jesus, the Reader and Reader-Response Criticism." *Journal of Literature and Theology* 1 (September 1987): 167–93.

Farmer, Craig S. "Changing Images of the Samaritan Woman in Early Reformed Commentaries on John." *Church History* 65 (September 1996): 365–75.

Fehribach, Adeline. *The Women in the Life of the Bridegroom: A Feminist Historical-Literary Analysis of the Female Characters in the Fourth Gospel.* Collegeville, Minn.: Liturgical, 1998.

Koester, Craig. "'The Savior of the World' (John 4:42)." *Journal of Biblical Literature* 109 (1990): 665–80. See also Koester's *Symbolism in the Fourth Gospel,* 48–51, 167–72. Minneapolis: Fortress, 1995.

Moore, Stephen. *Poststructuralism and the New Testament: Derrida and Foucault at the Foot of the Cross*, 43–64. Minneapolis: Fortress, 1994. Originally published as "Are There Impurities in the Living Water That the Johannine Jesus Dispenses?" *Biblical Interpretation* 1 (1993): 207–27; and reprinted in *A Feminist Companion to John*, edited by Amy-Jill Levine with Marianne Blickenstaff, 1:126–42. Sheffield: Sheffield Academic, 2003.

O'Day, Gail. "The Gospel of John," in *The New Interpreter's Bible*, vol. 9. Nashville: Abingdon, 1995.

———. "John," in *The Women's Bible Commentary*, edited by Carol A. Newsom and Sharon H. Ringe. Louisville, Ky.: Westminster/John Knox, 1992.

———. *The Word Disclosed: John's Story and Narrative Preaching*, 29–52. St. Louis: CBP, 1987. See also *The Word Disclosed: Preaching the Gospel of John*, rev. and expd., 33–61. St. Louis: Chalice, 2002.

Okure, Teresa. *The Johannine Approach to Mission: A Contextual Study of John 4:1–42*. Tübingen: J. C. B. Mohr (Paul Siebeck), 1988.

Schneiders, Sandra. A Case Study: Feminist Interpretation of John 4:1–42. Chap. 8 in *The Revelatory Text: Interpreting the New Testament as Sacred Scripture*, 180–99. San Francisco: HarperSanFrancisco, 1991. Reprinted in *Written That You May Believe*, 126–48 (noted below).

———. "Women in the Fourth Gospel and the Role of Women in the Contemporary Church." *Biblical Theological Bulletin* 12 (1982): 35–45. Reprinted in *Written That You May Believe*, 93–114 (noted below).

———. *Written That You May Believe: Encountering Jesus in the Fourth Gospel*. New York: Crossroad, 1999.

Webster, Jane. "Transcending Alterity: Strange Woman to Samaritan Woman." In *A Feminist Companion to John*, edited by Amy-Jill Levine with Marianne Blickenstaff, 1:126–42. Sheffield: Sheffield Academic, 2003.

Chapter Six

A Woman Accused of Adultery

John 7:53–8:11

Then each of them went home, while Jesus went to the Mount of Olives. Early in the morning he came again to the temple. All the people came to him and he sat down and began to teach them. The scribes and the Pharisees brought a woman who had been caught in adultery; and making her stand before all of them, they said to him, "Teacher, this woman was caught in the very act of commit-ting adultery. Now in the law Moses commanded us to stone such women. Now what do you say?" They said this to test him, so that they might have some charge to bring against him. Jesus bent down and wrote with his finger on the ground. When they kept on questioning him, he straightened up and said to them, "Let any-one among you who is without sin be the first to throw a stone at her." And once again he bent down and wrote on the ground. When they heard it, they went away, one by one, beginning with the elders; and Jesus was left alone with the woman standing before him. Jesus straightened up and said to her, "Woman, where are they? Has no one condemned you?" She said, "No one, sir." And Jesus said, "Neither do I condemn you. Go your way, and from now on do not sin again."

From its earliest history, the church has been ill at ease with matters of sexual impropriety. The text before us is a case in point. Scholars gen-erally agree that the story of the woman accused of adultery was not orig-inally part of the Gospel of John (for this reason, you may find it enclosed in double brackets in your Bible, or omitted altogether). It does not appear in the earliest Greek manuscripts of John; is more "Lukan" than "Johan-nine" in vocabulary, style, and theology; and interrupts the narrative in progress (you can skip from 7:52 to 8:12 without missing a beat). In later Greek manuscripts, the story appears in various locations—after John 7:36, John 7:52, John 21:25; even Luke 21:38. It is a truly homeless story! However, scholars also believe that the story is a truly ancient one based on the earliest oral traditions about Jesus—a story that has all the earmarks of an authentic incident from his life. Why, then, did it become a free-floating story without a secure canonical home? In all likelihood, because it was suppressed. The ease with which Jesus extended mercy to an adulterous woman embarrassed the earliest Christian communities and undermined their own more severe penitential practices.[1] Moreover, many interpreters (ancient and modern) have feared that Christian women would find encouragement in the story to live unchaste lives, to "sin with impunity."[2]

Nevertheless, the power of the story is such that it has been cherished and preserved through the centuries and is worthy of our close attention. Indeed, New Testament scholar Raymond Brown observes that "No apology is needed for this once independent story which has found its way into the Fourth Gospel and some manuscripts of Luke, for in quality and beauty it is worthy of either localization. . . . And the delicate balance between the justice of Jesus in not condoning the sin and his mercy in forgiving the sinner is one of the great gospel lessons."[3]

The unnamed woman, however, is not the only sinner who encounters Jesus in this story, or who hears a promise of new life. Indeed, the fact that the story is traditionally referred to as "the woman caught in adultery" tends to focus our attention solely on the woman and issues of sexual sin and obscures the significant role that others play in this scene. Religious persons and groups who would judge and condemn the one guilty of sexual sin are also addressed by Jesus—in strikingly parallel fashion[4]—and they, too, find their lives graced and transformed by the Word made flesh. Indeed, as Gail O'Day has demonstrated, the story unfolds in two parallel scenes in which Jesus bends down and writes on the ground (vv. 6, 8). Then Jesus stands up to speak to his conversation partners, first to the scribes and Pharisees in verse 7, and then to the woman in verse 10a. Finally, Jesus addresses words about sin to them both, to the scribes and Pharisees in verse 7c, and to the woman in verse 11b.[5] Let us look closely at both dimensions of this story.

Encountering the Text

The story is set in the temple precincts, where Jesus is interrupted as he teaches: "The scribes and the Pharisees brought a woman who had been caught in adultery; and making her stand before all of them, they said to him, 'Teacher, this woman was caught in the very act of committing adultery. Now in the law Moses commanded us to stone such women. Now what do you say?'" (vv. 3–5).

What's wrong with this picture? For one thing, where is the man who has been caught with the woman "in the very act of committing adultery"? Is his absence a reflection, perhaps, of the perennial double standard associated with women's sexuality? Or even an indication that the woman has been entrapped? Other irregularities appear as well. The religious authorities speak of only half the law of Moses, for they advise that it required them "to stone such women," when in fact the law prescribed the death penalty for both the man and woman involved (see Lev. 20:10; Deut. 22:22–24). Nor are witnesses produced who could verify the charge. Clearly neither the law nor the woman is the real focus of concern. In fact, "They said this to test him, so that they might have some charge to bring against him" (John 8:6).[6]

And how does Jesus respond to what is, in effect, a challenge to join a lynch mob in rendering judgment, to take part in a stoning? His first response is nonverbal: "Jesus bent down and wrote with his finger on the ground" (v. 6). We are not told what Jesus writes on the ground, and therefore speculation abounds. Recently, in a Bible study, a woman told me she knew exactly what Jesus was writing: "It takes two!" Others maintain that Jesus simply doodles to contain his anger or to buy time for reflection; still others imagine that he writes out either the sins of the accusers or words of Scripture, perhaps the Ten Commandments, Jeremiah 17:13, or Exodus 23:1b and 7.

> Jeremiah 17:13: "[T]hose who turn away from [me] shall be recorded in the underworld, for they have forsaken the fountain of living water, the LORD."

> Exodus 23:1b, 7: "You shall not join hands with the wicked to act as a malicious witness. . . . Keep far from a false charge, and do not kill the innocent and those in the right, for I will not acquit the guilty."

This is the only place in the New Testament where Jesus is presented as writing, which explains, in part, why scholars have been overly concerned to identify what he writes. But their efforts no doubt also reflect discomfort with the narrative, as Gail O'Day contends: "Attempts to find the interpretive key to John 7:53–8:11 in something outside the given story reveal a dissatisfaction with and distrust of the story as it is written. Such interpretations constitute a refusal to take the text seriously."[7]

Moreover, to fill in the blank is to miss the import of a dramatic action that speaks louder than words. By lowering himself, and thus refusing to stand with them, Jesus offers a visible sign of disengagement. As Patricia Klindienst Joplin observes:

> The gesture functions structurally: Jesus bends down to break the spell of unanimity generated among the crowd of men all of whom stand up, as one, before him. . . . The point is, he physically distinguishes his position from theirs. . . . He not only refuses to stand with the accusers, he lowers himself, uncontaminated by the crowd's desire or the very dirt he draws in, a sign of our common origin and end.[8]

Luise Schottroff contends that his gesture is also an "act of civil courage": "He resists the pressure of the group and of the presumably hysterical atmosphere of the stoning and refuses for himself to condemn and stone the woman."[9]

Nevertheless, his inquisitors persist in their challenge: "they kept on questioning him" (v. 7). He provides a verbal response as well: "he straightened up and said to them, 'Let anyone among you who is without sin be the first to throw a stone at her.' And once again he bent down and wrote on the ground" (vv. 7–8). Jesus' stunning counter challenge quite literally disarms a mob and is noteworthy in two important respects. First, it indicates that Jesus refuses to rank-order sins. He is not overly fascinated with sexual sin; nor does he seem to regard it as greater than other sins in the sight of God. Second, his counter challenge is addressed to individuals rather than to an undifferentiated crowd and directs their gaze inward, where they may discern from their own personal histories whether they are truly in a position to condemn. To their credit, none accepts the invitation to cast the first stone. None exempts himself from self-judgment.[10] And though they had arrived on the scene as an undifferentiated mob, they depart "one by one" (v. 9), as individuals who have been disarmed and redirected by the self-knowledge that emerges in encounter with the Word.

The woman finds herself left behind with Jesus,[11] and for the first time in the story she is personally addressed and summoned to speech: "Jesus straightened up and said to her, 'Woman, where are they? Has no one condemned you?' She said, 'No one, sir.' And Jesus said, 'Neither do I condemn you. Go your way, and from now on do not sin again'" (vv. 10–11). As O'Day observes, Jesus treats both the religious authorities and the woman as "theological equals, each as human beings to whom words about sin can be addressed."[12] Moreover, "Both the scribes and Pharisees and the woman are invited to give up old ways and enter a new way of life."[13] Though at the story's beginning she was a condemned woman, surrounded and threatened by violence, at its end she finds herself a free woman—free to go and to amend her ways. She is not to be imprisoned by her past, for the one before her refuses to let the guilt of sin define us and directs us toward an open future.

Angles of Vision

The text presents a number of lingering interpretive quandaries: the relevance of literary context for interpretation; presuppositions about the scribes and Pharisees, as well as the woman; and christological predicaments. It also bears profound contemporary implications. All of these matters provide vantage points for further reflection.

The Relevance of Literary Context for Interpretation

Chief among the interpretive quandaries the text presents is the relevance of literary context for interpretation. Normally, when engaging a biblical text it is advisable to attend closely to its literary context, the literary setting in which it appears. What precedes and follows the text, for example, and how does that context inform a reading of it? And what does the text itself contribute to the larger narrative of which it is an integral part? In the case of John 7:53–8:11, however, we have proceeded without much attention at all to matters of literary context, because, as we have observed, it is a free-floating story without a secure canonical home. Gail O'Day observes, "John 7:53–8:11 is a story without a time or place, a story to be read on its own terms without sustained reference to its larger literary context."[14]

Most scholars regard John 7:53–8:11 as not originally part of John but as an independent tradition, though also as a truly ancient one based on the earliest oral traditions about Jesus, a story that has all the earmarks of an authentic incident from his life. However, dissenting opinion exists on both "external" and "internal" grounds.

External evidence has to do with the ancient Greek manuscripts themselves. Most scholars agree that John 7:53–8:11 does not appear in the earliest and best Greek manuscripts of John and was unknown to many early church fathers. Bruce Metzger, for example, declares: "The evidence for the non-Johannine origin of the pericope of the adulteress is overwhelming."[15]

Some scholars, however, have challenged this conclusion. Zane Hodges, for example, points out that none of our surviving witnesses originated earlier than 200 C.E., and argues that the text may have been willfully omitted prior to that time because of its controversial nature and potential for offense.[16] Important manuscripts from the third and fourth centuries that omit the text[17] may rely on an earlier parental source that had already suffered textual corruption. Hodges also disagrees with Metzger's assertion that "No Greek Church Father prior to Euthymius Zigabenus (twelfth century) comments on the passage,"[18] noting positive testimonies to the story's presence in John in the writings of both Jerome (ca. 420) and Augustine (ca. 430) which Metzger overlooks.[19] There is no question that the story is massively attested in John in much later Greek manuscripts after the ninth century, and Hodges cautions against dismissing this evidence lightly:

> If after A.D. 200 a relatively conservative tendency set in which made it increasingly difficult to alter significantly the text in hand, the possibility that the disrupted passage was repeatedly and independently inserted into the manuscript tradition by scribes and editors in many scriptoria must rate rather low on the scale of probability. All the more is this true when it is remembered that the content of the pericope was controversial and potentially offensive. Indeed, the insertion of large blocks of noncanonical matter into *the great mass* of Gospel manuscripts is a phenomenon otherwise unknown in the history of their transmission and is in fact unlikely on its face.[20]

Such arguments remind us that textual criticism is an art rather than a science, with no assured results. Hodges hopes they will also persuade us, at the very least, that "the external evidence against the pericope is by no means as 'overwhelming' as it is sometimes made out to be."[21]

Internal evidence involves transcriptional probabilities and intrinsic probabilities. "Transcriptional probabilities" refer to how the interests, concerns, or accidents of scribes may have impacted transmission of John 7:53–8:11. "Intrinsic probabilities" have to do with whether John 7:53–8:11 conforms closely with the language, style, and theology of the Gospel of John.

It is sometimes suggested that this story was deliberately omitted from John because Jesus' closing words "were liable to be understood in a sense too indulgent to adultery," but as Metzger notes, there are no other instances of scribal excision of an extensive passage "because of moral prudence."[22] The fact that the story appears in a variety of locations (after John 7:35; John 7:52; John 21:25; and even Luke 21:38) is of more import; clearly, scribes who considered it too important to be lost were not at all sure where to place it. But the intrinsic considerations in John 7:53–8:11, in particular, are held to be compelling evidence against Johannine authorship. In terms of language, for example, 7:53–8:11 contains a number of words that appear frequently in the Synoptic Gospels (Matthew, Mark, Luke) but nowhere else in John. The text is also at odds with Johannine theology in an important respect. In this story, "sin" is linked to "actions," whereas the Fourth Gospel more typically links sin and "unbelief," with sin as the refusal to recognize Jesus as the revelation of God (see John 3:17–21; 8:24; 16:9). Finally, many observe that John 7:53–8:11 interrupts the flow of John's narrative.

Yet internal considerations, like external probabilities, have evoked dissenting opinion. John Paul Heil has made the most intriguing case for the Johannine character of the narrative on internal grounds,[23] noting significant linguistic links of style and vocabulary between John 7:53–8:11 and the rest of John's Gospel, including teaching in the Temple (8:2; 7:14), the narrator's asides (8:6; 6:6), and the concepts of "to throw a stone" (8:7; 8:59) and "sin no longer" (8:11; 5:14). Heil also argues that the story is not disruptive, but actually contributes to the narrative flow of John 7–8. He observes, for example, that John 7–8 contains many ominous notes concerning attempts to arrest and kill Jesus (see 7:1, 11, 19, 25, 30, 32, 44; 8:20, 37, 40) and that John 8 concludes by noting that the Jews "took up stones to throw at him" (8:59). "They tried," he argues, "to do to Jesus what he had prevented them from doing to the adulteress."[24] The story also coheres with the theme of judging and condemning that runs throughout John 7–8 (see 7:24, 51; 8:11, 15, 24, 26). In sum, Heil maintains that the story of Jesus and the adulteress in John 7:53–8:11 "fits perfectly well within its narrative context" in John's Gospel. "There are explicit linguistic links of vocabulary and style as well as thematic literary links between the story and the Johannine narrative. The story contributes to rather than detracts from the narrative flow in John 7–8."[25]

How important is this technical discussion? Textual criticism is a sophisticated scholarly discipline involving specialized procedures. Why bother? What difference does it make for the interpretation of John

7:53–8:11? Actually, the question of whether or not the story was originally part of the Gospel of John is significant, for it often bears on a decision about how interpretation should proceed. Whether we interpret
John 7:53–8:11 with or without reference to its larger literary context
makes quite a bit of difference,[26] and nowhere is this more evident than
in our construal of the Jewish religious leaders.

Presuppositions about the Scribes and Pharisees

Many of us read Gospel narratives expecting that the Jewish leaders will
be cast in the role of "villains," as they often are, opposing Jesus and seeking his destruction. Indeed, in this story, their motivation in bringing the
case of the adulteress before him is explicitly noted: "They said this to test
him, so that they might have some charge to bring against him" (v. 6).
However, in interpreting the text I have suggested that Jesus addresses
both the adulterous woman and the scribes and Pharisees about the reality of sin, in strikingly parallel fashion, and that both (as O'Day has noted)
are invited to turn from old ways and begin a new way of life.[27] Readers
often presume that the scribes and Pharisees make a shameful exit from
the scene, slinking off with their tails between their legs. However, I
would strongly caution against any such presupposition. I have suggested
that to their credit, none of the religious leaders accepts the invitation to
cast the first stone. When invited by Jesus to direct their gaze inward and
discern from their own personal histories whether they are truly in a position to condemn, none exempts himself from self-judgment. In our reading of the story, both the adulterous woman and the scribes and Pharisees
find their lives graced and transformed by the Word made flesh. Thus we
find in this story good news for those whose lives have been disfigured by
a judgmental spirit, as well as for those whose lives have been disfigured
by more self-evident expressions of sin. Neither is beyond the reach of
God's transforming grace in Jesus Christ. Both are directed toward a new
way of life and an open future.

The interpretive quandary is that such a reading can only be made if
the story is interpreted as a free-floating tradition, without reference to
its larger literary context. I find this to be an appropriate procedure and
defensible interpretation, because I am persuaded by the majority view
that the story was not originally a part of John's Gospel and that it is a
"homeless" story which has found a tentative resting place in John.
However, the dissenting opinions that hold that the story may well have
been a part of John's Gospel from the beginning and integral to its

narrative flow caution us against too much certainty about our position and procedure.

Thus, a question lingers. If one were persuaded that John 7:53–8:11 should be read with sustained reference to its larger literary context, what difference would this make for interpretation and, in particular, for a reading of "the Jews"? Quite a bit! One could hardly maintain that the Jewish religious leaders are set on new paths of righteousness by their encounter with Jesus—that their lives are "graced and transformed by the Word made flesh"—because their character portrayal throughout the Gospel of John is unrelievedly hostile. Nowhere is this portrayal more evident than within the context of chapters 7–8. Serious conflict between Jesus and "the Jews" surfaces for the first time in John's Gospel in chapter 5 over the matter of healing on the sabbath. At the end of that episode, "the Jews" receive their script for the rest of the narrative: "For this reason the Jews were seeking all the more to kill him, because he was not only breaking the sabbath, but was also calling God his own Father, thereby making himself equal to God" (5:18).

From that point on, hostility escalates steadily in John 5–10, reaching a fever pitch in John 7–8, where the real mudslinging begins. The Jews, for example, insinuate that Jesus' birth was illegitimate, and Jesus responds by calling their own father "the devil"—a murderer and a liar whose inclinations they share (see 8:39–47). Throughout John 7–8, Jesus' life is endangered by the hostility of "the Jews" (see 7:1, 11, 19, 25, 30, 32, 44; 8:20, 37, 40, 59). Indeed, chapter 7 begins by noting that Jesus "did not wish to go about in Judea because the Jews were looking for an opportunity to kill him" (7:1); the virulent exchange between Jesus and the Jews on the occasion of the Feast of Booths recorded in John 7–8 climaxes in Jesus' dramatic declaration "Very truly, I tell you, before Abraham was, I am"—to which the Jews respond with violence: "So they picked up stones to throw at him" (8:58–59). (Chapter 8 both begins and ends with an attempted stoning.) The Jews are not successful in their efforts on this occasion, but persist in their attempts to eliminate Jesus, and at the end of John's story Jesus finally faces his cross. Thus, if John 7:53–8:11 is read with sustained reference to its immediate and larger literary context, one can hardly escape the impression that the Jewish religious leaders (and indeed "the Jews" as a whole) are consistently portrayed as villains and bad guys.

Of course, historical realities account for the consistently negative portrayal of "the Jews" in John. The Christian community to which John's Gospel was first addressed had apparently suffered expulsion from the synagogue (9:22, 34; 12:42; 16:2), and the pain of their traumatic dislocation deeply colored John's telling of the story of Jesus' life and ministry and the portrayal of "the Jews." If we interpret John 7:53–8:11 with reference to its literary and historical context, it is hard to discern any redemptive possibilities in its presentation of "the Jews."

However, if we return to our earlier position, that John 7:53–8:11 is a free-floating tradition and interpret it as such without reference to its present context, a third interpretive possibility is available to consider—one that presents an altogether different way of understanding "the Jews" in this scene! What if we were to read the entire story without the evaluative aside from the narrator in 8:6a: "They said this to test him, so that they might have some charge to bring against him"? This aside provides damning commentary that guides the reader to a negative assessment of the scribes' and Pharisees' motivation. Would not the story read quite differently without it?

In an intriguing article, Brad H. Young, a scholar with special interest in first-century Judaism, explores this possibility.[28] He observes, first, that 8:6a is textually suspect, that a number of scholars have questioned whether it was originally included in ancient Greek manuscripts containing the story. Young traces a century-long debate about 8:6a, noting that many preeminent text critics have regarded the verse as a gloss or interpolation, that is, as an extraneous note or comment that later scribes or copyists have incorporated right into the biblical text.[29]

Young raises significant historical questions that further call into question the standard reading of the Pharisees here as a lynch mob, eager to use the death penalty against the adulteress and to entrap Jesus. He notes, "many of these traditional readings of the story of the adulteress seem in conflict with what is known about Pharisaic attitudes and practices both from non-Christian sources such as Josephus or rabbinic literature as well as from a NT source such as Luke-Acts."[30] Josephus, for example, a first-century Jewish historian, tells us that Pharisees sought to avoid using the death penalty and were "naturally lenient in the matter of punishments" (*Ant.* 13.294). Moreover, near the end of the first century, the rabbinic leader Johanan ben Zakkai cancelled the use of the humiliating ritual that involved drinking of bitter waters, which was employed to test a suspected adulteress (see Num. 5:11–31), a decision that "represented a strong trend which was based upon the high view of every human being in the thought of the Pharisees."[31]

New Testament evidence is also pertinent. In Luke 13:31, the Pharisees warn Jesus that Herod Antipas desired to kill him, and in Acts 5:33–39, the great Pharisaic teacher Gamaliel argues strongly for the defense of Peter and John, saving the lives of the apostles. Young concludes, "In all events, the historical sources indicate that the Pharisees were reluctant to use capital punishment."[32]

These thoughts lead Young to an interesting possibility: "Maybe the Pharisees had no intention of accusing Jesus at all. Perhaps they wanted to help the accused woman. When it becomes clear that John 8.6a is an addition to the text, the question of the Pharisees may be viewed from a fresh perspective."[33] Young suggests that the episode in 7:53–8:11 (once 8:6 is removed) actually describes a frequent occurrence in Jewish life: "When a difficult religious issue arises in the life of the community which affects faith and practice, it was an accepted custom to seek a *responsum*."[34] A *responsum* provided a forum in which questions and answers became a foundation of establishing accepted custom and official jurisprudence. Indeed, as Young notes, "Seeking answers to questions concerning biblical interpretation is a crucial part of the Jewish religious experience."[35]

How does this inform a reading of John 7:53–8:11? In Young's view,

> The Pharisees had a problem. The evidence against the woman was irrefutable. The Pharisees, however, did not want to execute her, but the law of Moses taught that an adulteress should be stoned to death. On the one hand they wanted to obey the law, but on the other, they wished to save her life. In an effort to accomplish two aims, they sought to find a loophole in the interpretation of the Torah which would guarantee her release or at least a more lenient and just ruling in her case. When they learned that Jesus, a young teacher with innovative ideas and a popular following, was in the Temple, they believed that he might be of assistance. As a recognized teacher coming from Galilee, he might possess fresh insight. The Pharisees decided to seek a *responsum* from Jesus.[36]

Thus, in John 7:53–8:11 the scribes and Pharisees ask Jesus a valid question relating to the interpretation of the Torah. Jesus writes in the dirt and then gives his answer in an oral form that challenged the listeners with the higher purpose of the Torah. In fact, Young observes that "the whole episode portrays the oral tradition as a living Torah which is adapted and applied in everyday life situations. Such a view is very close to the Pharisees.'"[37] Moreover, he interprets the writing on the ground as a parabolic action, signaling the fact that the oral law did not require written proof. When Jesus utters his wise and famous response, "Let anyone among you who is without sin be the first to throw a stone at her," the Pharisees apparently agree and accept his ruling. "It is doubtful," he observes, "that a lynch mob would be moved by such a remark."[38] In sum, he notes, "His reply is enough for the Pharisees, who are quite liberal in their innovative approaches designed to give application of the law in their daily lives. They wanted to save her and Jesus helped them."[39]

There is, of course, no way of proving the matter, but our understanding of the Pharisees is greatly in need of revision. The caricatures and stereotypes that have so often characterized our descriptions of them have been unduly influenced by early Christian polemics inscribed in the New Testament and do not always authentically reflect the Pharisaic historical reality. Given the sad Christian history of anti-Judaic interpretation, Young's alternative perspective provides a salutary question mark to linger in the corners of our minds.

Presuppositions about the Woman

We also need to examine our presuppositions about the woman in John 7:53–8:11. The Pharisees, Jesus, and most readers of the story all appear to share the assumption that she has in fact committed adultery. She is described, after all, as having been "caught in the very act" (8:4). However, no witnesses are produced to verify this claim, nor a partner in crime, and we are not made privy to her own reflections on what has transpired. The woman is not given a chance to speak in her own defense. We do not hear her voice until the end of the story, when Jesus asks if anyone remains to condemn her (to which she responds briefly, "No one, Lord") and sends her on her way with an admonition not to sin again.

Given the fact that the story provides no further details about the woman's circumstances, an appropriate assumption may well be that the accused has, in fact, committed adultery. Our purpose is not to dispute this claim, but rather to acknowledge the paltry information about her, and also to stretch our imaginations to consider whether there might not be other possibilities residing in the silences of the story and between its lines.

Given the dubious legalities represented in the scene (no trial, no witnesses, no partner in crime, and noninclusive reference to a law that actually includes both women and men in its purview), some interpreters have found cause to wonder if the woman might not have been entrapped.[40] Others detect intertextual echoes of the story of Susanna, an apocryphal addition to the book of Daniel, in which the young, wise Daniel intervenes to save a beautiful woman who has been condemned to death for adultery on the testimony of two false witnesses, lecherous "elders" of the Jews who have been rebuffed in their attempt to seduce her.[41]

In a profoundly unsettling reading of the text, Japanese feminist scholar Hisako Kinukawa stretches our minds further.[42] Kinukawa writes out of a cultural context in which she finds herself acutely aware of androcentrically biased consciousness regarding sexual morality, in which shame and sin for sexual immorality tends to be one-sidedly put on a woman. She also writes out of a social history which includes the story of more than two hundred thousand Asian women forced by the Japanese military government during World War II to serve as "comfort women" to soldiers—shamed and silenced victims of sexual crime. Consequently, Kinukawa urges us to extend our imaginations to the woman's social situation or background.

Jesus does not appear in an altogether positive light in her reading of the story:

> By identifying the scribes and Pharisees as sinners along with the woman, Jesus succeeds in saving her from punishment, but at the same time Jesus fails to let them see how much she has been objectified, ill-treated, and victimized. . . . By not taking any notice of the circumstances particular to the woman, Jesus—as he is presented in the Gospel—fails to reach the core of the issue: the question of why only the woman was dragged out, exposed before the public in shame, and accused of guilt worthy of death. It seems to me that if little attention is paid to this question, we lose the point of the story.[43]

Kinukawa rereads the story by standing on the side of the woman, trying to imagine what social or religious circumstances could have occasioned her tragic predicament:

> If she dared to have a sexual relationship with another man while being fully aware of the death sentence, and if we take into consideration the humiliating circumstances that hedged her in as her husband's property, there are only two possible interpretations for her action. One is that she was forced by a man and fell prey to his lust. While she was upset, he fled away. The other more plausible interpretation is that she took the action on her own initiative. Then her action could be called, in some respects, revolutionary. For a woman under such restrictions, adultery could have been her only form of protest or revolt. She might have spent years of tears enduring her

husband's sexual violence and finally passed the bearable limit. Adultery might have been the only means through which she could offer resistance to her husband. I can find no evidence for this in the text, but I cannot help but interpret the text in this way.[44]

From this perspective, Jesus' words to the woman, "Go your way, and from now on do not sin again," are a harsh sentence, for two reasons:

> First, as mentioned above, this "sinning" was possibly the only way she could manage to escape from her predicament. It might have been that she could gain her "liberation" only through committing the "sin." We cannot see in Jesus' words a perspective that is in solidarity with her desperate situation, nor do we find any help to get her out of her oppressed life. . . . Second, a question remains unanswered if Jesus, by his phrase "Go your way," is telling her to go back to her husband and continue her married life. She has not been liberated by these words if she is again bound by her husband, from whom she may have been trying to be freed.[45]

From Kinukawa's reading, how adultery might have effected "escape" for the woman, given the death sentence it carried, is not altogether clear. Moreover, as she notes, there is no evidence for her reading in the text. But her reflections direct our attention to the woman's circumstances and the importance of social analysis.

Jean K. Kim also attends to the woman's circumstances, pressing socio-historical analysis further and providing a compelling accounting of silences in the story.[46] Reading from a postcolonial perspective, Kim reminds us that Israel was a colonized nation, occupied by Roman military forces. Then, as now in military base areas such as Okinawa, Subic Bay in the Philippines, and South Korea, "sexually oppressed women are caught in a no-win situation between foreign and native men."[47] Moreover, when crimes are committed, occupying forces enjoy immunity from local prosecution. Thus, in Kim's view, the colonizing domination of the Roman Empire may explain why there is no mention of the man caught in adultery:

> From this historical point of view, if the adulterer was a Roman soldier (as we might assume), the Pharisees, scribes, and even Jesus could do nothing to accuse him because he, as a powerful patron, was beyond their control. In a patriarchal society, woman has thus been

simply the ground on which competing views of tradition or national identity are debated. In other words, it was only as a site of (im)purity that she was brought to the debate scene in order that the legitimate authority of the colonized Israel might be contested.[48]

Kim's reading, like Kinukawa's, leaves us pondering the silences in the story and with very disturbing questions.

One final perspective on the woman's circumstance, from Alan Watson, provides additional food for thought.[49] It is also an argument from silence, but one that is plausible. Watson considers the possibility that the woman may have been a remarried divorcée, and in so doing, places the story in a specific historical context: "Jesus had declared that a woman whose husband had divorced her and who remarried committed adultery (Matt. 5:31–32; 19:3–9; Mark 10:2–9)."[50] Thus, by Jesus' own claim, a remarried divorcée would have been an adulteress:

> Moses allowed divorce, Jesus forbade it. The trap of the Pharisees was this: the law of Moses demanded death by stoning for an adulteress; Jesus claimed remarried divorcées were adulteresses though Moses did not, and neither did the Pharisees. Would Jesus follow his argument to its logical conclusion and impose death on a remarried divorcée? The scribes and Pharisees brought the woman to Jesus very precisely to test him.[51]

Jesus had widened the scope of adultery and was thus "caught in a trap he himself had made."[52] How does he manage to escape it? By singling out an individual and transferring the possible crime of the adulteress to the sin of the husband who divorced her: "The one among you who is without sin (*anamartētos*), let him cast the first stone at her." Watson reads the Greek *anamartētos* as singular—"the *one* among you who is without sin"; it does not mean "anyone." Remember that in Jewish law, divorce proceeds from the husband.

The fascinating aspect of Watson's argument is that it does explain many of the troubling features of the story—for example, why the woman has not been formally tried or condemned for her crime; why Jesus accepts that she is guilty; why no evidence or witnesses are produced, nor a partner in crime; and why the woman is brought by the scribes and Pharisees to Jesus. For the Pharisees, there was no adultery, no catching in the act, and no male adulterer.

Why, then, does the text never explicitly state that the woman was a remarried divorcée? Watson speculates that as this story circulated orally among early Christians, "It presented problems that would be blurred in oral repetition. First, Jesus would appear more loving and forgiving if the context were generalized. Second, Jesus would not appear to be faced with a strong moral and legal dilemma of his own making if the context were generalized."[53] Indeed, the complicated textual history of the story may reflect "discomfort with the episode, an unwillingness to ignore it yet a reluctance to accept it."[54] Watson's scenario thus provides, in his view, "a plausible early setting" for the story, and an explanation of "why the pericope was changed yet retained."[55]

Again, we are faced with an argument that cannot be proved one way or the other. But we are also left with significant questions to ponder in our ongoing engagement with this story.

Christological Predicaments

As we have considered alternative perspectives on the story in John 7:53–8:11, several christological predicaments have surfaced. Hisako Kinukawa, for example, has suggested that Jesus fails to take notice of circumstances particular to the accused woman, and may even deliver a harsh sentence if his words "Go . . . and do not sin again" bind her to a husband from whom she needed to be freed. Alan Watson has raised the question of whether Jesus, by widening the scope of adultery to include remarried divorcées, might have found himself caught in a trap of his own making.

Holly J. Toensing has also articulated disconcerting questions, calling attention to dubious features of Jesus' response to the challenge before him. For example, Jesus places the woman's life at risk to avoid being trapped. As Toensing observes, "if one among them has not sinned—or, if someone lies purposely or even inadvertently—the stoning of the woman begins. . . . To initiate the woman's execution does not require all of them to be without sin, only one. The woman's death is set up to be determined by the life of one man."[56]

Moreover, Toensing argues that Jesus does not treat the Jewish leaders and the woman as equals, as O'Day, for example, has alleged. His responses to them differ in significant ways. Toensing explains:

> First, even though Jesus holds both the Jewish leaders and the woman accountable to the prevailing understanding of sin, he does not change the meaning of sin, which in patriarchal societies is defined differently for males and females. For example, married men could

have sex with any woman who was not married or engaged, whereas a married woman could have sex only with her husband. Hence, Jesus is not asking the Jewish leaders to give up or redefine aspects of their social and religious power. Men's definitions of sin are maintained.

Second, though Jesus gives power to both to take responsibility for their actions, this power is given to men in the form of a self-evaluation, while it is given to the woman in the form of commands. The scribes and Pharisees maintain the power to define, assess and guide for themselves. The woman is told what to do, what not to do, and how to interpret what she does! She is firmly reminded that she continues to be held accountable to prevailing definitions of sin, governed by men. . . .

Third and finally, Jesus' statements about sin to both guilty parties are different. When Jesus states, "The one among you without sin be the first to throw a stone," he implies—indeed likely knows—that no one can be without sin. However, when he responds to the woman by stating, "From now on no longer continue to sin," he prohibits sin altogether, as if one can refrain from sinning. This incongruity may suggest that, while the goal of not committing sin is worthy, it is rarely achieved. Or, this may reveal a double standard by which men and women in patriarchal societies are judged: it is not surprising when men do not live up to the standards of behavior set by laws, indeed it may not even be expected of them; but women bear the burden of being expected to keep these standards that are defined by men.[57]

Toensing appreciates the fact that Jesus prevented the woman's death and offered her a new lease on life. However, her point is that "often overlooked, even by feminists, is the kind of life that Jesus bestowed on her: it is a life that can be risked for a greater good, a life that remains confined to male definitions of reality, and in the larger context of John's gospel, a life that can never escape from the male gaze."[58]

Toensing's discussion of John 7:53–8:11 is part and parcel of the maturing of feminist scholarship, which has moved beyond its earliest impulse to establish women in the Bible and/or Jesus as role models in all respects. This approach can limit what texts can teach us. The dissonant notes that her reading has uncovered are important, if unsettling, contributions to christological reflection.

However, in the history of interpretation of John 7:53–8:11, the christological quandary of longest standing has been the question of whether or not Jesus actually forgives the adulterous woman. Why has this been called into question? For one thing, explicit Christian language of forgiveness (such as "Your sins are forgiven") does not appear on Jesus' lips. Moreover, the woman does not express faith, nor is she described as "repenting"—and repentance is held to be prerequisite to forgiveness. Above all, this interpretive quandary arises out of antinomian fears, that is, fears of the view that there is no need for the law of God in the Christian life. Surely Jesus should not be represented as letting an adulterous woman off the hook. In a study of prominent "misreadings" of John 7:53–8:11, Gail O'Day identifies fear and resistance to Jesus' perceived antinomianism as a perennial interpretive trend, citing John Calvin as a representative example. She notes that Calvin, in his commentary on John, reveals what is at stake:

> It is not related that Christ simply absolved the woman, but that he let her go free. And this is not surprising, for He did not wish to undertake anything that did not belong to his office. Those who deduce from this that adultery should not be punished by death must, on the same reasoning, admit that inheritances should not be divided, since Christ refused to arbitrate between two brothers. Indeed every crime will be exempt from the penalties of law if the punishment of adultery is remitted, for the door will then be thrown open to every kind of treachery.

Thus, Calvin resists finding grace in the story: "Yet the Popish theology is that in this passage Christ has brought in the law of grace, by which adulterers may be freed from punishment. . . . Why is this, but that they may pollute with unbridled lust nearly every marriage bed with impunity? This is the result of that diabolical celibacy." Calvin concludes that "although Christ remits men's sins, He does not subvert the social order or abolish legal sentences and punishments."[59] O'Day identifies Calvin as "an excellent example of the power of vested interests to reshape a text. What actually occurs in John 7:53–8:11 is secondary to what Calvin will allow to take place."[60]

Calvin is hardly alone among commentators, however. Other interpreters, ancient and modern, have also demonstrated antinomian concern.[61] In the fourth century, for example, Ambrose (ca. 397) bore witness to the distress the text could evoke: "At the same time also the Gospel which has been covered, could produce extraordinary anxiety in the inexperienced, in which you have noticed an adulteress presented to Christ and also dismissed without condemnation. . . . How indeed could Christ err? It is not right that this should come into our minds."[62]

In our own day, questions continue to be raised about the meaning of Jesus' concluding word to the accused woman. Barnabas Lindars, for example, writes that it "merely shows that he, too, dismisses the case."[63] Others press further, though stop short of admitting forgiveness. R. H. Lightfoot, for example, takes Jesus' final words to be "neither of condemnation nor of forgiveness, but a charge to forsake her former way of life."[64] Leon Morris apparently concurs: "He is calling the woman to amendment of life, the whole of life. It should not be overlooked that he says nothing about forgiveness. The guilty woman had as yet given no sign of repentance or faith. What Jesus does is to show mercy and to call her to righteousness."[65]

Why is it that so many commentators "hedge in their conclusions about this text and cannot allow Jesus' grace toward this woman"? Gail O'Day's compelling conclusion is this: "The possibility that in John 7:53–8:11 Jesus subverts the social status quo, particularly with regard to a woman's sexuality, is too dangerous for these interpreters. The need to depict Jesus as the maintainer of the social order (and it seems, to protect Jesus from himself) results in interpretation that reshapes the text."[66] Indeed, O'Day also persuasively argues that the canonical marginality of John 7:53–8:11 can be explained by the androcentric fears that the text evoked.[67]

A fascinating comment from Augustine (ca. 430) would appear to substantiate this claim: "Certain persons of little faith, or rather enemies of the true faith, fearing, I suppose, lest their wives should be given impunity in sinning, removed from their manuscripts the Lord's act of forgiveness toward the adulteress, as if He who had said 'sin no more' had granted permission to sin."[68] Moreover, as noted at the beginning of this chapter, other scholars, in addition to O'Day, are convinced that the text was suppressed as a result of the anxiety it evoked. The ease with which Jesus extended mercy to an adulterous woman embarrassed the earliest Christian communities and undermined their own more severe penitential practices.[69] Gary Burge, for example, notes that ethical perfection and penance were hallmarks of the patristic era, and that the church fathers were unequivocal in their judgment on adultery. Burge says, "It may even have been the case that adultery (along with homicide and apostasy) was treated in some areas as irremissible. This is at least true for Tertullian (c. 200), Origen (c. 250) and Cyprian. Sexual sins were especially heinous and without forgiveness."[70] Burge concludes, "It is against this background that we find our pericope struggling for recognition. Jesus' refusal to condemn the woman would have stood at odds with the mainstream of Church teaching."[71]

But is not the central christological claim of this text, and indeed the gospel as a whole, that Jesus has authority to forgive our sins? To bring us possibilities of new life?[72] To give our lives back to us with hope and direct us toward an open future? Adultery is a scandal, to be sure. But as continued wrestling with the text and its christological quandaries suggests, perhaps the even greater scandal is grace.[73]

Contemporary Implications

The implications of the story are many for any society that commonly judges sexual behavior more harshly than any other, the church being no exception. In *Adultery and Grace: The Ultimate Scandal*, C. Welton Gaddy argues:

> All too often, institutions of religion, notably local churches—ostensibly dispensaries of grace—compound the problems and intensify the trauma that plague people who have committed adultery. Ministers preach biblical grace, but practice vengeful judgment. Congregations invite "any and all" people to experience God's forgiveness, but turn away from their fellowships individuals guilty of "morals" charges. Undistinguished from other social bodies in this matter, the church tends to treat adultery as a sin so terrible that applying grace to it is unimaginable, thus demonstrating a scandalous misunderstanding of sin, adultery, and grace.[74]

Gaddy maintains that "to withhold grace and forgiveness from people guilty of adultery (or for persons guilty of adultery to withhold grace and forgiveness from themselves) constitutes a wrong equal in its severity to that of adultery."[75] He argues in the spirit of John 8, "Grace refuses to allow an episode of adultery to serve as the ultimate commentary on a person's character. Without in any way condoning the sin of adultery, grace seeks to halt negative reactions to an adulterer and create an opportunity for that person to enjoy a life that changes for the better."[76]

Other implications emerge when we consider the far-reaching effects of judgmentalism in human life. Church historian Roberta Bondi speaks of judgmentalism as one of the fundamental struggles of the Christian life:

Judgmentalism destroys community, it destroys those who do the judging, and, even more seriously . . . , it often destroys (and certainly excludes from community) the one who is judged. On a small scale judgmentalism destroys marriages, families, and churches. On a wider scale it provides the major fuel of racism, sexism, neglect of the poor, and national self-righteousness. Judgmentalism for this reason as a breach of love is as serious as any other sin we might commit against one another.[77]

How are we freed from a judging spirit? The story in John 8 suggests that self-knowledge plays a crucial role. Bondi, informed by the teachings of the early monastic writers, concurs:

Cultivating the virtue of seeing ourselves as sinners is a major source of heal-ing the wounds of judgmentalism in our hearts. . . . [K]nowing that I am a sinner means taking seriously the knowledge that we all do or at least are capable of terrible things. The monastic teachers were quite certain that it is not possible to love other people unless we under-stand at a very deep level that our human failings in the area of love put us all in the same boat.[78]

To know ourselves as sinners, and thereby to heal our judgmental hearts, would appear to be foundational to our ability to extend ourselves in love and compassion to others, and perhaps also to ourselves. We share a com-mon human struggle with sin, and are indeed all in the same boat—equally reliant on God's grace.

Susan Brooks Thistlethwaite, a minister and scholar who has worked with battered women, highlights another contemporary dimension of this ancient story. She observes that it is the biblical text with which many abused women find the most identification: "Women who have suffered physical violence hear that whatever human law or custom may legitimate violence against women, it cannot stand face to face with the revelation of God's affirmation of all humanity. Many abused women would echo the joy of the woman who exclaimed, 'That's right! He [Jesus] broke the law for her!' "[79]

For these and many other reasons we may be grateful that Christians through the ages have treasured and preserved this ancient, homeless story, and that it has found a tentative resting place in John. May it con-tinue to bear witness to the one who redeems lives that have been disfig-ured by a judgmental spirit, as well as lives that have been disfigured by more self-evident expressions of sin. There can scarcely be any better illustration of Paul's affirmation that anyone in Christ is a "new creation: everything old has passed away; see, everything has become new!" (2 Cor. 5:17). Our lives are given back to us with hope, for in the name of Jesus Christ our sins are forgiven.

Group Study Suggestions

Do a dramatic reading of John 7:53–8:11. Assign roles to a narrator, to Jesus, and to the woman. Have the rest of the group read collectively the lines of the scribes and Pharisees. Following the reading, share briefly: What most captures your attention as you hear the story? What questions does the story raise for you?

Proceed with any of the questions for discussion/reflection below.

Questions for Discussion or Reflection

Most scholars believe that the story was not originally part of the Gospel of John. Are you inclined to agree? Why or why not?

As we have noted, one of the non-Johannine features of the story is an understanding of sin that is linked to "actions." The Fourth Gospel more typically links sin and "unbelief." Sin is the refusal to recognize Jesus as the revelation of God (see John 3:17–21; 8:24; 16:9). Still, it can be argued that the story has found an appropriate resting place, for women are featured prominently in John, and the story illustrates key themes of the dialogues in John 7–8. You may wish to examine some of the thematic connections in John 7:19–24, 48–49, 51; John 8:15–16, 46. Does it matter to you that the story was not originally part of the Gospel of John? Why or why not? What difference does it make, in your view?

Do you think the story should be read with or without reference to its literary context?

With whom do you identify in this story, and why? Where have you encountered realities represented in the story in your own experience? How can the story inform your own practice of Christian discipleship and community?

How would you interpret Jesus' enigmatic gesture of writing on the ground?

Have you ever had an experience in which a gesture or posture may have spoken louder than words?

What do you make of the fact that only the woman caught "in the very act of committing adultery" is brought before Jesus?

The crowd disperses "one by one, beginning with the elders" (v. 9). Why do you think the elders were the first to leave?

Why do you think sexual misconduct is commonly judged more harshly than any other sin in both church and society? Should it be?

Do you think judgmentalism is a breach of love as serious as any other sin we might commit against one another? Why or why not?

What is your response to C. Welton Gaddy's observations? To those of Roberta Bondi? To those of Susan Brooks Thistlethwaite? What other contemporary implications of this ancient story come to mind?

As we have noted, the story is not simply one of "a woman caught in adultery," though it has traditionally carried this title. How would you retitle the story to more accurately reflect its dynamics? See if you can come up with a better title.

What are your presuppositions about the scribes and Pharisees as you hear this story?

What are your presuppositions about the accused woman? What do you imagine her circumstances to have been?

Do you think Jesus actually forgives the woman accused of adultery? Why or why not? Is this a christological quandary for you, as it has been for many throughout the history of interpretation?

What new insights have emerged from your consideration or discussion together of this story?

Resources for Further Study

Bondi, Roberta C. *To Pray and to Love: Conversations on Prayer with the Early Church*. Minneapolis: Fortress, 1991.

Gaddy, C. Welton. *Adultery and Grace: The Ultimate Scandal*. Grand Rapids: Eerdmans, 1996.

Heil, John Paul. "The Story of Jesus and the Adulteress (John 7:53–8:11) Reconsidered." *Biblica* 72 (1991): 182–91. See also Daniel Wallace's rebuttal of Heil's argument, "Reconsidering 'The Story of Jesus and the Adulteress Reconsidered.'" *New Testament Studies* 39 (1993): 290–96; and Heil's "Rejoinder." *Eglise et Théologie* 25 (1994): 361–66.

Hodges, Zane. "The Woman Taken in Adultery (John 7:53–8:11): The Text." *Bibliotheca Sacra* 136 (October–December 1979): 318–32.

Joplin, Patricia Klindienst. "Intolerable Language: Jesus and the Woman Taken in Adultery." In *Shadow of Spirit: Postmodernism and Religion*, edited by Philippa Berry and Andrew Wernick, 226–37. New York: Routledge, 1992.

Kim, Jean K. "Adultery or Hybridity? Reading John 7.53–8.11 from a Postcolonial Context." In *John and Postcolonialism: Travel, Space and Power*, edited by Musa W. Dube and Jeffrey L. Staley, 111–28. Sheffield: Sheffield Academic, 2002.

Kinukawa, Hisako. "On John 7:53–8:11: A Well-Cherished but Much-Clouded Story." In *Reading from This Place*, vol. 2, *Social Location and Biblical Interpretation in Global Perspective*, edited by Fernando F. Segovia and Mary Ann Tolbert, 82–96. Minneapolis: Fortress, 1995.

Kreiter, Larry, and Deborah Rooke, eds. *Ciphers in the Sand: Interpretations of the Woman Taken in Adultery (John 7:53–8:11)*. Sheffield: Sheffield Academic, 2000.

O'Day, Gail. "John 7:53–8:11: A Study in Misreading." *Journal of Biblical Literature* 111 (1992): 631–40.

Schottroff, Luise. *Lydia's Impatient Sisters: A Feminist Social History of Early Christianity*, 177–203. Louisville, Ky.: Westminster/John Knox, 1995.

Scott, J. Martin C. "On the Trail of a Good Story: John 7.53–8.11 in the Gospel Tradition." In *Ciphers in the Sand: Interpretations of the Woman Taken in Adultery (John 7.53–8.11)*, edited by Larry J. Kreitzer and Deborah W. Rooke, 53–82. Sheffield: Sheffield Academic, 2000.

Toensing, Holly J. "Divine Intervention or Divine Intrusion? Jesus and the Adulteress in John's Gospel." In *A Feminist Companion to the Gospel of John*, edited by Amy-Jill Levine with Marianne Blickenstaff, 1:159–72. Sheffield: Sheffield Academic, 2003.

Watson, Alan. "Jesus and the Adulteress." *Biblica* 80 (1999): 100–108.

Young, Brad H. "'Save the Adulteress!' Ancient Jewish *Responsa* in the Gospels?" *New Testament Studies* 41 (1995): 59–70.

Notes

Introduction

1. A phrase coined by Mary Jacobus, "Is There a Woman in This Text?" *New Literary History* 14 (1982): 119.
2. Marcion, a formidable second-century heretic, was the first to form a specifically Christian canon of Scripture. He rejected the Old Testament, substituting the letters of the apostle Paul. His canon also included an edited version of the Gospel of Luke, which he considered "Pauline" in its theology. The term "Marcionism" has come to describe interpretations of Christianity that devalue the Old Testament.
3. Rebecca West, *The Young Rebecca*, ed. J. Marcus (London: Macmillan, 1982), 219.
4. Katharine Sakenfeld, "Feminist Perspectives on Bible and Theology: An Introduction to Selected Issues and Literature," *Interpretation* 42 (January 1988): 5–6.
5. Letty M. Russell, *Church in the Round: Feminist Interpretation of the Church* (Louisville, Ky.: Westminster/John Knox, 1993), 22.
6. Elisabeth Schüssler Fiorenza, "Feminist Theology and New Testament Interpretation," *Journal for the Study of the Old Testament* 22 (1982): 42.
7. Ann J. Lane, "Do Women Have a History? Reassessing the Past and Present," in *With Both Eyes Open: Seeing Beyond Gender*, ed. Patricia Altenbernd Johnson and Janet Kalven (New York: Pilgrim, 1988), 59.
8. See Letty Russell's essay, "Authority and the Challenge of Feminist Interpretation," in *Feminist Interpretation of the Bible*, ed. Letty R. Russell (Philadelphia: Westminster, 1985), 138.
9. I am indebted to Rita Nakashima Brock for this important point; see Brock, "Dusting the Bible on the Floor: A Hermeneutics of Wisdom," in *Searching the Scriptures*, vol. 1, *A Feminist Introduction*, ed. Elisabeth Schüssler Fiorenza (New York: Crossroad, 1993), 72.

Chapter 1

1. Sharon Ringe, "A Gentile Woman's Story," in *Feminist Interpretation of the Bible*, ed. Letty Russell (Philadelphia: Westminster, 1985), 67–68.
2. John Meier, "Matthew 15:21–28," *Interpretation* 40 (October 1986): 397–402.

3. Elaine Wainwright, "A Voice from the Margin: Reading Matthew 15:21–28 in an Australian Feminist Key," in *Reading from This Place*, vol. 2, *Social Location and Biblical Interpretation in Global Perspective*, ed. Fernando F. Segovia and Mary Ann Tolbert (Minneapolis: Fortress, 1995), 143.

4. Meier, "Matthew 15:21–28," 397–99.

5. In the memories of the Jewish people, the district of Tyre and Sidon would also denote enemy territory. As Gail O'Day observes, Matthew's joint reference to Tyre and Sidon is significant: "In the prophetic literature of the Old Testament, Tyre and Sidon are more than place names; they were Israel's dangerous and threatening enemies (e.g., Isa 23; Ezek 26–28; Joel 3:4). The significance of the names Tyre and Sidon would not be lost on either Matthew or his readers" (Gail R. O'Day, "Surprised by Faith: Jesus and the Canaanite Woman," *Listening* 24 [1989]: 291. Reprinted in *A Feminist Companion to Matthew*, ed. Amy-Jill Levine with Marianne Blickenstaff [Sheffield: Sheffield Academic, 2001], 114–25). In Matthew, Jesus himself makes an earlier reference to Tyre and Sidon in order to underscore a polemical point, noting that the faith of which these Gentile cities were capable would far exceed that of Galilean Jewish towns: "Woe to you, Chorazin! Woe to you, Bethsaida! For if the deeds of power done in you had been done in Tyre and Sidon, they would have repented long ago in sackcloth and ashes. But I tell you, on the day of judgment it will be more tolerable for Tyre and Sidon than for you" (Matt. 11:21–22).

6. Jack Dean Kingsbury, *Matthew as Story*, 2d ed. (Philadelphia: Fortress, 1988), 149–50.

7. Robert Smith, *Matthew*, Augsburg Commentary on the New Testament (Minneapolis: Augsburg, 1989), 193. Indeed, a connective *kai* links the Canaanite's story to the preceding discussion of Jewish dietary laws.

8. Krister Stendahl made this remark in his spring convocation lecture at Gettysburg Lutheran Seminary in April 1995.

9. Elaine Wainwright, "The Gospel of Matthew," in *Searching the Scriptures*, vol. 2, *A Feminist Commentary*, ed. Elisabeth Schüssler Fiorenza (New York: Crossroad, 1994), 652; Wainwright, "A Voice from the Margin," 145.

10. Gail O'Day, in fact, has argued that Matt. 15:21–28 is a narrative embodiment of a lament psalm. See "Surprised by Faith," 290–301.

11. As Jack Kingsbury has demonstrated, Matthew's use of the title "Son of David" has a polemical edge in that it appears only on the lips of disenfranchised persons who count for nothing in Israel's society (9:27–31; 15:22; 21:15). Ironically, they recognize what Israel does not: that Jesus is Israel's Davidic Messiah. Thus they call attention to the guilt that is Israel's for not receiving Jesus as its Messiah. See Kingsbury, *Matthew*, Proclamation Commentaries, 2d ed., rev. and enl. (Philadelphia: Fortress, 1986), 58–59.

12. Frederick Dale Bruner, *Matthew: A Commentary* (Dallas: Word, 1990), 2:551.

13. Amy-Jill Levine rejects the "common interpretation . . . that the woman's appearance in public apart from her male protector and her addressing a strange man are actions that subvert propriety": "Matthew elsewhere depicts unaccompanied women" (9:20–22; 26:6–13; 27:55–56) "but never suggests they are anomalous" ("Matt. 15:21–28, Canaanite Woman," in *Women in Scripture: A Dictionary of Named and Unnamed Women in the Hebrew Bible, the Apocryphal/Deuterocanonical Books, and the New Testament*, ed. Carol Meyers [Boston: Houghton Mifflin, 2000], 413). However, this comment overlooks the continuous nature of the woman's cries and their decibel

level, which may be said to subvert propriety or decorum (as the disciples themselves suggest in v. 23).

14. Bruner, *Matthew: A Commentary*, 2:551.

15. The verb *apestalēn* is a "divine passive." In other words, God is the obvious agent. The passive voice is employed to avoid using the divine name, in deference to Jewish sensibilities.

16. Judith Gundry-Volf, "Spirit, Mercy, and the Other," *Theology Today* 51 (1994): 516.

17. I am indebted to Jon Sobrino for this insight. Sobrino writes, "Priestly service must be formally apostolic and missionary, in order to bring God to human beings, with the important nuance that it must be a spirituality that goes forth to seek the neediest of human beings. . . . It must be mindful of those most in need of salvation—of the poor, of the lost of the house of Israel, or the pagans of Paul's time, with today's translations of 'poor,' 'lost,' and 'pagans'" (*The Principle of Mercy: Taking the Crucified People from the Cross* [Maryknoll, N.Y.: Orbis, 1994], 123–24).

18. In this connection, Megan McKenna astutely observes:

    There are always needs that are greater than our individual ones. As Christians of one particular area we have needs of spirituality, of identity, of charity, justice, and compassion; yet we are Christians of the universal church as well, and that larger church has needs, massive needs related to health care, food, daily survival, persecution, devastating poverty, lack of education, pollution, declining resources, and lack of access to the dominant cultures that control the possibility of many peoples' future on the earth. Which needs take priority? How do we balance our needs as individuals and as church and as nation with others' needs as individuals and peoples? This story is about one such encounter (*Not Counting Women and Children: Neglected Stories from the Bible* [Maryknoll, N.Y.: Orbis, 1994], 128).

19. John Meier, *The Marginal Jew: Rethinking the Historical Jesus*, vol. 2, *Mentor, Message and Miracles*, The Anchor Bible Reference Library (New York: Doubleday, 1994), 660.

20. Sharon Ringe, "A Gentile Woman's Story, Revisited: Rereading Mark 7:24–31," in *A Feminist Companion to Mark*, ed. Amy-Jill Levine with Marianne Blickenstaff (Sheffield: Sheffield Academic, 2001), 89. As Ringe notes, there is no evidence for this oft-repeated assumption. It is a caricature that, in "addition to being inaccurate," becomes "part of a larger hermeneutic project of Christian anti-Judaism" (99).

21. T. A. Burkill, "The Story of the Syrophoenician Woman," *Novum Testamentum* 9 (1967): 173. Moreover, as Kathleen Corley notes, the "puppies" and "cozy household" interpretation "fails to take into account the conventional use of this diminutive in reference to women" (*Private Women, Public Meals: Social Conflict in the Synoptic Tradition* [Peabody, Mass.: Hendrickson, 1993], 99).

22. Here again, Matthean editorial fingerprints can be noted, for it appears that the evangelist added the word "yes" (*nai*) to the Canaanite's reply: "With the addition of *nai*, the woman's reply becomes an agreement with Jesus' statement, not the clever rebuttal that it seems in Mark" (Corley, *Private Women, Public Meals*, 168). The addition of "yes" to Mark 7:28 is due to assimilation to the parallel text in Matthew.

    Still, not all commentators would see this as simple acceptance of Israel's priority on the woman's part. O'Day, for example, reads her answer to Jesus as "rich in irony" and "a masterful use of overstatement": "she begins by granting the truth of

Jesus' maxim, but goes on to show that its truth is nonetheless irrelevant to her claim and request. Even the outsider deserves minimal attention" ("Surprised by Faith," 297).

Moreover, Elisabeth Schüssler Fiorenza reminds us that the text is uncertain at this point, as a number of manuscripts do not include the word "yes" (*nai*). She judges the "yes" to be a scribal insertion: "A substantial part of the manuscript tradition seeks to portray the woman as an example of humble submissiveness by inserting 'yes' into the text, and thereby downplaying the 'but' of the woman. . . . The word 'yes' (*nai*) is not found anywhere else in the Gospel and is missing from important manuscripts, such as Papyrus 45" (*But She Said: Feminist Practices of Biblical Interpretation* [Boston: Beacon, 1992], 12, 221n.29).

23. Theissen, *The Gospels in Context: Social and Political History in the Synoptic Tradition*, trans. Linda M. Maloney (Minneapolis: Fortress, 1991), 81.

24. I am indebted to Elizabeth Moltmann for this insight: "Jesus Christ—The Humanity of God," *Perspectives: A Journal of Reformed Thought* (September 1989): 9. Schüssler Fiorenza also makes this point: "The gracious goodness of the God of Jesus is abundant enough to satisfy not only the Jews but also the gentiles" (*In Memory of Her: Reconstruction of Christian Origins* [New York: Crossroad, 1983], 138).

25. Interestingly, Matthew speaks explicitly of the "masters' table" (compare Mark: "Sir, even the dogs under the table eat the children's crumbs"; Mark 7:28). The Canaanite woman has addressed Jesus as "Lord" three times (15:22, 25, 27).

26. Gundry-Volf, "Spirit, Mercy, and the Other," 518.

27. Stephenson Humphries-Brooks, "The Canaanite Women in Matthew," in *A Feminist Companion to Matthew*, ed. Amy-Jill Levine with Marianne Blickenstaff (Sheffield: Sheffield Academic, 2001), 143–44.

28. As Moltmann notes, "In her desperation, this woman has painted for Jesus another picture of God, a God of abundance and wealth with something to spare for all" ("Jesus Christ—The Humanity of God," 9).

29. As Joanna Dewey observes, "Matthew has transformed the woman from a model of creative intelligence in Mark to that of a persistent or nagging woman—a model more traditional and perhaps less of a threat to patriarchal norms" ("Jesus' Healings of Women: Conformity and Non-Conformity to Dominant Cultural Values as Clues for Historical Reconstruction," *Society of Biblical Literature 1993 Seminar Papers* 32, ed. Eugene H. Lovering Jr. [Atlanta: Scholars, 1993], 189).

30. Bruner, *Matthew: A Commentary*, 2:555.

31. Wainwright, "The Gospel of Matthew," 653.

32. Dewey, "Jesus' Healings of Women," 189. Italics and insert mine.

33. Gundry-Volf, "Spirit, Mercy, and the Other," 520–21.

34. Stendahl, spring convocation lecture, Gettysburg Lutheran Seminary, April 1995.

35. The verb *iathē* is a divine passive, indicating that Jesus is the channel of God's own healing and saving presence.

36. See Kingsbury, *Matthew*, 96–99, for further detail on these points and on the mixed character of the Matthean community.

37. Thus, non-Israelite women such as Tamar, Rahab, Ruth, and Bathsheba appear in the genealogy of Jesus in chap. 1, and "magi from the East" are the first to worship the newborn King of the Jews in chap. 2. See ibid., 98–99, for further discussion of the Gentile presence in Matthew's community.

38. See Ulrich Luz, *Matthew 1–7: A Commentary* (Minneapolis: Augsburg, 1985), 84.
39. David Hill, *The Gospel of Matthew*, New Century Bible (London: Oliphants, 1972), 254.
40. Smith, *Matthew*, 194.
41. Karl Barth, "The Jewish Problem and the Christian Answer," in *Against the Stream* (London: SCM Press, 1954), 200. See also Clark M. Williamson, *A Guest in the House of Israel: Post-Holocaust Church Theology* (Louisville, Ky.: Westminster/John Knox Press, 1993).
42. David Garland, *Reading Matthew: A Literary and Theological Commentary on the First Gospel* (New York: Crossroad, 1993), 165–66.
43. Theissen, *The Gospels in Context*, 64.
44. Warren Carter, *Matthew and the Margins: A Sociopolitical and Religious Reading* (Maryknoll, N.Y.: Orbis, 2000), 305.
45. Ibid., 326.
46. See, for example, *Sermons of Martin Luther*, ed. John Nicolas Lenker (Grand Rapids: Baker, 1988), 2:148–54.
47. Roy A. Harrisville, "The Woman of Canaan: A Chapter in the History of Exegesis," *Interpretation* 20 (July 1966): 285.
48. F. Gerald Downing, "The Woman from Syrophoenicia, and Her Doggedness: Mark 7:24–31 (Matthew 15:21–28)," in *Women in the Biblical Tradition*, ed. George J. Brooke, Studies in Women and Religion 31 (Lewiston, N.Y.: Edwin Mellen, 1992), 133.
49. Though the Roman centurion (8:5–13) and the Canaanite woman are both Gentiles with faith in Jesus who make similar requests of him, Jesus responds to the centurion immediately and without any hesitation. More than gender considerations may be at work. Musa Dube makes a persuasive case that this is part and parcel of the implied author's accommodating stance toward the Roman Empire and its agents. She finds this stance reflected also in Matthew's discussion of the imperial tribute (22:15–22) and in the presentation of Pilate, Pilate's wife, and Roman soldiers in the trial and death of Jesus (26:57–28:15), where they are compared favorably to the religious leaders (Musa Dube, *Postcolonial Feminist Interpretation of the Bible* [St. Louis: Chalice, 2000], 130–41).
50. Wainwright, "The Gospel of Matthew," 653.
51. Ibid., 670. On the role of public-private gender ideology in Mediterranean society, see also Karen Jo Torjesen, "Reconstruction of Women's Early Christian History," in *Searching the Scriptures*, vol. 1, *A Feminist Introduction*, ed. Elisabeth Schüssler Fiorenza (New York: Crossroad, 1993), 290–310.
52. Wainwright, "The Gospel of Matthew," 670; and "A Voice from the Margin," 145.
53. Wainwright employs the redaction-critical approach of transparent reading, assuming that editorial fingerprints must reflect and address some situation in the Matthean community. However, redaction critics have made diverse and conflicting claims about the Gospel communities based on such evidence, which recommends caution against a quick leap from text to context. I find the cumulative nature of the evidence Wainwright presents compelling, but we are in the realm of speculation.
54. Wainwright, "The Gospel of Matthew," 654.
55. Schüssler Fiorenza, *But She Said*, 97. See also Schüssler Fiorenza, *In Memory of Her*, 138.
56. Schüssler Fiorenza, *But She Said*, 13.

57. Ibid., 103.

58. Ibid., 162.

59. Fernando F. Segovia, *Decolonizing Biblical Studies: A View from the Margins* (Maryknoll, N.Y.: Orbis, 2000), 125.

60. Dube, *Postcolonial Feminist Interpretation of the Bible*, 140. For further discussion of the text's mission ideology see Kwok Pui-Lan, *Discovering the Bible in the Non-Biblical World* (Maryknoll, N.Y.: Orbis, 1995), 71–83; and R. S. Sugirtharajah, "The Syrophoenician Woman," *Expository Times* 98 (1986): 13–15.

61. Dube, *Postcolonial Feminist Interpretation of the Bible*, 147–55.

62. Leticia A. Guardiola-Sáenz, "Borderless Women and Borderless Texts: A Cultural Reading of Matthew 15:21–28," *Semeia* 78 (1997): 79.

63. Ada María Isasi-Díaz, "*La Palabra de Dios en Nosotras*—the Word of God in Us," in *Searching the Scriptures*, vol. 1, *A Feminist Introduction*, ed. Schüssler Fiorenza, 88.

64. Downing, "The Woman from Syrophoenicia and Her Doggedness," 129. Downing's investigation of this bold and outspoken approach leads him to conclude that the woman is characterized as a Cynic: "To allow oneself to be called 'dog,' 'dog of the table,' in the Greco-Roman world of late antiquity is obviously to render oneself liable to be interpreted as a Cynic . . . and Jesus of this story was aware of at least some aspects of Cynicism and at least one Cynic *topos*. He challenges the woman in light of this awareness, she accepts his assessment, and wins the encounter—and her request" (146).

65. O'Day, "Surprised by Faith," 299, 300.

66. Theissen, *The Gospels in Context*, 70.

67. Interestingly, the Jewish-Christian *Pseudo-Clementine Homilies*, dating from the third century C.E., contain a later version of the story. In them, the woman is named "Justa" (Latin for "just") and depicted as an honorable, well-educated, and upper-class woman, who adopted two brothers of Clement of Rome and brought them up "very attentively in all the departments of Greek learning" (*Ps.-Clem. Hom.* 13.7.3). As Theissen notes, "This is certainly a novelistic composition, but it well illustrates what one could expect, in the third century C.E., of a 'Greek woman of Syrophoenician origin'" (*The Gospels in Context*, 69). See also Schüssler Fiorenza, *But She Said*, 100. While many scholars have found Theissen's analysis compelling, not all would agree with his identification of the Syrophoenician/Canaanite as a high-status woman. Warren Carter notes that "The woman comes not from the cities of Tyre and Sidon but from that region, suggesting perhaps her poverty as a rural peasant" (*Matthew and the Margins*, 322).

68. Theissen, *The Gospels in Context*, 79.

69. Ibid.

70. Ibid., 75.

71. Ibid., 79–80.

72. Ringe, "A Gentile Woman's Story, Revisited," 86.

73. Ibid., 91.

74. Ernesto Cardinal, *The Gospel of Solentiname*, trans. Donald D. Walsh (Maryknoll, N.Y.: Orbis Books, 1978), 2:210. Ringe draws attention to this quote in "A Gentile Woman's Story, Revisited," 93.

75. Gundry-Volf, "Spirit, Mercy, and the Other," 508.

76. Moltmann, "Jesus Christ—The Humanity of God," 8–9.

77. Theissen, "Dealing with Religious Prejudices: The Example of the Canaanite Woman (Matthew 15:21–28)," *The Open Door: Variations on Biblical Themes*, trans. John Bowden (Minneapolis: Fortress, 1991), 41.

78. Bruner, *Matthew: A Commentary*, 2:552.

79. Ringe, "A Gentile Woman's Story," 69.

80. Theissen, *The Gospels in Context*, 63–64.

81. Ringe, "A Gentile Woman's Story," 68. See also Joanna Dewey, "Jesus' Healings of Women," 190–91.

82. Ringe, "A Gentile Woman's Story," 69.

83. John Meier, *A Marginal Jew: Rethinking the Historical Jesus*, vol. 1, *The Roots of the Problem and the Person*, The Anchor Bible Reference Library (New York: Doubleday, 1991), 168.

84. Ibid., 1:170.

85. Theissen, "Dealing with Religious Prejudices," 46. See also Daniel Patte, "The Canaanite Woman and Jesus: Surprising Models of Discipleship (Matt. 15:21–28)," in *Transformative Encounters: Jesus and Women Re-viewed*, ed. Ingrid Rosa Kitzberger (Leiden: Brill, 2000), 33–53. Patte finds Jesus to be an appropriate model for discipleship: "For many of us it is very easy to identify ourselves with Jesus in this passage. His insensitivity, that might be shocking from a high-christological perspective, makes him very human—one of us. . . . We European-American males—and many others with us!—can readily recognize that, more often than we care to admit, we similarly ignore desperate cries for help, especially if they come from people who are different from us, be it in terms of class, race, culture, religion, and/or gender." In his view, "imitating Jesus as disciples means, a) recognizing and affirming as persons of great faith those who, like the Canaanite woman, obstinately importune us by challenging our domesticated understandings of discipleship, and b) allowing them to re-define our vocation, so that we might recognize that all of us struggle to feed our respective children with the same bread (15:27), or, in other words, that all of us 'struggle for the kingdom and God's justice'" (35).

86. Ringe, "A Gentile Woman's Story," 71. A contextual and intertextual observation further supports the view that the woman changed Jesus' mind. As Amy-Jill Levine notes, there are points of commonality between the stories of Rahab and Tamar (both of whom appear in Matthew's genealogy) and the Canaanite woman in Matt. 15: "All three Canaanite women overcome hesitancy or lack of initiative in Hebrew/Israelite/Jewish men; all three acknowledge, whether implicitly or explicitly, Israel's priority in salvation history; all three achieve their goals through clever speech and action" (Levine, "Matt 15:21–28, Canaanite Woman," 412).

87. O'Day, "Surprised by Faith," 294, 297. Likewise, P. Pokorny maintains that "Dialogue and even controversy with God has a good tradition in the Bible beginning with Abraham (Gen 18) to the prophets (e.g. Jer 12) and later writings like Sirach (35.17ff.). In Luke 18.1–8 we have explicit instruction on how to persuade God through prayer. It is expressed in a parable, and it is again a woman who eventually persuades a key person to help her. . . . For understanding the origin of our pericope this is the most important spiritual tradition—a phenomenon typical for Hebrew and Christian experience, a symptom of an encounter with the living God who communicates with humans as a person" ("From a Puppy to the Child: Some Problems of

Contemporary Biblical Exegesis Demonstrated from Mark 7.24–30/Matt 15.21–8," *New Testament Studies* 41 [1995]: 328).

88. O'Day, "Surprised by Faith," 298.
89. Ibid., 299–300.
90. Megan McKenna, *Not Counting Women and Children*, 133.
91. Bruner, *Matthew: A Commentary*, 2:556.
92. Theissen, "Dealing with Religious Prejudices," 45.

Chapter 2

1. Although the stories are intertwined in all three Synoptic Gospels (Matt. 9:18–26; Mark 5:21–43; Luke 8:40–56), Mark presents the oldest, longest, and most detailed version. The word "synoptic" means "to view together," to have the same point of view. The first three Gospels (Matthew, Mark, and Luke) are referred to as "Synoptic Gospels" because their similarities are so pronounced that they appear to be interrelated. Most scholars believe that Mark was the first Gospel to be written and that it served as a source for the evangelists Matthew and Luke. Mark's graphic 374-word account of the story of Jairus's daughter and the hemorrhaging woman is streamlined by both Matthew and Luke. Matthew uses 138 words, and Luke 280, to narrate the same events. However, Matthew and Luke follow Mark in insisting that the two stories be heard together. We do not know whether it was Mark or an earlier tradition that linked these miracles. Whatever the case may be, the sandwiching of episodes occurs throughout Mark's story and appears to have been among the evangelist's favorite patterns in storytelling (cf. 2:1–12; 3:19–35; 6:7–30; 11:12–25; 14:1–11; 14:53–72).

2. Susan Lochrie Graham makes this suggestion in "Silent Voices: Women in the Gospel of Mark," *Semeia* 54 (1991): 151.

3. Mary Ann Tolbert makes this suggestion in *Sowing the Gospel: Mark's World in Literary-Historical Perspective* (Minneapolis: Fortress, 1989), 168n.58.

4. Richard A. Horsley, *Jesus and Empire: The Kingdom of God and the New World Disorder* (Minneapolis: Fortress, 2003), 109. See also Horsley's *Hearing the Whole Story: The Politics of Plot in Mark's Gospel* (Louisville, Ky.: Westminster/John Knox, 2001), 208–12. As Horsley notes, the story follows directly on the heels of a symbolic exorcism and destruction of the alien force named "Legion" (occupying Roman troops).

5. Ched Myers, *Binding the Strong Man: A Political Reading of Mark's Story of Jesus* (Maryknoll, N.Y.: Orbis, 1988), 202. In Myers's view, the number twelve symbolizes the twelve tribes of Israel, and "these 'daughters' represent the privileged and the impoverished respectively" within the family of Israel (Ched Myers, "Mark's Gospel: Invitation to Discipleship," in *The New Testament: Introducing the Way of Discipleship*, ed. Wes Howard-Brook and Sharon H. Ringe [Maryknoll, N.Y.: Orbis, 2002], 59). Richard Horsley argues, however, that the two women are not opposites but similar in social status, noting that an *archisynagōgos* was not a Jewish "ruler" but a leader of a local Galilean village assembly, "a community leader, but not wealthy or powerful. The twelve-year-old's father is thus not a representative of the elite" (*Hearing the Whole Story*, 211). It is worth noting, however, that a large group of mourners and musicians gather at Jairus's house for a funeral. These details may provide a glimpse of Jairus's economic status, as Marie-Eloise Rosenblatt suggests ("Gender, Ethnicity, and Legal Considerations in the Haemorrhaging Woman's Story Mark 5:25–34," in *Transformative Encounters: Jesus and Women Re-viewed*, ed. Ingrid Rosa Kitzberger [Leiden: Brill, 2000], 141).

6. Gerald West, "Constructing Critical and Contextual Readings with Ordinary Readers," *Journal of Theology for Southern Africa* 92 (Spring 1995): 61.

7. Francis J. Moloney, *The Gospel of Mark: A Commentary* (Peabody, Mass.: Hendrickson, 2002), 98.

8. Tolbert, *Sowing the Gospel*, 170.

9. John Meier, *A Marginal Jew: Rethinking the Historical Jesus*, vol. 2, *Mentor, Message, and Miracles* (New York: Doubleday, 1994), 784–85.

10. Joanna Dewey, "Jesus' Healings of Women: Conformity and Non-Conformity to Dominant Cultural Values as Clues for Historical Reconstruction," *Society of Biblical Literature 1993 Seminar Papers* 32, ed. Eugene H. Lovering Jr. (Atlanta: Scholars, 1993), 186–87.

11. John Meier notes that "No other miracle story in the Gospels centers on the delicate question of a gynecological problem" (*A Marginal Jew*, 2:709)! Perhaps this "delicacy" accounts for the discomfort and imprecision many (male) commentators evince in discussions of the woman's medical difficulties. While the story is traditionally referred to as "the woman with the hemorrhage," this characterization probably overspecifies the diagnosis. As Mary Rose D'Angelo notes, ancient physicians made a distinction between hemorrhage and various female "fluxes" or discharges, what we call irregular bleeding ("Gender and Power in the Gospel of Mark: The Daughter of Jairus and the Woman with the Flow of Blood," in *Miracles in Jewish and Christian Antiquity*, Notre Dame Studies in Theology 3 [Notre Dame: University of Notre Dame Press, 1999], 93). Thus, she prefers "flow of blood" as a more accurate translation of the ambiguous diagnosis. John R. Donahue and Daniel J. Harrington also note that the traditional title is not entirely accurate: "continual hemorrhaging over twelve years would have caused death" (*The Gospel of Mark*, Sacra Pagina [Collegeville, Minn.: Liturgical, 2002], 174).

See D'Angelo for a discussion of the two miracles in Mark 5:21–43 in the context of ancient medicine, which evinced concern with the appropriate opening and closing of the womb. She speculates that for an ancient audience, there may have been an inherent connection or symmetry between the two stories: "The two stories belong together because they record healings/wonders that offset two opposing dangers to the female body. The woman with a flow of blood for twelve years suffers from a womb that is inappropriately open. The twelve-year-old girl may well represent the young girl who dies because her womb is closed; at twelve, she is just at the age for marriage in Roman law" ("Gender and Power in the Gospel of Mark," 95).

12. Myers, *Binding the Strong Man*, 201. Wendy Cotter finds the lengthy and detailed description of the woman's problem "almost defensive, an excuse for unfitting behavior," for she violates the modesty expected of the Greco-Roman woman by deliberately touching a strange man in the streets ("Mark's Hero of the Twelfth-Year Miracles: The Healing of the Woman with the Hemorrhage and the Raising of Jairus's Daughter [Mark 5:21–43]," in *A Feminist Companion to Mark*, ed. Amy-Jill Levine with Marianne Blickenstaff [Sheffield: Sheffield Academic, 2001], 57–59).

13. Mary Ann Tolbert, "Mark," in *The Women's Bible Commentary*, ed. Carol A. Newsom and Sharon H. Ringe (Louisville, Ky.: Westminster/John Knox, 1992), 268.

14. Karen A. Barta, "'She Spent All She Had . . . But Only Grew Worse': Paying the Price of Paternalism," in *Where Can We Find Her? Searching for Women's Identity in the New Church*, ed. Marie-Eloise Rosenblatt (New York: Paulist, 1991), 31.

15. Tolbert, "Mark," 268.

16. Elizabeth Struthers Malbon, "Fallible Followers: Women and Men in the Gospel of Mark," *Semeia* 28 (1983): 29–48.

17. Donald Juel, *Mark*, Augsburg Commentary on the New Testament (Minneapolis: Augsburg, 1990), 84.

18. James L. Bailey and Lyle D. Vander Broek, *Literary Forms in the New Testament: A Handbook* (Louisville, Ky.: Westminster/John Knox, 1992), 142.

19. Cotter, "Mark's Hero of the Twelfth-Year Miracles," 59–60.

20. An extreme example of this view is found in Helmut Thielicke's sermon on the text, which describes the woman's "crazy, mixed-up attempt" to come in contact with Jesus:

> To put it mildly, this woman is operating under a terrific misunderstanding. . . . Jesus can only come to a person and help him when that individual achieves personal fellowship with him. This woman, however, doesn't want a personal relationship; she is intent on remaining an anonymous atom in the crowd. For that reason she does not step up to him in face-to-face encounter; she moves in on him from behind. She is not interested in his face or in his message. She only wants the magic contact with his robe that will shower her with sparks of healing power. . . . She believes that a single touch with her finger will complete the circuit of magical radiation. In other words, this woman moves within the tenacious thought-patterns of heathenism. She is caught in the thought-patterns of heathendom. . . . It is actually grotesque that, in this woman's eye, Jesus of Nazareth is some sort of enchanted figure from the world of witchcraft. No misunderstanding could be stranger or further from the truth. Even a not-too-bright confirmand could tell her that much" (*How to Believe Again* [Philadelphia: Fortress, 1970], 53–54).

Ben Witherington also assumes that "the woman had a magic-tainted belief about Jesus," and that Jesus questions her "to elevate the woman's faith" (*The Gospel of Mark: A Socio-Rhetorical Commentary* [Grand Rapids: Eerdmans, 2001], 187). See also Ben Witherington, *Women in the Ministry of Jesus: A Study of Jesus' Attitudes to Women and Their Roles as Reflected in His Earthly Life* (Cambridge: Cambridge University Press, 1984), 73.

21. Tolbert, "Mark," 268.

22. Mitzi Minor, "Old Stories through New Eyes: Insights Gained from a Feminist Reading of Mark 5:25–34," *Memphis Theological Seminary Journal* 30 (Spring 1992): 9.

23. Ibid., 8.

24. Ibid., 10.

25. Meier, *A Marginal Jew*, 2:786.

26. Ibid., 2:787.

27. Cotter, "Mark's Hero of the Twelfth-Year Miracles," 73, 75.

28. Lamar Williamson, *Mark*, Interpretation (Atlanta: John Knox, 1983), 109. See Dan. 12:2; 1 Cor. 15:6; 1 Thess. 5:10.

29. I am indebted to Gerald West for this observation ("Constructing Critical and Contextual Readings with Ordinary Readers," 62).

30. Morna Hooker, *The Gospel according to St. Mark*, Black's New Testament Commentary (London: A. & C. Black, 1991), 151.

31. Bruce J. Malina and Richard Rohrbaugh make this point in *Social-Science Commentary on the Synoptic Gospels* (Minneapolis: Fortress, 1992), 210.
32. Mary Rose D'Angelo, "Gender and Power in the Gospel of Mark: The Daughter of Jairus and the Woman with the Flow of Blood," in *Miracles in Jewish and Christian Antiquity*, ed. John C. Cavadini, Notre Dame Studies in Theology 3 (Notre Dame: University of Notre Dame Press, 1999), 85.
33. David Rhoads, "Social Criticism: Crossing Boundaries," in *Mark and Method: New Approaches in Biblical Studies*, ed. Janice Capel Anderson and Stephen D. Moore (Minneapolis: Fortress, 1992), 147.
34. Ibid.
35. Ibid., 144.
36. Ibid., 154.
37. Ibid., 154–55.
38. Dewey, "Jesus' Healings of Women," 187–88.
39. Ibid., 188.
40. See Marcus Borg, *Meeting Jesus Again for the First Time: The Historical Jesus and the Heart of Contemporary Faith* (San Francisco: HarperSanFrancisco, 1994), 58. For an important critique of Borg's treatment of purity issues, see Paula Fredriksen, "Did Jesus Oppose the Purity Laws?" *Bible Review* 11 (June 1995): 20–25, 42–45.

    Jesus' negation of purity regulations also figures prominently in interpretations of the text set forth by Marla J. Selvidge and Hisako Kinukawa. Selvidge argues that "Mark 5:25–34 may stand preserved because it remembers an early Christian community's break with the Jewish purity system, which restricted and excluded women from cult and society" ("Mark 5:25–34 and Leviticus 15:19–20: A Reaction to Restrictive Purity Regulations," *Journal of Biblical Literature* 103 [1984]: 619–23). See also Selvidge, *Woman, Cult, and Miracle Recital: A Redactional Critical Investigation on Mark 5:24–34* (Lewisburg, Pa.: Bucknell University Press, 1990). Kinukawa maintains that "Even though [Jesus] does not attack the purity laws directly, he negates them by ignoring them. He identifies himself with the polluted. Thus, her liberation is completed" ("The Story of the Hemorrhaging Woman [Mark 5:25–34] Read from a Japanese Feminist Context," *Biblical Interpretation: A Journal of Contemporary Approaches* 2 [1994]: 292). Moreover, Kinukawa suggests that the text is relevant to the situation of Japanese women who for centuries have endured discrimination engendered by purity codes: "In our society also, just as in first-century Palestine, religious purity codes have contributed to establishing cultural identity and to supporting the power-structure and various kinds of discrimination against women. Women have been 'labeled' polluted. Even though for the last 50 years, these teachings discriminating against women have not been enforced, institutionally or legally, the prejudice against women has never disappeared and has been reflected in long-established social conventions in our daily life. Thus, women's experiences in our country have been very close to those of the hemorrhaging woman. Women have been alienated as unclean and culturally despised and have endured the status of non-persons for centuries. I identify myself with her in this sense" (287). See also Kinukawa, *Women and Jesus in Mark: A Japanese Feminist Perspective* (Maryknoll, N.Y.: Orbis, 1994), 29–50. As we will have occasion to note, these interpretations are problematic. Both Selvidge and Kinukawa present harshly anti-Judaic readings.
41. I wish to thank Amy-Jill Levine for bringing this important point to my attention.

See Levine's clear articulation of this concern in "Discharging Responsibility: Matthean Jesus, Biblical Law, and Hemorrhaging Woman," in *Treasures New and Old: Recent Contributions to Matthean Studies*, ed. David R. Bauer and Mark Allan Powell (Atlanta: Scholars, 1996), 379–97. Reprinted in *A Feminist Companion to Matthew*, ed. Amy-Jill Levine with Marianne Blickenstaff (Sheffield: Sheffield Academic, 2001), 70–87.

42. "Discharging Responsibility," in *Treasures New and Old*, 381.

43. Fredriksen, "Did Jesus Oppose the Purity Laws?" 23.

44. See Jacob Milgrom, "Sin-Offering or Purification Offering?" in *Studies in Cultic Theology and Terminology*, Studies in Judaism in Late Antiquity 36 (Leiden: Brill, 1983), 67–69. See also Milgrom, *Leviticus 1–16*, The Anchor Bible (New York: Doubleday, 1991), 253–54; and E. P. Sanders, *Judaism: Practice and Belief 63 B.C.E.–66 C.E.* (Philadelphia: Trinity, 1992), 108ff.

45. Fredriksen, "Did Jesus Oppose the Purity Laws?" 23.

46. Ibid.

47. Shaye J. D. Cohen, "Purity and Piety: The Separation of Menstruants from the Sancta," in *Daughters of the King: Women and the Synagogue*, ed. Susan Grossman and Rivka Haut (Philadelphia: The Jewish Publication Society, 1992), 106 (italics mine).

48. Shaye J. D. Cohen, "Menstruants and the Sacred in Judaism and Christianity," in *Women's History and Ancient History*, ed. Sarah B. Pomeroy (Chapel Hill: University of North Carolina Press, 1991), 279.

49. Wegner, "Leviticus," in *The Women's Bible Commentary*, ed. Carol A. Newsom and Sharon H. Ringe (Louisville, Ky.: Westminster/John Knox, 1992), 40.

50. Levine, "Discharging Responsibility," 387. The quotation she references is from Jacob Milgrom's commentary, *Leviticus 1–16*, The Anchor Bible (New York: Doubleday, 1991), 936. Milgrom, a prominent Leviticus scholar, provides further commentary on the legislation in Lev. 15:

> The implicit assumption of the pericope on the menstruant is that she lives at home, communicating with her family and performing her household chores. How is this possible, considering the severity of her impurity: . . . she can contaminate an object she does not even touch if her bed or seat connect them (v. 23)! The answer, the ingenious answer of the legislators, was to restrict her impurity to that which was underneath her, in effect, whatever might receive a drop of menstrual blood. Of course, she herself was rendered impure and, in turn, could render persons and objects impure. Thus anyone touching her is contaminated (v. 19b). But *what if she touches someone? The text is silent. . . . The conclusion is inescapable: the menstruant may touch.* As long as she is scrupulous about rinsing her hands, she may clean the house, cook and serve the food, and perform whatever other chores she desires. All she needs is a separate bed, a separate chair, and the discretion to stay out of her family's reach (952–53, italics mine).

These comments, relating to the menstruant, are also pertinent to the woman with an irregular flow of blood, for the legislation indicates that women with abnormal discharges were treated the same as menstruants, except that extension of the impurity beyond seven days required sacrificial expiation (Lev. 15:28–30).

51. Charlotte Fonrobert, "The Woman with a Blood-Flow (Mark 5.24–34) Revisited: Menstrual Laws and Jewish Culture in Christian Feminist Hermeneutics," in *Early*

Christian Interpretation of the Scriptures of Israel: Investigations and Proposals, ed. Craig A. Evans and James A. Sanders, Journal for the Study of the New Testament Supplement Series 148 (Sheffield: Sheffield Academic, 1997), 130.

52. Levine, "Discharging Responsibility," 386.
53. Cohen, "Menstruants and the Sacred in Judaism and Christianity," 279. Interestingly, in this fascinating article Cohen provides evidence that "Christianity excluded menstruants from the church long before Judaism excluded them from the synagogue. The earliest attested exclusion of women from the sancta in Christianity is from the mid-third century; in post-70 Judaism it is from the sixth or seventh" (287). See Cohen, 288–90, for the three oldest references to the separation of Christian menstruants in Hippolytus (Rome), Dionysius of Alexandria, and the Didascalia (Syria). See also Charlotte Fonrobert on this point ("The Woman with a Blood-Flow").
54. Amy-Jill Levine, "Mark 5:25–34, Woman with a Twelve-Year Hemorrhage," in *Women in Scripture: A Dictionary of Named and Unnamed Women in the Hebrew Bible, the Apocryphal/Deuterocanonical Books, and the New Testament*, ed. Carol Myers (Boston: Houghton Mifflin, 2000), 424.
55. Levine, "Discharging Responsibility," 386.
56. Charlotte Fonrobert, however, astutely observes that this may not be the case. The identity of the woman with the blood-flow is not specified ("The Woman with a Blood-Flow," 129). If she is a Gentile, Jewish purity regulations cannot be said to bear upon her. See also Marie-Eloise Rosenblatt, who notes that the text is silent on the question of the woman's ethnicity and thus permits the reader to consider her a Gentile, which has important theological implications in Rosenblatt's reading: "the compassion of Jesus in this instance transcends ethnic, linguistic, geographical, economic and religious boundaries" ("Gender, Ethnicity, and Legal Considerations in the Haemorrhaging Woman's Story Mark 5:25–34," in *Transformative Encounters: Jesus and Women Re-viewed*, ed. Ingrid Rosa Kitzberger [Leider: Brill, 2000], 160). Moreover, "If the haemorrhaging woman was understood as a gentile, she represented the majority of Mark's hearers. Her alliance with a young Jewish girl, Jairus' daughter, represented a sisterhood among women, no matter what their ethnicity. Their stories were intertwined because they represented the hope of a united community. As a gentile woman healed and a Jewish girl awakened, they witnessed to a healing greater than the healing of any physical ailment: the overcoming of ancient hatreds between ethnic groups, and discrimination based on racial heritage" (161).
57. This point is underscored by Levine, Graham, Selvidge, and Kinukawa, for example.
58. Kinukawa, *Women and Jesus in Mark*, 34.
59. Graham, "Silent Voices," 149. The quotation within Graham's quotation is from Marla Selvidge, "'And Those Who Followed Feared' (Mark 10:32)," *Catholic Biblical Quarterly* 45 (1983): 396. It must be admitted that this observation entails "psychologizing" of the text.
60. Levine, "Discharging Responsibility," 380.
61. In 5:28, the woman speaks to herself.
62. Graham, "Silent Voices," 149–50.
63. Ibid., 150.
64. Ibid.
65. Ibid., 156.

66. This verb is found only four times in Mark's Gospel, to describe the ministries of angels (1:13), of Simon's mother-in-law (1:31), of Galilean women who follow Jesus to the cross (15:41), and of Jesus himself (10:45), but never those of any other persons.

67. Graham, "Silent Voices," 153.

68. Ibid., 155. Graham's article employs the methodology of "deconstruction": "By listening to the silence, giving it a voice, bringing it in from the margin to the center, we reverse the opposition and allow it to stand, on its head" (155).

69. Barta, "She Spent All She Had," 32.

70. Ibid., 31.

71. Ibid.

72. Ibid., 31–32.

73. Dewey, "The Gospel of Mark," in *Searching the Scriptures*, vol. 2, *A Feminist Commentary*, ed. Elisabeth Schüssler Fiorenza (New York: Crossroad, 1994), 481–82.

74. Dewey, "Jesus' Healings of Women," 190.

75. Antoinette Clark Wire, "The Structure of the Gospel Miracle Stories and Their Tellers," *Semeia* (1978): 83–113. Joanna Dewey references this important article, noting its implications for a reading of Jesus' healings of women as countercultural narratives (Dewey, "Jesus' Healings of Women," 182–83).

76. Wire, "The Structure of the Gospel Miracle Stories and Their Tellers," 100.

77. Ibid., 106.

78. Ibid., 108.

79. Dewey, "Jesus' Healings of Women," 183.

80. D'Angelo, "Gender and Power in the Gospel of Mark," 101.

81. Ibid. On the relational nature of Jesus' divine healing power in Mark, see also Rita Nakashima Brock's important discussion in *Journeys by Heart: A Christology of Erotic Power* (New York: Crossroad, 1988), 81–87.

82. I wish to thank Lamar Williamson for this insight. See Williamson, *Mark*, 112.

83. Myers, *Binding the Strong Man*, 201–2.

84. Henri J. M. Nouwen, *Reaching Out: The Three Movements of the Spiritual Life* (Garden City, N.Y.: Doubleday, 1975), 36.

85. William Willimon, "Ready for Interruptions (Mark 5:21–43)," *The Christian Century* (May 29–June 5, 1991): 587.

86. Williamson, *Mark*, 113.

Chapter 3

1. See Jack Dean Kingsbury, *Jesus Christ in Matthew, Mark, and Luke*, Proclamation Commentaries (Philadelphia: Fortress, 1981), 105.

2. Joseph Fitzmyer, for example, denies a connection between the story of Martha and Mary and its immediately preceding context: "It is an episode unrelated to the preceding passages" (*The Gospel According to Luke X–XXIV*, The Anchor Bible [Garden City, N.Y.: Doubleday, 1985], 891). See also Barbara E. Reid, *Choosing the Better Part? Women in the Gospel of Luke* (Collegeville, Minn.: Liturgical, 1996), 147–48. Other commentators, however, discern a complementary relationship between the parable of the Good Samaritan in 10:25–37 and Martha and Mary's story: see Charles Talbert, *Reading Luke: A Literary and Theological Commentary on the Third Gospel* (New York: Crossroad, 1984), 120–26; Alan Culpepper, "The Gospel of Luke," in *The New Interpreter's Bible* (Nashville: Abingdon, 1995), 9:226, 231–32; and Robert W. Wall,

"Martha and Mary (Luke 10:38–42) in the Context of a Christian Deuteronomy," *Journal for the Study of the New Testament* 35 (1989): 19–35.

3. Alan Culpepper highlights this similarity ("The Gospel of Luke," 231). See also John Donahue, *The Gospel in Parable* (Philadelphia: Fortress, 1988), 134–35. Barbara E. Reid, however, maintains that this formula frequently introduces characters in Luke-Acts, and thus does not prove a connection. She also notes that Luke's gender "pairs" typically reiterate the same point, rather than different and complementary points (as in Luke 10:25–43; *Choosing the Better Part?* 148). Luke's penchant for pairing male and female examples is considered later in this chapter.

4. Warren Carter, "Getting Martha Out of the Kitchen: Luke 10:38–42 Again," *Catholic Biblical Quarterly* 58 (1996): 267–68. Reprinted in *A Feminist Companion to Luke*, ed. Amy-Jill Levine with Marianne Blickenstaff (Sheffield: Sheffield Academic, 2002), 24–31.

5. Kathleen Corley, *Private Women, Public Meals: Social Conflict in the Synoptic Tradition* (Peabody, Mass.: Hendrickson, 1993), 154.

6. Ibid., 138.

7. One other individual is positioned at Jesus' feet in Luke's Gospel: in 8:41, a desperate father named Jairus falls at Jesus' feet and begs him to heal his dying daughter. While it is not as clear in this case that Jairus is a disciple of Jesus, his posture and words do convey his confidence that Jesus can heal his daughter if only he arrives in time. In Acts 10:25, Cornelius falls at Peter's feet, worshiping him, and Peter protests, saying, "Stand up; I am only a mortal." In Acts 22:3 Paul defends his Jewish upbringing by insisting that he was brought up "at the feet of Gamaliel," thereby identifying himself as a disciple of the great teacher.

8. Adele Reinhartz, "From Narrative to History: The Resurrection of Mary and Martha," in *"Women Like This": New Perspectives on Jewish Women in the Greco-Roman World*, ed. Amy-Jill Levine (Atlanta: Scholars, 1991), 169.

9. See Elisabeth Schüssler Fiorenza, *But She Said: Feminist Practices of Biblical Interpretation* (Boston: Beacon Press, 1992), 51–76. Schüssler Fiorenza's chapter 2 on Martha and Mary is an expanded and revised version of an article that appears in two different versions: "A Feminist Critical Interpretation for Liberation: Martha and Mary (Luke 10:38–42)," *Religion and Intellectual Life* 3 (1986): 16–36; and "Theological Criteria and Historical Reconstruction: Martha and Mary (Luke 10:38–42)," in *Protocol of the Fifty-Third Colloquy: 10 April 1986*, ed. Herman Waetjen (Berkeley, Calif.: Center for Hermeneutical Studies in Hellenistic and Modern Culture, 1987), 1–12, 41–63.

10. It might appear anachronistic to speak of Martha, at this point in the narrative, as engaged in eucharistic table service (prior to the death and resurrection of Jesus). However, the story is addressed to Luke's postresurrection community, in which women may well have been engaged in such service.

11. *A Greek English Lexicon of the New Testament and Other Early Christian Literature*, 3d ed., rev. and ed. F. W. Danker (Chicago: University of Chicago Press, 2000), 804.

12. Turid Karlsen Seim, *The Double Message: Patterns of Gender in Luke-Acts* (Nashville: Abingdon, 1994), 103.

13. Barbara E. Reid maintains that "Martha's anxiety should not be equated with that denounced in other Lukan texts," for her anxiety concerns "much serving" rather than the riches and pleasures of life (8:14), worry about what to say when brought

before authorities (12:11), and concerns about daily life (21:34) (*Choosing the Better Part?* 146). However, in what sense is anxiety about service any less regrettable or debilitating than anxiety evoked by riches and pleasures, testimony before authorities, or the concerns of daily life? The Lukan Jesus consistently admonishes disciples not to worry or be anxious—whatever anxiety's source.

14. Luke Timothy Johnson, *The Gospel of Luke*, Sacra Pagina (Collegeville, Minn.: Liturgical, 1991), 174. In many ancient manuscripts, *thorybazē* is replaced by the more common verb *tyrbazein* ("to trouble" or "stir up"; middle and passive "to trouble oneself" or "to be troubled").

15. Corley, *Private Women, Public Meals*, 140. See Acts 17:5; 19:40–20:1; 21:34; 24:12 and 18.

16. Carter, "Getting Martha Out of the Kitchen," 275.

17. Frederick W. Danker, *Jesus and the New Age According to St. Luke: A Commentary on the Third Gospel* (St. Louis: Clayton Publishing House, 1972), 133.

18. Seim, *The Double Message*, 104. See Gordon D. Fee for a defense of the longer reading: "'One Thing is Needful'? Luke 10:42," in *New Testament Textual Criticism. Its Significance for Exegesis. Essays in Honour of Bruce M. Metzger*, edited by Eldon Jay Epp and Gordon D. Fee (Oxford: Clarendon, 1981), 61–75. Fee argues that "few things are necessary or only one" is actually the more difficult and thus preferred reading: "If so, then the text is not so much a 'put down' of Martha, as it is a gentle rebuke for her anxiety. For a meal, Jesus says, there is no cause to fret over *polla*, when only *oliga* are necessary" (75).

19. One criterion by which text-critical decisions are made is that "in general, the more difficult reading is to be preferred" (i.e., "'more difficult' to the scribe, who would be tempted to make an emendation" (Bruce Metzger, *A Textual Commentary on the Greek New Testament*, 2d ed. [Stuttgart: United Bible Societies, 1994], 12–13). The date and character of the witnesses supporting any given reading is also an important factor. In the case of Luke 10:41–42, both considerations point to "there is need of only one thing" as the best reading.

20. Ibid., 129.

21. See n.9, this chapter.

22. Schüssler Fiorenza, *But She Said*, 68.

23. Carter, "Getting Martha Out of the Kitchen," 271. See also Reid, *Choosing the Better Part?* 147.

24. Again, as noted in n.10, it might appear anachronistic to speak of Martha, at this point in the narrative, as engaged in "eucharistic table service" (prior to the death and resurrection of Jesus) and of "house-churches" (prior to Pentecost). However, the story is addressed to Luke's postresurrection community that no doubt gathered in house-churches and may well have been familiar with women's eucharistic leadership.

25. Schüssler Fiorenza, "Theological Criteria and Historical Reconstruction," 7.

26. Schüssler Fiorenza, *But She Said*, 68.

27. Mary Rose D'Angelo, "Women in Luke-Acts: A Redactional View," *Journal of Biblical Literature* 109 (1990): 455.

28. Barbara E. Reid, *Choosing the Better Part?* 157.

29. Ibid.

30. Ibid.

31. Ibid., 158.
32. Corley, *Private Women, Public Meals*, 140.
33. Reid, *Choosing the Better Part?* 154.
34. Ibid., 54.
35. Ibid., 205.
36. Schüssler Fiorenza, *But She Said*, 69.
37. Robert C. Tannehill, *Luke*, Abingdon New Testament Commentaries (Nashville: Abingdon, 1996), 185–86.
38. See Seim, *The Double Message*, 72.
39. See Carter, "Getting Martha Out of the Kitchen," 268–76.
40. John N. Collins, "Did Luke Intend a Disservice to Women in the Martha and Mary Story?" *Biblical Theology Bulletin* 28 (1998): 110. See also John N. Collins, *Diakonia: Reinterpreting the Ancient Sources* (New York: Oxford University Press, 1990), 335–37, where he argues that *diakon*-words were not common in the first-century cultural context, and that they do not have to do mainly with the task of waiting at table. Instead, they denote "activity of an in-between kind," engaged in by a spokesperson, by one who acts on behalf of another, or by one commissioned to a special task. "Waiting at table" is "merely one expression of the notion of 'go-between'—that is, the table attendant goes between diner and kitchen" (335).
41. Collins, "Did Luke Intend a Disservice to Women in the Martha and Mary Story?" 110.
42. Seim, *The Double Message*, 100.
43. Tannehill, *Luke*, 186.
44. Herman Waetjen makes this point in his response to Schüssler Fiorenza's presentation in "Theological Criteria and Historical Reconstruction," in *Protocol of the Fifty-Third Colloquy: 10 April 1986*, ed. Herman Waetjen (Berkeley, Calif.: Center for Hermeneutical Studies in Hellenistic and Modern Culture, 1987), 36.
45. See Jane Schaberg, "Luke," in *The Women's Bible Commentary*, ed. Carol A. Newsom and Sharon H. Ringe (Louisville, Ky.: Westminster/John Knox, 1992), 289; Reid, *Choosing the Better Part?* 153–54.
46. Schüssler Fiorenza, *But She Said*, 69.
47. See Mary Ann Tolbert, "Protestant Feminists and the Bible: On the Horns of a Dilemma," *Union Seminary Quarterly Review* 43 (1989): 1–18, for an insightful discussion of the discomfort many Protestant feminists experience when their "sola scriptura" commitment is challenged.
48. Only Luke features the stories of Elizabeth (chap. 1); Mary (chaps. 1–2); Anna (2:36–38); the widow of Nain (7:11–17); the forgiven woman who shows great love (7:36–50); Mary Magdalene, Joanna, Susanna, and the other Galilean women who minister (8:1–3); Martha and Mary (10:38–42); the woman bent double (13:10–17); and the women of Jerusalem who lament Jesus en route to the cross (23:26–31). Luke shares several other stories featuring women with Mark and Matthew: Simon's mother-in-law (4:38–39); the woman with a hemorrhage and Jairus's daughter (8:40–56); a woman baking bread (13:20–21); a widow who gives her all (21:1–4); and the Galilean women who witness Jesus' death and burial (23:49, 55–56) and who discover the empty tomb (24:1–12).
49. Only Luke tells the parable of the woman searching for a lost coin (15:8–10) and the parable of the widow demanding justice (18:1–8).

50. For excellent summaries, see D'Angelo, "Women in Luke-Acts," 441–61; Schaberg, "Luke," 275–92; Reid, *Choosing the Better Part?* 1–53; and Turid Karlsen Seim, "The Gospel of Luke," in *Searching the Scriptures*, vol. 2, *A Feminist Commentary*, ed. E. Schüssler Fiorenza (New York: Crossroad, 1994), 728–62. See also Seim's *The Double Message*.

Feminist biblical scholars are by no means the only proponents of a revisionist position. Stevan Davies, for example, acknowledges that he once assumed the traditional view of Luke as a sympathetic liberator of women, but now finds "the whole house of cards collapsed. Indeed, together with the unstable peak of the house, its base—my set of assumptions about Luke's particular concern for women—crumbled as well." (See Davies, "Women in the Third Gospel and the New Testament Apocrypha," in *"Women Like This,"* 185.)

51. Schaberg, "Luke," 282.
52. Seim, "The Gospel of Luke," 731.
53. D'Angelo, "Women in Luke-Acts," 452.
54. Schaberg, "Luke," 279. See also D'Angelo, "Women in Luke-Acts," on this point.
55. Seim, *Double Message*, 249.
56. Schüssler Fiorenza, *But She Said*, 70.
57. Loveday Alexander, "Sisters in Adversity: Retelling Martha's Story," in *Women in the Biblical Tradition*, ed. George J. Brooke, Studies in Women and Religion 31 (Lewiston, Me.: Edwin Mellen, 1992), 171. Reprinted in *A Feminist Companion to Luke*, ed. Amy-Jill Levine with Marianne Blickenstaff (Sheffield: Sheffield Academic, 2002), 197–213.
58. Alexander, "Sisters in Adversity," 173.
59. Sharon H. Ringe, *Luke*, Westminster Bible Companion (Louisville, Ky.: Westminster/John Knox, 1995), 161–62.
60. Alexander, "Sisters in Adversity," 186.
61. Reinhartz, "From Narrative to History," 171.
62. Ibid., 184.
63. Schüssler Fiorenza, *But She Said*, 60–61.
64. Ibid.
65. Danker refers to Martha as such in *Jesus and the New Age According to St. Luke*, 133.
66. Blake R. Heffner, "Meister Eckhart and a Millennium with Mary and Martha," *The Lutheran Quarterly* 5 (1991): 172.
67. Alexander, "Sisters in Adversity," 170.
68. Elisabeth Moltmann-Wendel, *The Women around Jesus* (New York: Crossroad, 1993), 19.
69. Heffner, "Meister Eckhart and a Millennium with Mary and Martha," 173.
70. Ibid.
71. Ibid., 174.
72. Ibid.,174–75.
73. Ibid., 176.
74. Ibid., 178–79.
75. Ibid., 181.
76. John Calvin, *Commentary on a Harmony of the Evangelists, Matthew, Mark, and Luke* (Grand Rapids: Eerdmans, 1949), 2:143.
77. Ibid., 2:144.

78. Mary Rose D'Angelo, "Women Partners in the New Testament," *Journal of Feminist Studies* 6 (1990): 78–80.

79. The change from "*who also*" to "*and she*" involves the omission of a single letter (*hē*). Although D'Angelo acknowledges that the omission is supported by some of the earliest and best witnesses (p45, p75, the uncorrected Sinaiticus, and the second corrector of Vaticanus), she maintains that the omission is "quite easy to explain": "The expression 'sat at the feet of' Jesus came to be less widely understood as an expression of discipleship, and taken as a literal description of the scene, the story made no sense if Martha also was sitting down. The reading 'who also' suggests that the author of Luke still understood the story as presenting two women disciples, and strengthens my suggestion that they were a pair" (ibid., 79).

80. Ibid., 79.

81. Ibid., 80.

82. Ibid., 85. D'Angelo maintains that the evangelist Luke modifies the story in order that it may serve his own purposes and concerns: "Luke's story exploits an unequal definition of the roles of *diakonos* and *adelphē* into a tension between the two women. . . . The literary structure of Luke has also exerted influence on the telling of the story, as has this author's preference for silent women" (80–81).

83. Carter references Acts 1:17, 25; 6:1–6; 11:29–30; 12:25; 20:24; 21:19 in "Getting Martha Out of the Kitchen," 270–71.

84. Ibid., 276. Italics mine.

85. Ibid., 280. If Jesus is indeed instructing both Martha and Mary (both of whom threaten partnership in ministry), we might wish that he had addressed Mary more explicitly!

86. Alexander, "Sisters in Adversity," 177.

87. Martha is the subject of three finite verbs in main clauses, with one participle, and is accorded direct speech. Mary is described in a relative clause.

88. Alexander, "Sisters in Adversity," 178.

89. Ibid., 183.

90. Ibid., 182.

91. Ibid., 184.

92. Ibid., 185.

93. Ibid.

94. Ibid., 182.

95. Seim, *The Double Message*, 105. Reid reads this point differently, as an indication that Luke portrays Jesus authoritatively siding against Martha in the dispute: "[I]n his reproach the word *diakonia* no longer appears. Whereas Martha had expressed concern about *pollēn diakonian*, her 'much service,' Luke's formulation of Jesus' response, 'you are anxious and worried about much' in itself obliterates her diaconal ministry. It is the silent, passive Mary who has 'chosen the better part'" (*Choosing the Better Part?* 158).

96. I wish to thank the Rev. Anne Dichtel Dwiggins, a former student at Gettysburg Lutheran Seminary, for this astute observation.

97. Fred B. Craddock, *Luke*, Interpretation (Louisville, Ky.: John Knox, 1990), 152.

98. Alison M. Cheek, "Shifting the Paradigm: Feminist Bible Study," in *Searching the Scriptures*, vol. 1, *A Feminist Introduction*, ed. Elisabeth Schüssler Fiorenza (New York: Crossroad, 1993), 341.

Chapter 4

1. See, for example, Elisabeth Schüssler Fiorenza, *But She Said: Feminist Practices of Biblical Interpretation* (Boston: Beacon, 1992), 196–217.
2. See, for example, Joel Green, "Jesus and a Daughter of Abraham (Luke 13:10–17): Test Case for a Lucan Perspective on Jesus' Miracles," *Catholic Biblical Quarterly* 51 (1989): 643–54, who argues for the unity of the story.
3. Charles B. Clayman, ed., *The American Medical Association Encyclopedia of Medicine* (New York: Random House, 1989), 111–12. See also John Wilkinson, *The Bible and Healing: A Medical and Theological Commentary* (Grand Rapids: Eerdmans, 1998), 131–41.
4. Horst Balz and Gerhard Schneider, eds., *Exegetical Dictionary of the New Testament* (Grand Rapids: Eerdmans, 1990), 1:170.
5. Schüssler Fiorenza, *But She Said*, 202.
6. Joel B. Green, *The Theology of the Gospel of Luke*, New Testament Theology (Cambridge: Cambridge University Press, 1995), 78.
7. Mark Allan Powell, "Salvation in Luke-Acts," *Word and World* (Winter 1992): 8.
8. Joel Green, *The Gospel of Luke*, The New International Commentary on the New Testament (Grand Rapids: Eerdmans, 1997), 521.
9. Sharon H. Ringe, *Luke*, The Westminster Bible Companion (Louisville, Ky.: Westminster/John Knox, 1995), 187.
10. Ibid.
11. Robert O'Toole, "Some Exegetical Reflections on Luke 13, 10–17," *Biblica* 73 (1992): 87.
12. Claudia J. Setzer, "Rulers of the Synagogue," *Anchor Bible Dictionary* (New York: Doubleday, 1992), 5:841–42; Green, *The Gospel of Luke*, 523.
13. Barbara E. Reid, *Choosing the Better Part? Women in the Gospel of Luke* (Collegeville, Minn.: Liturgical, 1996), 167.
14. Turid Karlsen Seim, *The Double Message: Patterns of Gender in Luke and Acts* (Nashville: Abingdon, 1994), 42–57.
15. Ibid., 48.
16. Ibid.
17. M. Dennis Hamm, "The Freeing of the Bent Woman and the Restoration of Israel: Luke 13.10–17 as Narrative Theology," *Journal for the Study of the New Testament* 31 (1987): 34.
18. Ibid.
19. O'Toole, "Some Exegetical Reflections on Luke 13, 10–17," 96.
20. Ibid.
21. Schüssler Fiorenza, *But She Said*, 209.
22. See, for example, Marcus Borg, who makes this a central thesis in his reconstruction of the historical Jesus in *Meeting Jesus Again for the First Time: The Historical Jesus and the Heart of Contemporary Faith* (San Francisco: HarperSanFrancisco, 1994), 58.
23. See Bernadette Brooten, *Women Leaders in the Ancient Synagogue: Inscriptional Evidence and Background Issues*, Brown Judaic Studies 36 (Chico, Calif.: Scholars Press, 1982).
24. See Joseph B. Tyson, *Luke, Judaism, and the Scholars: Critical Approaches to Luke-Acts* (Columbia: University of South Carolina Press, 1999).
25. Walter Brueggemann, *Reverberations of Faith: A Theological Handbook of Old Testament Themes* (Louisville, Ky.: Westminster/John Knox, 2002), 180.

26. Judith Plaskow, "Anti-Judaism in Feminist Christian Interpretation," in *Searching the Scriptures*, vol. 1, *A Feminist Introduction*, ed. Elisabeth Schüssler Fiorenza (New York: Crossroad, 1993), 124.

27. See Turid Karlsen Seim, *The Double Message*. Seim's contribution is also discussed on pp. 64–72.

28. Turid Karlsen Seim, "The Gospel of Luke," in *Searching the Scriptures*, vol. 2, *A Feminist Commentary*, ed. Elisabeth Schüssler Fiorenza (New York: Crossroad, 1994), 738–39.

29. Schüssler Fiorenza, *But She Said*, 199–200.

30. Reid, *Choosing the Better Part?* 167.

31. Schussler Fiorenza, *But She Said*, 216. In addition to these observations, perhaps Luke is more likely to see women than men as objects of demonic possession. Joanna Dewey argues this point, noting that Mark and Matthew include only one such female character (the Syrophoenician/Canaanite's daughter in Mark 7/Matt. 15). Luke, however, unlike Mark and Matthew, attributes Simon's mother-in-law's fever to an evil spirit (4:39), adds the story of the bent woman who is Satan-bound (13:10–17), and describes the women following Jesus as formerly demon-possessed: "The twelve were with him, as well as some women who had been cured of evil spirits and infirmities: Mary, called Magdalene, from whom seven demons had gone out" (8:1–2). Moreover, in his redaction of Mark and Q material and in his own special material, the evangelist Luke adds no additional references to males possessed of demons. Dewey speculates "that this is part of Luke's general pattern of rendering women visible in his narrative, but at the same time restricting them to subordinate roles. It is one of his ways of discrediting the authority of women" (Joanna Dewey, "Jesus' Healings of Women: Conformity and Non-Conformity to Dominant Cultural Values as Clues for Historical Reconstruction," in *Society of Biblical Literature 1993 Seminar Papers* 32, ed. Eugene H. Lovering Jr. [Atlanta: Scholars, 1993], 181). However, I am not as certain of this point, as Luke does retain stories in the tradition that present men as objects of demonic possession (4:31–37, 40–41; 6:17–19; 7:21; 8:26–39; 9:37–43). Thus, perhaps by increasing the number of stories in which women suffer demonic affliction, he seeks to make women equally visible as objects of possession.

32. Powell, "Salvation in Luke-Acts," 8.

33. Peggy Orenstein, *SchoolGirls: Young Women, Self-Esteem, and the Confidence Gap* (New York: Doubleday, 1994), xvi.

34. Susan Dunfee Nelson, "The Sin of Hiding: A Feminist Critique of Reinhold Niebuhr's Account of the Sin of Pride," *Soundings* (Fall 1982): 317.

35. See Carol Lakey Hess, *Caretakers of Our Common House: Women's Development in Communities of Faith* (Nashville: Abingdon, 1997), 34–35; and the pioneering works of Valerie Saiving ("The Human Situation: A Feminine View," in *Womanspirit Rising: A Feminist Reader in Religion*, ed. Carol Christ and Judith Plaskow [San Francisco: Harper and Row Publishers, 1979]) and Judith Plaskow (*Sex, Sin, and Grace: Women's Experience and the Theologies of Reinhold Niebuhr and Paul Tillich* [Washington, D.C.: University Press of America, 1980]).

36. Elizabeth A. Johnson, *She Who Is: The Mystery of God in Feminist Theological Discourse* (New York: Crossroad, 1992), 64.

37. See Mary Elise Lowe, "Woman-Oriented Hamartiologies: A Survey of the Shift from

Powerlessness to Right Relationship," *Dialog* 39 (Summer 2000): 119–39. The quote is from Lowe's concluding observations on 136.

38. Schüssler Fiorenza, *But She Said*, 199.
39. Megan McKenna, *Leave Her Alone* (Maryknoll, N.Y.: Orbis, 2000), 53.
40. Ibid.
41. Ibid.
42. Richard A. Horsley, *Jesus and Empire: The Kingdom of God and the New World Disorder* (Minneapolis: Fortress, 2003), 20–22.
43. Walter Rauschenbusch, *Prayers of the Social Awakening* (New York: Pilgrim, 1925), 65–66.
44. See Kathy Black, *A Healing Homiletic: Preaching and Disability* (Nashville: Abingdon, 1996), 43–44.
45. Ibid., 44.
46. Ibid., 184–85.
47. Simon Horne, "'Those Who Are Blind See': Some New Testament Uses of Impairment, Inability, and Paradox," in *Human Disability and the Service of God: Reassessing Religious Practice*, ed. Nancy L. Eiseland and Don E. Saliers (Nashville: Abingdon, 1998), 96–97.
48. Ibid., 96.
49. Horne quotes the form used by Disabled Peoples International, in ibid., 97.
50. Horne, "'Those Who Are Blind See,'" 97.
51. John Dominic Crossan, *Jesus: A Revolutionary Biography* (San Francisco: Harper-Collins, 1994), 81.
52. Ibid.
53. Black, *A Healing Homiletic*, 53–54.
54. Nancy Eiesland, *The Disabled God: Toward a Liberatory Theology of Disability* (Nashville: Abingdon, 1994), 116.
55. Ibid., 100.
56. Martin Luther King Jr., "Letter from Birmingham Jail" (April 16, 1963), in *Why We Can't Wait* (New York: New American Library, 1963), 77.
57. Ibid., 80–81.
58. Ibid., 86.
59. Reid, *Choosing the Better Part?* 163.
60. Ibid., 168.
61. Ibid.

Chapter 5

1. Fred B. Craddock, "The Witness at the Well," *The Christian Century* (March 7, 1990): 243.
2. For a compelling historical reconstruction of the Johannine community, see Raymond E. Brown, *The Community of the Beloved Disciple: The Life, Loves, and Hates of an Individual Church in New Testament Times* (New York: Paulist, 1979).
3. Teresa Okure persuasively argues this point in *The Johannine Approach to Mission: A Contextual Study of John 4:1–42* (Tübingen: J. C. B. Mohr, 1988), 83–86.
4. Gail R. O'Day, *The Word Disclosed: John's Story and Narrative Preaching* (St. Louis: CBP, 1987), 29. See also Margaret M. Beirne's discussion of Nicodemus and the Samaritan Woman as a "Johannine gender pair" in *Women and Men in the Fourth*

Gospel: A Genuine Discipleship of Equals, Journal for the Study of the New Testament Supplement Series 242 (Sheffield: Sheffield Academic, 2003), 67–104.

5. Much has been made of the fact that the woman appeared at the well at noon, at the hottest hour of the day. Indeed, a common assumption is that the hour conveys the contempt in which the woman was held by others—that is, that she comes to the well at noon to avoid public humiliation. This assumption is highly questionable. See the discussion question on page 133 for arguments against it.

6. On the ambiguity of Nicodemus's subsequent appearances in John's Gospel, see Jouette Bassler, "Mixed Signals: Nicodemus in the Fourth Gospel," *Journal of Biblical Literature* 108 (1989): 635–46.

7. Adele Reinhartz, "The Gospel of John," in *Searching the Scriptures,* vol. 2, *A Feminist Commentary,* ed. Elisabeth Schüssler Fiorenza (New York: Crossroad, 1994), 573.

8. Robert Alter, *The Art of Biblical Narrative* (London: George Allen and Unwin, 1981), 50–51.

9. Lyle Eslinger, "The Wooing of the Woman at the Well: Jesus, the Reader and Reader-Response Criticism," *Journal of Literature and Theology* 1 (1987): 167–93; reprinted in *The Gospel of John as Literature: An Anthology of Twentieth-Century Perspectives,* ed. Mark Stibbe (Leiden: Brill, 1993), 165–82. Jane Webster also finds the encounter between Jesus and the Samaritan woman to be sexually suggestive, yet provides an alternative intertextual reading. Reading John 4 alongside the Old Testament Wisdom tradition, she argues that the presence of the Samaritan woman echoes that of the "strange woman" in Proverbs, Lady Wisdom's negative counterpart, in that she, too, is (1) adulterous, (2) foreign, and (3) unknowing. In Webster's view, these characteristics are transcended through the Samaritan woman's encounter with Jesus, as she emerges as one who has a spiritual relationship with Jesus, who is a member of a universal community, and who knows the truth about Jesus and collaborates with him in his work, bringing others to belief (see "Transcending Alterity: Strange Woman to Samaritan Woman," in *A Feminist Companion to John,* ed. Amy-Jill Levine with Marianne Blickenstaff [Sheffield: Sheffield Academic, 2003], 1:126–42).

10. Sandra M. Schneiders, *The Revelatory Text: Interpreting the New Testament as Sacred Scripture* (San Francisco: HarperCollins, 1991), 187.

11. Craig Koester makes this point in *Symbolism in the Fourth Gospel: Meaning, Mystery, Community* (Minneapolis: Fortress, 1995), 49.

12. Schneiders, *The Revelatory Text,* 190. See also Webster, "Transcending Alterity," 135.

13. Koester, *Symbolism in the Fourth Gospel,* 49.

14. Schneiders, *The Revelatory Text,* 191.

15. For compelling readings of these stories in John 3 and 9 as representative or symbolic in function, see David Rensberger, *Johannine Faith and Liberating Community* (Philadelphia: Westminster, 1988), 37–86. See also Koester's discussion of "Symbolic and Representative Figures" in John in *Symbolism in the Fourth Gospel,* 32–73.

16. Stephen D. Moore, *Poststructuralism and the New Testament: Derrida and Foucault at the Foot of the Cross* (Minneapolis: Fortress, 1994), 48–49. The essay on John 4 that appears in this volume was originally published as "Are There Impurities in the Living Water That the Johannine Jesus Dispenses?" in *Biblical Interpretation* (1993): 207–27. It is reprinted in *A Feminist Companion to John,* vol. 1, ed. Amy-Jill Levine with Marianne Blickenstaff (Sheffield: Sheffield Academic, 2003), 126–42.

17. Jane Webster, who inclines toward the view that the Samaritan woman is an adulter-

ess, argues that the reference to five husbands may be both literal and symbolic: "It is possible that the Samaritan woman mirrors in her own life—or is a symbolic representation of—the Samaritan people as a nation." Thus, "One need not exclude the possibility that the woman is both adulterous herself and a representative of 'adulterous Samaria'. These two interpretations reinforce each other and make the allusion stronger" ("Transcending Alterity," 135).

18. Calvin's interpretation of the Samaritan woman's story is found in his *Commentary on the Gospel According to John* (Grand Rapids: Eerdmans, 1949), 1:143–77. These quotations are found on 153 and 168. Italics mine.

19. Gail O'Day, "John," in *The Women's Bible Commentary*, ed. Carol Newsom and Sharon Ringe (Louisville, Ky.: Westminster/John Knox, 1992), 296. Luise Schottroff notes that "the Bible often speaks of women's consecutive marriages without regarding them as immoral" ("The Samaritan Woman and the Notion of Sexuality in the Fourth Gospel," in *"What Is John?"* vol. 2, *Literary and Social Readings of the Fourth Gospel*, ed. Fernando F. Segovia [Atlanta: Scholars, 1998], 162). Scott Spencer concurs: "the Sadducees posed the presumably plausible case of a *seven*-time widow in similar circumstances" (Mark 12:18–23; "'You Just Don't Understand' [Or Do You?]: Jesus, Women and Conversation in the Fourth Gospel," in *A Feminist Companion to John*, ed. Amy-Jill Levine with Marianne Blickenstaff [Sheffield: Sheffield Academic, 2003], 1:35).

20. Linda McKinnish Bridges, "John 4:5–42," *Interpretation* (April 1994): 173–76.

21. O'Day, *The Word Disclosed*, 41–42. Italics mine.

22. Ibid.

23. See Okure, "The Johannine Approach to Mission," 96–98, for a discussion of interpretive possibilities. Okure persuasively argues that Jesus himself is the gift of God (3:16), though others note that 7:37–39 equates "rivers of living water" with "the Spirit." I see no reason that both the gift (Jesus) and the medium by which the new life available in him is received (the Spirit) cannot be in view.

24. Raymond E. Brown, *The Gospel according to John I–XII*, The Anchor Bible (Garden City, N.Y.: Doubleday, 1966), 176.

25. Schneiders, for example, identifies it as such (*The Revelatory Text*, 192).

26. See Gail R. O'Day, *Revelation in the Fourth Gospel* (Philadelphia: Fortress, 1986), 75.

27. Craddock, "The Witness at the Well," 243.

28. In Greek, the question begins with the interrogative particle *mēti*, which signals her uncertainty. *Ou* is used in direct questions when an affirmative answer is expected.

29. Schneiders, *The Revelatory Text*, 195.

30. Calvin, *Commentary on the Gospel according to John*, 176.

31. Robert Kysar, *John: The Maverick Gospel*, rev. ed. (Louisville, Ky.: Westminster/John Knox, 1993), 151.

32. Gary A. Phillips, "The Ethics of Reading Deconstructively, or Speaking Face-to-Face: The Samaritan Woman Meets Derrida at the Well," in *The New Literary Criticism and the New Testament*, ed. Elizabeth Struthers Malbon and Edgar V. McKnight, Journal for the Study of the New Testament Supplement Series 109 (Sheffield: Sheffield Academic, 1994), 293. "Aporias" represent "gaps" in a narrative (where something is missing) that must be "filled" by a reader. Phillips notes that the "undecidability of a text" is Derrida's way of referring to "the structural capacity of all texts to generate more than one meaning" (293).

33. Schneiders, *The Revelatory Text*, 188.

34. Craig S. Farmer, "Changing Images of the Samaritan Woman in Early Reformed Commentaries on John," *Church History* 65 (September 1996): 367.

35. Ibid., 366.

36. Ibid., 366, 374.

37. Ibid., 374.

38. Ibid.

39. Ibid.

40. Ibid., 375.

41. Ibid.

42. Schneiders, *The Revelatory Text*, 188.

43. Stephen Moore, in an intriguing deconstructionist reading of John 4, even argues that the Samaritan woman is "the more enlightened partner in the dialogue" (*Poststructuralism and the New Testament*, 50). Deconstruction dismantles "binary oppositions" such as the one Jesus emphasizes in John 4 between figurative and literal, heavenly and earthly, material and spiritual water. As Moore points out, "What Jesus *says* is contradicted by what he *is*," for as the Word made flesh, he "dissolves the partition between heaven and earth, spirit and matter, figure and letter" (59). The female student outstrips her male teacher, for "what Jesus *is* is affirmed by what the Samaritan woman says" (59), in that she insists that "the earthly and the heavenly, flesh and Spirit, figurative and literal, are symbiotically related categories" (62).

44. Schneiders, *The Revelatory Text*, 195.

45. Adeline Fehribach, *The Women in the Life of the Bridegroom: A Feminist Historical-Literary Analysis of the Female Characters in the Fourth Gospel* (Collegeville, Minn.: Liturgical, 1998), 80.

46. Ibid., 71.

47. Ibid., 78–79.

48. Ibid., 81.

49. Sandra Schneiders, *Written That You May Believe: Encountering Jesus in the Fourth Gospel* (New York: Crossroad, 1999), 93–94n.3.

50. Fehribach, *The Women in the Life of the Bridegroom*, 179.

51. Okure, *The Johannine Approach to Mission*, 291.

52. Ibid., 290.

53. Ibid., 294.

54. Ibid., 287.

55. Ibid., 292–93.

56. Ibid., 186.

57. Ibid.

58. Ibid., 187.

59. Robert Kysar, *John*, Augsburg Commentary on the New Testament (Minneapolis: Augsburg, 1986), 71–72.

60. Craddock, "The Witness at the Well," 243.

61. Schneiders, *Written That You May Believe*, 216.

62. Ibid., 229–30.

63. Musa W. Dube, "Reading for Decolonization (John 4:1–42)," *Semeia* 75 (1996): 38.

64. Ibid.

65. Ibid., 49.

66. Ibid., 50.

67. Ibid., 51.
68. Ibid., 42.
69. Ibid., 51.
70. Ibid., 52.
71. Ibid., 49.
72. Ibid., 56.
73. Ibid., 57.
74. Luise Schottroff notes this possibility in "The Samaritan Woman and the Notion of Sexuality in the Fourth Gospel," 165–66.
75. Alan Culpepper, *Anatomy of the Fourth Gospel: A Study in Literary Design* (Philadelphia: Fortress, 1983), 192.

Chapter 6

1. This point has been persuasively argued by Gail O'Day, "John 7:53–8:11: A Study in Misreading," *Journal of Biblical Literature* 111 (1992): 631–40. See also Harald Riesenfeld, *The Gospel Tradition*, trans. E. Margaret Rowley (Philadelphia: Fortress, 1970), who makes the case that "In all probability the contents of the account came to contrast in a disturbing and embarrassing way with the praxis of church discipline regarding offenses against the sixth commandment" (98–99). Raymond Brown concurs: "The ease with which Jesus forgave the adulteress was hard to reconcile with the stern penitential discipline in vogue in the early Church. It was only when a more liberal penitential practice was firmly established that this story received wide acceptance" (*The Gospel according to John I–XII*, The Anchor Bible [Garden City, N.Y.: Doubleday, 1966], 335).
2. In the fifth century, for example, Augustine observed that "certain persons of little faith, or rather enemies of the true faith, fearing, I suppose, lest their wives should be given impunity in sinning, removed from their manuscripts the Lord's act of forgiveness toward the adulteress, as if He who had said 'sin no more' had granted permission to sin" ("Adulterous Marriages" [2.7], trans. Charles T. Huegelmeyer, in *Augustine's Treatises on Marriage and Other Subjects*, trans. Charles T. Wilcox [and others]; ed. Roy J. Deferrari [New York: Fathers of the Church, 1955], 107).
3. Brown, *The Gospel according to John I–XII*, 336–37.
4. O'Day, "John 7:53–8:11," 633.
5. Ibid.
6. What is the nature of the "test"? Commentators assess the matter in various ways. At the least, the test pits the judgment of Jesus against the teaching of Moses. O'Day maintains that "The narrator's commentary in verse 6a ["they said this to test him"] explains why the scribes and Pharisees only speak of half the law" ("John 7:53–8:11," 632). Raymond Brown articulates a traditional explanation: "If he decides the case in favor of the woman and releases her, he violates the clear prescriptions of the Mosaic Law; if he orders her to be stoned, he will be in trouble with the Romans," for it appears that the Sanhedrin's power to impose death sentences was removed by Roman decree around the year 30 (*The Gospel according to John I–XII*, 337).
7. O'Day, "John 7:53–8:11," 636.
8. Patricia Klindienst Joplin, "Intolerable Language: Jesus and the Woman Taken in Adultery," in *Shadow of Spirit: Postmodernism and Religion*, ed. Philippa Berry and Andrew Wernick (New York: Routledge, 1992), 232. Paul S. Minear reads the

dramatic action differently. In his view, Jesus' use of his finger on the ground may be an implicit claim to divine authority (see Exod. 31:18; Deut. 9:10; Mark 2:6–11; Luke 11:20; "Writing on the Ground: The Puzzle in John 8:1–11," *Horizons in Biblical Theology* 13 [1991]: 23–27).

9. Luise Schottroff, *Lydia's Impatient Sisters: A Feminist Social History of Early Christianity* (Louisville, Ky.: Westminster John Knox, 1995), 184.

10. Joplin, "Intolerable Language," 232–33.

11. While it is usually assumed that the woman is left "alone" with Jesus, the language is ambiguous, as Martin Scott notes: "On the one hand we are told that Jesus is left 'alone' (*monos*) with the woman. Yet on the other hand, she is still curiously described as being 'in the middle' (*en mesō*). This echoes back to verse 3, where the reader is conscious that two distinct groupings are present: scribes and Pharisees who have dragged the woman in, and the crowd who were listening and learning before the others arrived. The narrator has thus left open the possibility that the accusers, those morally responsible, have departed the scene, while the seekers after the truth, the crowd, remain as witnesses to the entire event" ("On the Trail of a Good Story: John 7.53–8.11 in the Gospel Tradition," in *Ciphers in the Sand: Interpretations of the Woman Taken in Adultery [John 7.53–8.11]*, ed. Larry J. Kreitzer and Deborah W. Rooke [Sheffield: Sheffield Academic, 2000], 53–82, 69). Holly Toensing also makes this point ("Divine Intervention or Divine Intrusion? Jesus and the Adulteress in John's Gospel," in *A Feminist Companion to John*, ed. Amy-Jill Levine with Marianne Blickenstaff [Sheffield: Sheffield Academic, 2003], 1:166n.17).

12. O'Day, "The Gospel of John," in *The New Interpreter's Bible* (Nashville: Abingdon, 1995), 19:630.

13. O'Day, "John 7:53–8:11," 637.

14. Gail O'Day, "John," in *The Women's Bible Commentary*, ed. Carol A. Newsom and Sharon H. Ringe (Louisville, Ky.: Westminster/John Knox, 1992), 297.

15. Bruce M. Metzger, *A Textual Commentary on the Greek New Testament*, 2d ed. (Stuttgart: United Bible Societies, 1994), 187.

16. See Zane Hodges, "The Woman Taken in Adultery (John 7:53–8:11): The Text," *Bibliotheca Sacra* 136 (October–December 1979): 318–32.

17. Important papyri (p66 and p75) and the major codices dating from the fourth century (Sinaiticus and Vaticanus) are usually cited. Because these manuscripts are all early Egyptian manuscripts, their textual independence cannot be demonstrated.

18. Metzger, *A Textual Commentary*, 188.

19. According to Jerome, "in the Gospel according to John in many manuscripts, both Greek and Latin, is found the story of the adulterous woman who was accused before the Lord" (Hodges, "The Woman Taken in Adultery," 330). Augustine's quotation is noted above in n.2.

20. Hodges, "The Woman Taken in Adultery," 326.

21. Ibid., 332.

22. Metzger, *A Textual Commentary*, 189.

23. See John Paul Heil, "The Story of Jesus and the Adulteress (John 7:53–8:11) Reconsidered," *Biblica* 72 (1991): 182–91; Daniel Wallace's rebuttal of Heil's argument, "Reconsidering 'The Story of Jesus and the Adulteress Reconsidered,'" *New Testament Studies* 39 (1993): 290–96; and Heil's "Rejoinder," *Eglise et Théologie* 25 (1994): 361–66.

24. Heil, "The Story of Jesus and the Adulteress," 187.
25. Ibid., 191.
26. See Martin Scott for a recent intriguing reading of the story within its literary context: "On the Trail of a Good Story," 53–82.
27. O'Day, "John 7:53–8:11," 637.
28. Brad H. Young, "'Save the Adulteress!' Ancient Jewish *Responsa* in the Gospels?" *New Testament Studies* 41 (1995): 59–70.
29. David Flusser, for example, "has suggested that it is a gloss, partly based on its similarity to Luke 6:7 and Matthew 22:15, and partly on the fact that the style of the verse does not fit the rest of the passage" (Young, "Save the Adulteress!" 59). Moreover, alternative placing and wording of the verse can be observed in various Greek manuscripts. Thus, in the twenty-fifth edition of the standard Nestle-Aland Greek New Testament, sufficient doubt about the authenticity of 8:6a led the editors to enclose it in single brackets, denoting its "dubious claim to authenticity" as part of the original text.
30. Young, "Save the Adulteress!" 63.
31. Ibid., 64.
32. Ibid., 65.
33. Ibid.
34. Ibid.
35. Ibid., 67.
36. Ibid., 68.
37. Ibid., 67.
38. Ibid., 69.
39. Ibid., 70.
40. See, for example, Luise Schottroff, *Lydia's Impatient Sisters*, 181. Schottroff claims that "the text reflects a social praxis of getting rid of women by means of accusing them of adultery" (181).
41. See, for example, J. Ian H. McDonald, "The So-Called *Pericope de Adultera*," *New Testament Studies* 41 (1995): 420–22. Martin Scott also takes parallels with the Susanna story into account. Indeed, Scott's reading of the story leads him to the conclusion that the woman was not guilty of adultery, but innocent and released from injustice by Jesus ("On the Trail of a Good Story," 53–82).
42. Hisako Kinukawa, "On John 7:53–8:11: A Well-Cherished but Much-Clouded Story," in *Reading from This Place*, vol. 2, *Social Location and Biblical Interpretation in Global Perspective*, ed. Fernando F. Segovia and Mary Ann Tolbert (Minneapolis: Fortress, 1995), 82–96.
43. Ibid., 92.
44. Ibid., 94.
45. Ibid., 95.
46. Jean K. Kim, "Adultery or Hybridity? Reading John 7:53–8:11 from a Postcolonial Context," in *John and Postcolonialism: Travel, Space, and Power*, ed. Musa W. Dube and Jeffrey L. Staley (Sheffield: Sheffield Academic, 2002), 111–28.
47. Ibid., 125.
48. Ibid., 126.
49. Alan Watson, "Jesus and the Adulteress," *Biblica* 80 (1999): 100–108.
50. Ibid., 102.

51. Ibid., 102–3.
52. Ibid., 107.
53. Ibid., 106.
54. Ibid., 107.
55. Ibid., 108.
56. Toensing, "Divine Intervention or Divine Intrusion?" 165. Martin Scott also notes that Jesus adopts a "high-risk strategy" with regard to the woman's welfare: "Jesus here runs the risk of encouraging his opponents to carry out their barbaric intentions towards the woman" ("On the Trail of a Good Story," 67).
57. Toensing, "Divine Intervention or Divine Intrusion?" 170.
58. Ibid., 172. Toensing's last comment about the "male gaze" is in reference to the fact that the Gospel of John presents Jesus and the Father as one; thus "divine male eyes will be watching her every move, private and public, intimate and mundane" (171). In Toensing's view, Jesus' unity with the Father qualifies him to render judgment, for it fulfills the requirement of the law for two witnesses.
59. John Calvin, *The Gospel according to St. John*, ed. D. W. Torrance and T. F. Torrance; trans. T. H. L. Parker (Grand Rapids: Eerdmans, 1959), 209. Referenced by O'Day in "John 7:53–8:11," 634–35.
60. O'Day, "John 7:53–8:11," 635.
61. In addition to O'Day's survey, see also Thomas O'Loughlin, "A Woman's Plight and the Western Fathers," in *Ciphers in the Sand: Interpretations of the Woman Taken in Adultery (John 7.53–8.11)*, ed. Larry J. Kreitzer and Deborah W. Rooke (Sheffield: Sheffield Academic, 2000), 83–104.
62. Quoted in Hodges, "The Woman Taken in Adultery," 331; and O'Day, "John 7:53–8:11," 639.
63. Barnabas Lindars, *The Gospel of John* (London: Oliphants, 1972), 312.
64. R. H. Lightfoot, *St. John's Commentary: A Commentary* (London: Oxford University Press, 1957), 348.
65. Leon Morris, *The Gospel According to John*, The New International Commentary on the New Testament, rev. ed. (Grand Rapids: Eerdmans, 1995), 786. See also Ben Witherington III, who shares the view that repentance (which the woman does not demonstrate) is necessary for salvation: *Women in the Ministry of Jesus: A Study of Jesus' Attitudes to Women and Their Roles as Reflected in His Early Life* (London: Cambridge University Press, 1984), 23.
66. O'Day, "John 7:53–8:11," 635.
67. Ibid., 639.
68. Augustine, "Adulterous Marriages," 107.
69. See n.1. See also Gary M. Burge, "A Specific Problem in the New Testament Text and Canon: The Woman Caught in Adultery (John 7:53–8:11)," *Journal of the Evangelical Theological Society* 27 (1984): 146–48. Raymond Brown also raises the question: "Many think . . . that [John 7:53–8:11] was an early Jesus story. Why was this story a problem to scribes? Was it because it ran contrary to the early Christian practice of refusing public forgiveness to adulterers?" (*An Introduction to the New Testament* [New York: Doubleday, 1997], 53).
70. Burge, "A Specific Problem in the New Testament Text and Canon," 147. Burge directs attention to J. N. D. Kelly, *Early Christian Doctrines*, 5th ed. (London: A. & C. Black, 1977), 217–19.

71. Burge, "A Specific Problem in the New Testament Text and Canon," 147.
72. O'Day, "The Gospel of John," 630.
73. See C. Welton Gaddy, *Adultery and Grace: The Ultimate Scandal* (Grand Rapids: Eerdmans, 1996), for a compelling treatment of this probability.
74. Ibid., xii–xiii.
75. Ibid., xiii.
76. Ibid., 155.
77. Roberta C. Bondi, *To Pray and to Love: Conversations on Prayer with the Early Church* (Minneapolis: Fortress, 1991), 109.
78. Ibid., 112. Italics mine.
79. Susan Brooks Thistlethwaite, "Every Two Minutes: Battered Women and Feminist Interpretation," in *Feminist Interpretation of the Bible*, ed. Letty M. Russell (Philadelphia: Westminster, 1985), 101–2.

Index of Authors